European Series   *Series Editor :*   *Cheryl Robson*

PLAYS BY MEDITERRANEAN WOMEN

Editor: *Marion Baraitser*
Consultant: *Susan Croft*

P l a y w r i g h t s

MARIA AVRAAMIDOU
LLUISA CUNILLÉ
MIRIAM KAINY
DACIA MARAINI
ARIANE MNOUCHKINE
NAWAL EL SAADAWI

T r a n s l a t o r s

MARION BARAITSER
RHEA FRANGOFINOU
HELEN KAYE
CHERYL ROBSON
LOLA LOPEZ RUIZ
TIMBERLAKE WERTENBAKER
SIÂN WILLIAMS

AURORA METRO PRESS

Dedication to: Michael, with a full heart and to Paula, Lisa,
Vanessa and Alexandra from a full heart.

FINANCIALLY ASSISTED BY THE ARTS COUNCIL OF ENGLAND,
SPANISH MINISTRY OF CULTURE (DIRECCION GENERAL DEL
INSTITUTE LIBRO Y BIBLIOTECHAS), ISRAELI EMBASSY, ITALIAN
INSTITUTE, PAUL HAMLYN FOUNDATION.

Cover illustration by: Alexandra Baraitser

Book Production: Claire Pearson, Mary Connolly, Jessica Carney, Lisa Baraitser, Simon Bailey.

Thanks to: Bintou Cisse, Psyche Hughes, Sue Brill., Ruth Christie, Saliha Paker, Seamus Finnegan, Dvora Ben-David, Sian Evans, Sian Williams, Jessica Carney.

Printed by: POLPRINT, 63 Jeddo Rd, W12 .

CAUTION: All rights whatsoever in theses plays are strictly reserved. Application for performance, including professional, amateur, recitation, lecturing, public reading, broadcasting, television and the rights of translation into foreign languages should be addressed to:

"Twelve Women in A Cell" Curtis Brown Ltd. 162-8 Regent St., W1R 5TB.
"Mephisto" Michael Imison Playwrights Ltd., 28 Almeida St, N.1 / S.A.C.D.,11 bis rue Ballu, 75442, Paris/ Rowohlt Verlag, Hamburger Strass 17, 21465 Reinbek.
Other plays: Write to Author/Translator c/o AURORA METRO PUBLICATIONS, Interchange Studios, 15 Dalby St. London NW5 3NQ.

CONTENTS

INTRODUCTION

by Marion Baraitser

This collection of Mediterranean women playwrights is the first in a series that brings to light the rich diversity of talent by women playwrights throughout Europe. The fascination of this collection lies in the fact that not only do the plays range across geographic and cultural boundaries from Spain to Italy, from Egypt to Israel, but that they move across the shifting ground of feminine consciousness.[1] The word *'woman'*, has different meanings in various parts of the Mediterranean ranging from *'ideal mother'* or *'virgin/whore,'* to *'witch'*, *'not-there'*, *'negative'* or *'superwoman'*. These plays allow us to reverse the position and lift the veil on ancient civilisations - Jewish, Muslim and Christian - and view them in the light of a liberating female gaze.

This selection of six plays can only act as an introduction to the fine work within the Mediterranean region. We would particularly like to acknowledge the work of Turkish women playwrights, such as Adalet Agaöglu, Bilgèsu Erenus and Melissa Gürpinar, working in a culture where the novel takes precedence over theatre and many women novelists are proving highly successful.[2] The plays in this collection were written under conditions that women playwrights share - an economic climate that favours the market-place, a backlash against

4

Dacia Maraini is perhaps best-known for her novel '*The Silent Duchess*' and she places language at the centre of her playwriting, unlike Franco Rame whose work draws more directly from Italian performance-based 'street theatre'. Maraini began her career as a dramatist by founding *Teatro della Maddalen* in the early 70's, a left-wing community theatre for women.[5] She went on to write over forty sceptical and provocative plays about women, three of which won major awards in Italy. She wanted to write political theatre that was neither too literary nor too performance-based, but was what she called 'drama' : i.e. what was missing in the gap between the two. '*Veronica Franco, Courtesan and Poet*' is about a sixteenth century Venetian courtesan who is shown to be a product exchanged in a political economy. Veronica cleverly uses her sexual servitude as experience which she turns into poetry for her own pleasure but her sexuality is never allowed full expression, depriving her of equality and respect, a position that Maraini sees as true for most women, even today.

As a playwright of Mediterranean ancestry, it is with pleasure that I offer these courageous and passionate plays by Mediterranean women to a wider public of readers, directors and performers.

(1) Dolan, J, *'The Feminist Spectator as Critic'*, Univ. Michigan Press '88.

(2) Paker, S,' *Unmuffled voices in the shade and beyond: women's writing in Turkish'*, *Textual Liberation: European Women Writers in the Twentieth Century'* ed. Forsas-Scott,Routledge, 1991.

(3) el Saadawi, N, *'Egypt:Women &Censorship'*, Index on Censorship 9;'90,

(4) Lamar, C, *'Our Voices, Ourselves: Women Writing for the French Theatre'*, Peter Lang,1991, **(5) Bassnett, S**, *'Feminist Experiences: the Women's Movement in Four Cultures'*, Allen & Unwin, 1986, passim.

Marion Baraitser took an M.A. in Literature at Witwatersrand University, then worked as a teacher and journalist before settling in London .She retrained and worked for several years as a Tutor in English Literature for Birkbeck, London University and taught Creative Writing for Morley College, the City Lit. and the Women's Theatre Workshop. Her playwriting includes: *"Winnie"* Bristol Express Theatre Co,*"Mr Bennett and Miss Smith"* Old Red Lion Theatre, Islington and *"Elephant in a Rhubarb Tree"* Etcetera Theatre, Camden. She lives in London with her husband and four children.

TWELVE WOMEN IN A CELL

by Nawal el Saadawi

Translated by Marion Baraitser and Cheryl Robson

"There I was with eleven other prisoners, because Sadat had decided to put a stop to the opposition and silence all those whose voices didn't agree with his own. I remember the day of my arrival, September 6th 1981, one of those Muslim sisters called out, on seeing me: "Nawal el Saadawi, you deserve to be hung for your writing". However, several days later, this woman had become a friend. Reaching an understanding of each other which seemed impossible at the outset became more of a reality day by day."

CHARACTERS:

SALMA Abou Khalil, young uneducated girl from the streets
ALIA Ibrahim Chawky, young woman, a freethinker, divorcee
SAMIRA el Fichawy, elderly teacher and fundamentalist Muslim
BASSIMA Charafel Din, elderly teacher and progressive Muslim
AZZA Mortada, slim, pretty, around 40, researcher, westernised
LABIBA Tewfik, clerical worker, non-political, unhappily married
MADIHA Abdel Azim, atheist
NAGAT Soleiman, young Christian girl
HADIA Marzouk, unveiled Muslim
ETEDAL el Cheikh, high-school student and devout Muslim
NEFFISSA el Charkawy, university student and government spy
RACHIDA Zakaria, pregnant, devout Muslim
WARDEN, Fahima
ZOUBA the prostitute
ZEINAB the criminal
SABAH the beggar
POLICEMAN
GOVERNOR
INSPECTOR
RUBBISH COLLECTOR

ACT ONE

Darkness, silence, an empty stage. The portrait of a man is hanging in a huge golden frame decked with a string of fairy lights. The facial features are stern, the eyes piercing, the smile is broad and sardonic. A faint spot of light signals the dawn. Birds sing. All is calm. SABAH enters limping. She is wearing a threadbare djellaba; her hair dishevelled. Her face is stained with dark blotches, mud and tar. She sits on the ground to rummage through a pile of rubbish, singing sadly.

SABAH:*(sings)* Sad times these,
           Bending double those who once lived well,
           Giving myrrh to him to drink at his ease,
           And the son-of-a-bitch ruling as he pleases,
           Patience. Wisdom.
           The pretender's unmasked.
           A real charmer but his heart's full of smoke.
           Patience...patience...
           Everything in its time.

(SABAH gets up, moves bent over and limping. She continues her lament in the same sad tone.)

SABAH: Honest people thrown in the mud,
           The son-of-a-bitch ruling as he pleases,

(A POLICEMAN suddenly appears, seizes her violently by the neck.)

POLICEMAN: Come here you, beggar, daughter of a beggar. You've been told a thousand times that begging's against the law. And the law's what counts. Here's for you. *(He gives her a beating.)* What do you mean, eh? Take that and that. *(He continues to hit her.)*
SABAH: *(moans)* Sing for the daughter. What does the bastard care?
POLICEMAN: What daughter? What bastard? Move on.

SABAH: They're going to take her in again. Whenever they see her they lock her up. They've got nothing else to do.

(The POLICEMAN pulls SABAH off. Sound of boots and police siren. Lights fade. The sound of a large key turning three times in a lock. A metal door opens and clanks shut.)

SABAH: Nothing else to do...

(A faint light. We find SABAH next to a small barred door in the prison's outer yard. The door leads to an inner yard and a second barred cell. SABAH puts her hand through the bars and tries to grab a tuft of watercress but she cannot reach it. The prison walls are very high, topped with barbed wire. The sound of a curlew singing - SABAH looks up.)

SABAH: *(Sings)* Patience...patience...Everything in its own good time

(A RUBBISH COLLECTOR enters and sweeps up, leaving some of the rubbish behind.)

RUBBISH COLLECTOR: Clear off, you're a gonner if the Warden sees you.
SABAH: Where will she go?...She has nowhere to go?
RUBBISH COLLECTOR: What? Nowhere to go? Aren't there enough rooms for you here?
SABAH: There's nowhere for her: not inside or outside.
RUBBISH COLLECTOR: There's plenty of room, why are you sitting there?
SABAH: This is her place.
RUBBISH COLLECTOR: Used to be for the likes of you, now it's for them, the politicals.
SABAH: It's her place, it's her cress, they've taken it.

(The RUBBISH COLLECTOR shoves her with his broom. She goes out singing. The dawn fades up and we see the beggars' cell. It is divided by a clothes line. Suitcases and boxes, a gas stove, a rubbish bin, beds and mattresses on the floor. To the right, sit the

13

veiled politicals, an old cloth spread as a prayer mat on the floor.
SAMIRA kneels. praying face to the wall. Behind her, kneel
RACHIDA, NEFFISSA and ETEDAL, praying. HADIA, unveiled
and with her hair loose sits reading the Koran. SALMA stands on
guard at the gate, watching the yard. To the left BASSIMA and
AZZA lie on the beds. MADIHA and NAGAT make tea and
LABIBA sits alone, head in hands)

(The PRISON WARDEN enters hurriedly.)

SALMA: *(Rushing back.)* The warden!

(The veiled women stop praying. LABIBA calmly crosses her arms.
MADIHA and NAGAT hide the stove in a box. BASSIMA stands
and lights a cigarette and AZZA puts rollers in her hair.)

WARDEN: The Governor and the Inspector are coming today. There
might be a search: I'll let you know. The police inspector has been in
this morning. No hassle. I don't want them finding anything or they'll
be down on me - and you. Won't they Madame Bassima?
BASSIMA: Of course, of course, God willing, there'll be no
problems.
WARDEN: Get rid of that mirror.
SALMA: *(naively)* Why?
WARDEN: A woman died last year.
SALMA: Why?
RACHIDA: *(Gives SALMA a nudge.)* Don't you know why people
kill themselves in prison, idiot?
(WARDEN continues to search)
WARDEN: No money, no newspapers, no radio, no paper and no pen
- with politicals - worse than a gun.
SALMA: I haven't got one. Don't know how to read or write.
(The WARDEN goes to inspect the bathroom.)
BASSIMA: *(worried)* If you've got something - hide it.
LABIBA: *(angry)* Inspections, searches, haven't they anything better
to do than give us this shit?
(The WARDEN comes back.)
WARDEN: The washroom's filthy and the yard has to be swept and

watered - I've been here for twenty years and I'm not lowering my standards now, am I Salma?

SALMA: Why me? Why don't you ask Etedal or Hadia?

HADIA: You do absolutely nothing all day.

SALMA: And what do you do?

HADIA: I read the Koran.

SALMA: So it's work to read the Koran, is it?

SAMIRA: What are you saying? May God forgive you. To read the words of God is the finest work there is.

WARDEN: But if you're all reading the Koran, who's going to clean the washroom?

SAMIRA: Some people do nothing, they don't read the Koran or pray - Let them clean the washroom.

(BASSIMA lights a cigarette.)

BASSIMA: *(ironic)* Look Madame Fahima, I'm far too old to clean the floor. I never cleaned it at home, so why should I start here?

AZZA: It's unthinkable one of us should have to do it.

LABIBA: I have three domestics at home, Madame Fahima.

WARDEN: I didn't mean...I know you're all educated and come from good families.

SALMA: Does that mean I'm not from a good family?

WARDEN: You're still young, my little Salma, you can't compare yourself to them.

SAMIRA: Salma is the same as the rest of us and perhaps even better than some. At least she covers her head and respects God.

LABIBA: How dare you?

WARDEN: Calm down, ladies. I'll find someone else.

(The WARDEN exits.)

SAMIRA: *(imitates LABIBA)* "I have three domestics, Madame Fahima!" Look at who's sticking up for the working classes.

LABIBA: Look at who's got nothing to do except read the Koran.

SAMIRA: The world passes, only God remains.

LABIBA: And who's going to work to feed you? God?

RACHIDA: May God forgive you.

NEFFISSA: The real food is from God and the real cleanliness is from your faith and dirt comes from...

SAMIRA: Sinners!

BASSIMA: Calm down. We've got more important things to worry

15

about. Like the search.

(PRISON WARDEN enters.)

WARDEN: I've found someone, from the prostitutes' cell. She's very clean.

SAMIRA: *(Sits up.)* A prostitute? That's impossible.

RACHIDA/NEFFISSA: *(together)* Outrageous!

WARDEN: What's wrong with prostitutes? They're the cleanest of the lot. I've seen 'em all: Criminals, drug dealers, thieves and some of them are good people, it's life that's let them down. Lots of innocent people inside, ladies. Bet you never thought you'd land up in here.

(SAMIRA shrieks.)

ALL: What is it?

SAMIRA: Cockroach.

(SALMA squashes it with her slipper.)

WARDEN: Cockroaches, beetles and lizards. You'll get them all in here if you don't clean up. I'll get Zouba, she's a good girl.

SAMIRA: Why stop there? Why not a thief or a murderer?

WARDEN: They're just ordinary people, they simply had a moment of anger. Feel sorry for them.

(SABAH appears at the bars.)

SABAH: Give her a pinch of cress.

SALMA: *(to the WARDEN)* Who's that?

WARDEN: It's forbidden to speak to the other prisoners. Clear off,

SABAH: Get your filthy face out of here. *(Pointing to her face.)* That's life.

WARDEN: Dead right. Get it out of here. The governor's coming.

SABAH: This is the beggar's cell. She's here because she lives here. She planted the cress.

WARDEN: Salma, give her a bit of cress.

(SALMA gives her some watercress. SABAH eats it.)

WARDEN: Now go and get Zouba!

(SABAH goes off and calls out loudly.)

SABAH: Zouba! Zouba!

WARDEN: I forgot to tell you, Madame Bassima, once Zouba's cleaned up, give her a couple of cigarettes.

BASSIMA: In that case, we need some more. I've only got my own and I can't give those up.

16

(NEFFISSA stands in front of the door watching the yard. SALMA wanders around and stops in front of the portrait.).

SALMA: *(Pointing to the portrait)* Who's that man?
WARDEN: Good God. That's not a man, girl. That's the Governor, at the top.
SALMA: Top of what?
WARDEN: On top, on top, on top.
(She indicates much higher than herself.)
SALMA: As high as the sky?
WARDEN: Even higher.
SALMA: Higher than the sky? Higher than God?
WARDEN: Heavens above! Who's higher than God? You're joking.
RACHIDA: Don't be stupid, he's the one who's put you here.
SALMA: *(even more naively)* Does he know me? I don't know him. Reminds me of someone.
RACHIDA: *(mocking)* Perhaps he looks like your dad?
SALMA: *(hurt)* I don't remember what he looks like. All I remember is my mum's old man - I used to call him dad. He looked like this one.
(Everyone laughs.)
WARDEN: I don't know why they've put you in with the politicals.
SAMIRA: I'll give my right hand if she's not putting it on.
BASSIMA: *(whispers to AZZA)* I can't stand being in the same cell as them.
(NEFFISSA screams.)
WARDEN: What's up? Another cockroach?
NEFFISSA: No. A man.
(NEFFISSA runs to put on her veil and the others do the same.)
WARDEN: My God! It's the Governor!

*(The **PRISON WARDEN** rushes to open the gate to the outer yard. The **GOVERNOR** appears, holding his cane regally. Behind him, the **POLICE INSPECTOR**, wearing dark glasses. The **POLICE INSPECTOR** raises his glasses and looks at the yard.*
)
INSPECTOR: *(to the WARDEN)* Nobody's cleaned in here!
WARDEN: Sorry Sir. Right away Sir.

(The GOVERNOR looks around. The WARDEN tries to stop him going into the cell.)

WARDEN: *(spluttering)* A moment, Excellency, just give them time to cover themselves.
GOVERNOR: Nonsense. Let me in.
INSPECTOR: This isn't just any man. Move aside, woman.

(The WARDEN steps aside, the GOVERNOR goes toward the cell, then stops at the entrance, hesitates.)

GOVERNOR: *(to WARDEN)* You're a woman. You check they've covered themselves.
(The WARDEN goes into the room. The veiled women are seated to the right. SAMIRA is alone reading the Koran. RACHIDA and NEFFISSA are completely covered. HADIA and ETEDAL, reveal only their eyes, even their hands are covered. SALMA is sitting next to them, her head veiled, wearing a djellaba. To the left, on a bedcover are seated BASSIMA, AZZA, LABIBA, MADIHA and NAGAT. They are unveiled and have not covered their hair. They wear either djellabas or dresses. BASSIMA smokes. The GOVERNOR waits outside, nervously tapping his cane.)

INSPECTOR: *(apologetically)* It's because they're...
GOVERNOR: I don't understand them. How can they be political? Overturn a government with their veils on?

(The WARDEN appears behind the barred door.)

WARDEN: Ready, Sir.
(The GOVERNOR enters first. He surveys the cell, closely inspecting the walls and staring attentively at the faces. He twiddles his cane. The women remain seated and silent, watching the GOVERNOR and his retinue. They all stare at the prisoners, the INSPECTOR scrutinises each of them in turn.)

GOVERNOR: *(Still whirling his cane.)* I hope that you're happy here...with us.

18

(Silence.)

WARDEN: Very happy, monsieur, very happy to see you.
GOVERNOR: Silence, woman, I'm not addressing you.
INSPECTOR: Silence Fahima.
GOVERNOR: Anyone need anything?
(SALMA gets up and goes to him.)
SALMA: Yes, me.
GOVERNOR: Name?
SALMA: Salma Abou Khalil.
GOVERNOR: Well, Salma?
SALMA: I want to know why I'm here.
(The WARDEN turns away to hide her smile, the INSPECTOR twitches, looks embarrassed.)
GOVERNOR: You're asking me? You don't know why you're here?
SALMA: *(naively)* No, I don't know.
WARDEN: It's not for him to say.
SALMA: Then who'll tell me?
INSPECTOR: Tomorrow. At the interview.
SALMA: What interview? Tomorrow? It's always tomorrow.

(The WARDEN turns her face to the wall. The INSPECTOR whispers to SALMA. SALMA goes back to sit next to HADIA and ETEDAL.)

GOVERNOR: Any more questions?
BASSIMA: *(Gets up.)* Monsieur, none of us know what we're accused of or why we've been put in this Beggar's cell.
INSPECTOR: It's the best room in the prison. It's the only one with a washroom.
AZZA: Monsieur, conditions are appalling; no visits, no food, no papers, no radio and all day the chimney smokes us out.
SAMIRA: And all night cockroaches and bugs...
ETEDAL: *(small, tearful voice)* We haven't seen our parents and they don't even know where we are.
BASSIMA: *(nervously)* Monsieur, no-one should have to put up with this life. We're all tired. Very tired.
MADIHA: *(calmly)* We haven't even been questioned or allowed to

19

see our lawyers.

GOVERNOR: Nothing to do with me. Not my department.

LABIBA: Whose job is it, Monsieur?

GOVERNOR: I don't know. We'll sort something out, eh?

(He looks at the INSPECTOR.)

INSPECTOR: *(politely)* We're waiting for instructions from the top.

SALMA: *(Gets up quickly and looks up.)* From the top, from the top? Up there?

(The WARDEN hides her face in her hands. The INSPECTOR takes SALMA by the hand.)

INSPECTOR: Sit down next to the others, Salma.

GOVERNOR: Any other questions?

ETEDAL: *(feebly)* I'd like a pen and paper to write to my mother.

GOVERNOR: *(hardens)* All contact with the outside world is forbidden. No letters in or out until we have orders that permit it.

WARDEN: They're well aware of it, Monsieur. They're very good really. It's the best cell in the prison.

INSPECTOR: Of course they're educated and respect the law.

AZZA: *(whispers to LABIBA)* What law? If they kept to the law, we wouldn't be here.

LABIBA: Stop or I'm going to explode.

AZZA: Calm down, it's all right. Ssh...

(GOVERNOR talks to the INSPECTOR.)

GOVERNOR: The Inspector tells me the food's good here.

(He smiles at SALMA.) Isn't that so Salma?

(SALMA gets up.)

WARDEN: Excellent, better than they get at home.

SALMA: I'm always hungry here, two pieces of bread a day isn't enough.

GOVERNOR: Why only two pieces? They should be getting three!

WARDEN: It's because -

GOVERNOR: No excuses. From today you must give them three.

WARDEN: Yes, sir.

LABIBA: *(coughing)* The chimney smokes all day, it's choking us. If we go on coughing we'll end up with pneumonia or T.B.

GOVERNOR: Professor Labiba perhaps you're allergic, not quite adjusted to your new life here. The air's a little different to what you're used to, that's all. If you've a complaint, we can call the specialist in to see you.

(GOVERNOR walks round twirling his cane.)

Everybody happy then?

(Silence.)

We'll take your silence as a yes, then. Always the way with women, isn't it? *(He laughs.)*

INSPECTOR: Too right, too right.

GOVERNOR: Since everything's in order, we can go.

INSPECTOR: Sir, if you don't need me, I'll stay on. I want some information.

GOVERNOR: Good. Carry on.

(GOVERNOR exits, WARDEN following. INSPECTOR remains.)

INSPECTOR: I need some more details, ladies. Bassima Charaf El Din?

(He takes out a notebook and pen.)

BASSIMA: Yes.

INSPECTOR: You're married, aren't you?

BASSIMA: My husband's dead.

INSPECTOR: *(coldly)* I'm sorry.

BASSIMA: Don't be. It was ten years ago.

INSPECTOR: You have a place in Heliopolis?

BASSIMA: A four-storey house.

INSPECTOR: How did you get this house?

BASSIMA: Thanks to God.

INSPECTOR: Surely you inherited it from your husband?

BASSIMA: I've never inherited anything. I've worked for the government for thirty years.

INSPECTOR: So you bought it with your savings?

BASSIMA: Doesn't the government encourage savings?

LABIBA: It's all she's got, that house.

(INSPECTOR goes over to AZZA.)

INSPECTOR: Azza Mortada?

AZZA: Yes.

INSPECTOR: Married?

AZZA: No, I'm not married.

INSPECTOR: A widow perhaps, like Madame Bassima?

AZZA: No.

INSPECTOR: Then what are you?

AZZA: Divorced.

INSPECTOR: I do beg your pardon. And you have a daughter - sixteen years old?

AZZA: Apparently, you know everything about me.

INSPECTOR: Wouldn't you be better off staying at home looking after your daughter?

AZZA: I'm best left here.

INSPECTOR: Welcome then.

(INSPECTOR goes to RACHIDA and NEFFISSA.)

INSPECTOR: I can't tell one from the other. *(To RACHIDA.)* Who are you?

(Silence.)

SAMIRA: They can't unveil in front of a man.

INSPECTOR: But you do.

SAMIRA: Each sect has its own rules. As the Prophet has written.

RACHIDA, ETEDAL, HADIA, NEFFISSA:*(together)* As the Prophet has written.

INSPECTOR: *(to RACHIDA)* Who are you?

SAMIRA: She's not allowed to speak either.

INSPECTOR: But you can speak as much as you want to. Who are you anyway?

SAMIRA: *(with dignity)* Professor Samira El Fichawy.

INSPECTOR: *(indifferent)* Delighted. Are you married, divorced or widowed?

SAMIRA: None of them. I have devoted myself to God.

INSPECTOR: Spinster.

SALMA: *(Whispers)* What's that?

(INSPECTOR goes to ETEDAL.)

INSPECTOR: Name?

ETEDAL: Etedal Mohamed El Cheikh.

INSPECTOR: What do you do, Etedal?

ETEDAL: I'm still at school.

INSPECTOR: The law forbids the veil at school.

(ETEDAL looks down and says nothing.)

NEFFISSA: We can do without school.

INSPECTOR: Who said that?

(NEFFISSA says nothing.)
INSPECTOR: Who said that?
NEFFISSA: I did.
INSPECTOR: Who are you?
NEFFISSA: Neffissa Mohamed el Charkawy.
INSPECTOR: Occupation?
NEFFISSA: Student, at the University.
INSPECTOR: But you no longer go to the University do you
Neffissa? You have to choose the veil or the University?
(NEFFISSA says nothing.) What's it to be?
NEFFISSA: The veil.
SAMIRA: There's no education to be had at the schools or the
Universities.
INSPECTOR: Really? Then where?
SAMIRA: Only the Koran can teach us. As the Prophet has written.
*The **MUSLIM SISTERS** together*: As the Prophet has written.
(INSPECTOR goes to SALMA.)
INSPECTOR: And where have you come from?
SALMA: From my house.
INSPECTOR: Which school do you go to?
SALMA: I don't go to school.
INSPECTOR: Can you read or write?
SALMA: No.
INSPECTOR: What does your father do?
SALMA: I dunno. I've never seen him. He left.
INSPECTOR: And have you got any brothers or sisters?
SALMA: Lots and lots.
INSPECTOR: How many?
SALMA: I dunno. My Dad's had a lot of kids, my Mum says.
INSPECTOR: You live with your mother?
SALMA: *(sad)* She's got a new man and they've had so many kids,
she can't look after me.
INSPECTOR: Don't you see her?
SALMA: I go and see her sometimes. Or she comes to see me. She'd
come here if she knew where I was.
INSPECTOR: Who do you live with?
SALMA: My Granny. She's blind so she can't come unless someone
comes with her. She's probably looking for me now.

(NAGAT cries. The INSPECTOR puts his notebook away.)

LABIBA: Stop it. You're driving us crazy!

INSPECTOR: All right. I'm going.

AZZA: You've nothing better to do than bother us, have you?

INSPECTOR: You're not the only ones here, you know. I want to see you all out of here safe and sound, believe me. *(Kindly.)* Let me know if there's anything you want, ladies...Madame Bassima?

BASSIMA: *(touched)* No, thank you.

(INSPECTOR exits. Silence.)

SAMIRA: They're all the same. Real jokers. Snakes in the grass.

BASSIMA: It's true. A few minutes ago he implied I was some sort of criminal.

AZZA: He told me to stay at home and mind my daughter.

SAMIRA: He called me a spinster.

(RACHIDA takes off her veil, her long hair falls about her shoulders.)

RACHIDA: *(Mimics INSPECTOR.)* Which one are you?

NEFFISSA: *(Unveils and mimics INSPECTOR.)* The veil or the University? What's it to be? May you burn in hell.

(SALMA takes off her veil and imitates the INSPECTOR'S walk.)

SALMA: And you, where do you live? None of your business. I live where I like. *(She bursts into laughter.)*

SAMIRA: Listen, girl. We don't believe a word of it. What did he whisper in your ear?

SALMA: When?

SAMIRA: Why did he take you aside? What did he say?

AZZA: Go on, Salma. Tell us.

SALMA: I don't know what he said so how can I tell you?

BASSIMA: You have to. The last thing we need is a spy.

SALMA: What's that?

SAMIRA: Someone who spies on others.

SALMA: I'm not a spy. I swear it. I haven't done anything. I haven't...I haven't...

(She bursts into tears.)

(The WARDEN enters with ZOUBA the prostitute, wearing a white

*low-cut djellaba. She is slim and vivacious. **ZOUBA** enters, broom in hand. The **WARDEN** closes the door behind her and speaks through the bars.)*

WARDEN: Sweep the yard and water the cress, it looks half-dead. Don't go near the politicals or speak to any of them. Understood?
ZOUBA: *(Chewing gum.)* Understood, Foufou. No worries.
*(**WARDEN** leaves.)*

ZOUBA: *(Singing and sweeping.)*
> Whoever wants to marry me,
> Show me what you can do,
> Don't bore me to death,
> With your life history.

*(**RACHIDA** sees her through the bars.)*
RACHIDA: Look what she's wearing. Showing off all she's got.
*(**NEFFISSA**, **HADIA** and **ETEDAL** come over to watch. **SALMA** follows them.)*

ZOUBA:*(sings)*
> Whoever wants to marry me,
> Show me what you can do,
> Don't bore me to death,
> With your life history.

SALMA: I've heard that on the radio. Who sings it?
RACHIDA: We never listen to the radio.
LABIBA: She might have picked up some disease.
ETEDA : Or A.I.D.S.
SALMA: What's that?
HADIA: You don't want to know, Salma.
SALMA: I do.
RACHIDA: A whore in here!
HADIA: She could lead us astray.
AZZA: Can't be that difficult then.
SAMIRA: *(angry)* We're too strong for that.
AZZA: I wasn't thinking of you.

SAMIRA: Why not? I'm as good as them.

BASSIMA: Calm down. We'll ask the Warden to send us someone else. The prison's full of them.

RACHIDA: Full of them.

NEFFISSA: There must be honest prisoners, at least some with more self-respect than a whore.

HADIA: Anything's better than a whore.

AZZA: Really? You don't think stealing or murder is worse?

HADIA: Selling oneself is the worst crime of all.

AZZA: How can you tell which is worse?

HADIA: There are major crimes and minor crimes. The sins I commit are small and God forgives me.

SAMIRA: Nonsense. If you're a believer, any sin is a crime.

HADIA: I know what I'm saying.

RACHIDA: You know nothing at all, Hadia!

HADIA: I know more than you.

NEFFISSA: Calm down, the lot of you. And Hadia, shut up.

HADIA: I can say what I think.

NEFFISSA: Shut up!

HADIA: Why should I?

SAMIRA: We don't want to know.

HADIA: Then put your fingers in your ears.

BASSIMA: Come on, prostitutes and criminals, they're all as bad as each other.

HADIA: You can't compare a thief and a murderer. God permits a hungry man to steal -

SAMIRA: God permits us to kill the infidels. A sin of any kind is a crime against God.

(ZOUBA is heard singing and sweeping.)

ZOUBA: Oh my love, come and see,
               Since you left, what's become of me.
               I watch and wait
               Hiding my heart -
               It's tearing me apart
               Crying to myself
               Crying for you
               Again, my love.

(RACHIDA and NEFFISSA cover their ears. SAMIRA counts her beads and reads the Koran. ZOUBA stands at the entrance.)

ZOUBA: If you'll let me ladies, I'd like some water for the cress. *(Nobody responds.)*
AZZA: Come in. The bucket's under the sink.
(ZOUBA goes and gets the bucket, waters the cress, then comes back to wash the floor. SAMIRA shrieks.)
ZOUBA: What's up?
SAMIRA: A cockroach.
(ZOUBA stamps on it, carries on sweeping.)
ZOUBA: Afraid of roaches? Let's hope whoever put you in here gets what he deserves.
(She gestures to the portrait. ZOUBA rolls up her sleeves and scrubs the floor.)

(RACHIDA, NEFFISSA and ETEDAL read the Koran. SAMIRA reads alone to one side. HADIA sits in the corner thinking. The rest talk among themselves. HADIA gets up, goes to the bars and starts to scream.)

ZOUBA: What is it? Another roach?
HADIA: A man!
(The women rush to put on their veils. ZOUBA rushes to the door.)
ZOUBA: No men in here.

(The INSPECTOR and the PRISON WARDEN enter carrying a small case.)

ZOUBA: God it's the boss. Quick.

(She hides in the washroom. The WARDEN opens the door and goes in, leaving the INSPECTOR in the entrance for some moments.)

INSPECTOR: Check they're decent, Fahima.
WARDEN: Ladies, are you ready?
SAMIRA: Yes.

WARDEN: O.K., monsieur.

INSPECTOR: Which one is Madame Bassima?

BASSIMA: Here. What is it?

INSPECTOR: There's someone outside, says he's your uncle. Brought you this.

BASSIMA: Where is he?

INSPECTOR: In my office.

BASSIMA: Can I see him?

INSPECTOR: Visits are forbidden, as you know. Do you want me to tell him something?

BASSIMA: Tell him I'm well...he's an old man, he's sick, he musn't... *(She wipes away tears, lights a cigarette.)*

INSPECTOR: Give her the case. It's been checked.

(He exits, followed by WARDEN. ZOUBA comes out. BASSIMA sits down and opens the case, breathes in the smell of fresh clothes and bursts into tears.)

BASSIMA: It's the smell of home.

(ZOUBA and AZZA try to console her.)

ZOUBA: You'll be free tomorrow, God willing. Home in no time.

BASSIMA: My uncle's very old with a bad heart. He couldn't bear it.

AZZA: He'll be all right, don't worry. I tell myself the same thing. Don't let yourself get in a state. What can I say? I've left my own kid on her own.

MADIHA: I'll light the stove for tea. That will calm us all down.

ZOUBA: *(sympathetically)* You have a daughter, like me, Madame Azza? How old is she?

AZZA: Sixteen years and all alone.

ZOUBA: Lucky for her - my girl's only eleven and she's going with a man.

AZZA: What man?

ZOUBA: The man who ruined my life and hers. I'd kill him if I could.

AZZA: What's he done to you?

ZOUBA: He makes me work. Makes me do this, dirty work. But he's not worth swinging for. Without my Yasmine, I'd have done away with meself long ago. I've got her photo, look, she's pretty;

look, look...

(She shows them all the photograph.)

BASSIMA: She is lovely.

MADIHA: Like her mother.

SALMA: May God keep her safe, Zouba.

(HADIA and ETEDAL look at the photo, but say nothing.
SAMIRA looks away, embarrassed.)

ZOUBA: Don't you like it?

SAMIRA: I don't want to look at pictures.

RACHIDA: It's not allowed.

NEFFISSA: Never go in houses with dogs or pictures.

ZOUBA: Good lord...what's wrong with dogs?

SAMIRA: These are God's words.

BASSIMA: Don't get involved Zouba. Just carry on...

ZOUBA: Learn something new every day.

(She goes to get the bucket from the washroom.)

(Silence. MADIHA pours tea into glasses.)

BASSIMA: God knows when we'll get out of here.

LABIBA: God didn't put us in here.

BASSIMA: Who else can we ask for help?

AZZA: There are people outside, you know. No one person can change the law when there are fifty million who believe in it.

BASSIMA: There's the one that's to blame. Up there.

(She points to the portrait.)

AZZA: He can't break all the laws and get away with it.

BASSIMA: You'd think so, but who's to stop him?

AZZA: Who knows? Last night I had a bad dream. I was in our old house at Zagazig and there was my dead father in front of me with his hands up, like this. Then I was outside the Pyramids near the Sphinx and she had her hand raised too. On the stone there were hieroglyphics and people were asking me what they meant. But I couldn't read a single word. Then I heard Samira calling me for prayer and I woke up.

BASSIMA: Samira and her friends don't go through it like we do. Day and night it's the Koran. Inside or out, it's the same for them. They're probably freer in here. They can meet with other people, they

29

can talk. And the food here's probably better than they get at home.

AZZA: It's true, life's so busy for us - committees, meetings, trips, conferences. I don't know how to get by without a newspaper, or the radio, or even a pen and paper.

BASSIMA: Stop it. I can't go on like this.

AZZA: You have to.

BASSIMA: I can't.

AZZA: Yes, you can. Just think how much we'll laugh when we get out of here.

BASSIMA: I don't think so. That man takes everything and spares no-one.

AZZA: We have to hope.

BASSIMA: We have to pray.

AZZA; What? Next you'll be taking the veil and when you get out of here no-one will recognise you.

(They laugh.)

BASSIMA: Louder, louder. Samira will tell us it's a sin to laugh - a crime to be happy.

(AZZA laughs even louder. BASSIMA lights a cigarette. ZOUBA comes out of the washroom.)

ZOUBA: Spick and span. Give us a fag, love.

(BASSIMA gives ZOUBA a cigarette.)

ZOUBA: Worth a million pounds this fag. I'd give up everything for one puff.

AZZA: Just one?

ZOUBA: It's the only drug I need. Some of the others are at it all night.

SALMA: What does that mean?

SAMIRA: Quiet. I don't want to know.

ZOUBA: All right. I'm going. Open up, Foufou, and let me out. It's all real spotless.

WARDEN: Well done, Zouba. It's nearly four o'clock. Time to lock up for the night. *(She lets ZOUBA through and shuts the door.)* 'Night ladies.

TOGETHER: 'Night, Madame Fahima.

WARDEN: Don't need anything?

BASSIMA: Some paraffin for the stove and I'm almost out of cigarettes.

WARDEN: All right.

*(She locks up and leaves. They lie down. The **MUSLIM SISTERS** go back to reading the Koran. **ETEDAL** stares our through the bars.)*

LABIBA: We can't sleep now!

MADIHA: Let's do something.

AZZA: What?

MADIHA: You could talk politics, Bassima. And you could tell us about France, Azza.

AZZA: Well, I could tell you about my research...

MADIHA: Great. Come and listen everyone. What's up, Nagat?

(NAGAT sits and cries in a corner.)

NAGAT: I miss my mother.

MADIHA: Come over here, with us.

*(NAGAT goes to sit with them. **ETEDAL** suddenly falls on the floor and has a fit.)*

ETEDAL: Maman! Maman!

*(ETEDAL loses consciousness. **MADIHA** tries to bring her round with some Eau de Cologne but **SAMIRA** pushes her violently away.)*

SAMIRA: Take that away from her.

MADIHA: It's only a little cologne.

SAMIRA: It's got alcohol in it.

MADIHA: She's not going to drink it - just smell it.

SAMIRA: Doesn't matter.

LABIBA: Oh, my head! It's bursting.

(They all go back to their places wearily and lie down to go to sleep. The light fades. Silence for some minutes.)

SAMIRA: *(cries out)* Praise be to Allah! Praise be to Allah!

LABIBA: I can't stand it. I can't stand being woken up like this.

SAMIRA: Prayers before bed or you'll sleep with the devil.

LABIBA: I can sleep with whoever I want to.

SAMIRA: And I can pray whenever I want to.

AZZA: Yes, but not so loud. We're trying to sleep.

SAMIRA: You don't praise God in whispers. You use your whole voice.

AZZA: You could try.

SAMIRA: If you don't like it - ask for another room - how about solitary confinement?

(SAMIRA turns to the wall and continues.)

SAMIRA: Praise be to Allah! Praise be to Allah!

(RACHIDA, NEFFISSA and ETEDAL sit behind her and pray.
HADIA prays alone in a corner.)

RACHIDA: Come and join in, Hadia.

HADIA: No, I prefer it this way.

RACHIDA: You can't pray alone.

HADIA: Why not?

RACHIDA: You can't.

SAMIRA: Let her. She's a Faramawia.

HADIA: I'm not. You bloody Khomeiniste.

AZZA: *(to BASSIMA)* We're in a madhouse.

BASSIMA: My body's numb and I can't breathe. I think I'm having an attack.

AZZA: It's all those cigarettes.

BASSIMA: I can hardly breathe.

AZZA: You'll have to give up.

BASSIMA: I couldn't cope.

AZZA: You could try Valium -

BASSIMA: Let me be, will you?

AZZA: Let's have some tea. Labiba, tell us about your job, what you were doing.

LABIBA: With this headache?

AZZA: Well, tell us what your dream was.

LABIBA: It's always the same nightmare.

AZZA: Well, what about your bloke? He must be missing you.

LABIBA: You're joking. I only stay with him for my daughter's sake.

AZZA: She's grown up now. She's working. My daughter's still young, her life's ahead of her.

BASSIMA: Thank God I've got no worries - no husbands, no sons and no daughters!

AZZA: We're all daughters and mothers, Bassima

(The MUSLIM SISTERS finish praying and set to reading the
Koran. ETEDAL goes to get tea.)

MADIHA: Better now, Etedal?

ETEDAL: Yes, thanks.

MADIHA: Come here a minute.

ETEDAL: I'm worried about my mother. She'll die if she finds out I'm in here.

MADIHA: She won't. She's all right, I'm sure. Come on, give us a smile.

AZZA: You smile like an angel, Etedal. *(ETEDAL smiles.)* Tell us about your dreams.

(ETEDAL drinks her tea.)

ETEDAL: I see my mother out shopping for my wedding dress, but whenever she goes into a shop, they say they've none left. In the end, she can't go on and so she says, "Why? Why can't you sell me a dress for my daughter?";-"We don't have any for jail birds," they tell her.

AZZA: Why are you dreaming of that?

ETEDAL: Because if they ban the veil at school, I have to stay at home and be married. A priest has asked for me.

MADIHA: A priest?

ETEDAL: I have to marry a man of God.

AZZA: And not finish school?

ETEDAL: I hate school. If I go there I'll burn in hell forever.

AZZA: Forever?

ETEDAL: I feel sorry for you. Why don't you pray? You'll go through agony, you know.

MADIHA: I grew up in a house where no-one prayed. One side of the family were Muslim, the others Coptic.

ETEDAL: Coptic? Infidels?

(NAGAT gets upset, moves away.)

MADIHA: You've upset her.

ETEDAL: I forgot she's a Christian.

LABIBA: How could you forget?

ETEDAL: She looks exactly the same as us.

LABIBA: Well, she's not. They're not like us.

ETEDAL: Sorry.

SAMIRA: There's only one God, the prophet Mohamed, the greatest of them all, has said so. Come here, Etedal, don't waste your time with them.

(ETEDAL rejoins the others reading the Koran. NAGAT weeps and MADIHA goes over to sit with her.)

MADIHA: Don't listen to them, Nagat. What do they know,

anyway?

NAGAT: I say my prayers. I always go to Church, how can they call me that?

MADIHA: God alone knows who believes and who doesn't. I've never read the Koran. I know how to read French, English, German but not Arabic.

NAGAT: Samira looks at me as though she hates me. I can't bear it. I want to ask them to move me.

MADIHA: That's what they want us to do. Why do you think they've put us all together in here?

NAGAT: At school I was the only one, too. "Infidel! Infidel!" I've heard it all my life. *(She starts to cry again.)*

MADIHA: Come on, let's get some fresh air.

AZZA: We have to stop all this moaning. Someone please tell me something new and interesting. My brain's seized up.

BASSIMA: My mind's numb - and my body. We'll never get out of here. The whole country's asleep.

AZZA: People aren't mad.

BASSIMA: Then, why don't they protest?

AZZA: We're not forgotten. The whole world knows about us. Someone will speak up -

BASSIMA: Organise a demonstration perhaps? Come off it.

AZZA: We have to hope, Professor. Help each other get through this. We're not going to die in here.

LABIBA: I think I'll die in here. I do.

(She stares out. An uneasy atmosphere prevails. We hear the sounds of cries from outside. ETEDAL, SALMA, HADIA and MADIHA run towards the door and look through the bars.)

ETEDAL: God, let me out of here!

MADIHA: You'll be the first to go, Etedal.

SALMA: Me too. I'm getting out with her.

(SALMA jumps about then falls down laughing. SAMIRA gives her a dirty look.)

SAMIRA: You're a disgrace, Salma. Why don't you cover your head in front of the door?

SALMA: Nobody's out there. Not a single man. Not even Mohamed, the rubbish collector.

SAMIRA: You know his name then?

SALMA: Yes, Mohamed. It's the name of the prophet, okay?

SAMIRA: How do you know that? Did anyone else know his name?

(Everyone keeps quiet.)

RACHIDA: How could we? We don't talk to men, do we?

SALMA: I heard him talking to Sabah in the yard.

ETEDAL: Who's Sabah?

SALMA: The beggar woman. I heard them talking. What could I do? Shut my ears?

RACHIDA: He could have seen you.

SALMA: He had his back to me.

RACHIDA: He could have turned round.

NEFFISSA: They all try to look in.

SALMA: Who? There are no men out there.

RACHIDA: This Mohamed's a man.

SALMA: He only comes once a week.

RACHIDA: How do you know? Do you count the days, then?

SALMA: I've seen him once in a while, that's all.

SAMIRA: You'd do better to read the Koran than to waste time with such nonsense.

(SALMA goes and sits next to HADIA and stares at the Koran.)

LABIBA: When will God save us from this?

BASSIMA: I can't take much more.

AZZA: They won't forget us. I know it.

MADIHA: We have to think of something.

LABIBA: We've nothing to read except the Koran.

MADIHA: Then let's read it.

BASSIMA: You can read it. I'll give it a miss.

AZZA: Then tell us, something else.

BASSIMA: I'm too tired. I want to sleep. Sleep my way through all this. *(She lies down on the mattress.)* Before they arrested me, I was in hiding for some time. You can't imagine how tired I was. All I wanted to do was find a bed and sleep.

AZZA: I thought of hiding too. But then I said, "What have I done wrong?" Nothing. When they take everything away, what can we do? We have to speak out. Against him.

MADIHA: He wants even more than God.

LABIBA: More than God...more than God...

(Silence and sadness descend.)

SAMIRA:*(Takes her rosary and prays in a low voice.)*
Allah is beyond all. Allah is beyond all. Allah is beyond all.
(Suddenly she starts to scream - ETEDAL joins in too.)
MADIHA: Oh! What is it now? A cockroach or a man?

(Lights fade.)

ACT TWO

Darkness and silence. Heavy knocks on a wooden door can be heard, becoming louder until the door opens. The sound of marching boots approaching. A woman's voice screams out,"No!" Silence returns. Cries of a new-born child are heard. The sound of boots going away. Sounds of a key turning in a lock and a metal door opening. Slow, heavy footsteps can be heard then a metal door closes. Silence. A light fades up on the same cell. A new prisoner, ALIA, stands in front of the door. She is tall, young, with long hair and a simple white dress. She seems nervous and examines the room intensely. A washing-line divides the room in two. On the right side are the MUSLIM SISTERS, on the left, the other prisoners are sleeping. SALMA gets up and goes over to ALIA.

SALMA: Who are you?
ALIA: Alia Ibrahim Chawky.
SALMA: Where you from?
ALIA: From home. What about you?
SALMA: They took me from the street. I was going to see my mother.
ALIA: They broke down the door. They knocked for a long time but I wouldn't let them in.
SALMA: Why should you?
ALIA: They had no orders, no warrant, nothing.
SALMA: They don't tell you anything. "Where are you going, love?" they said. "Come with us, we'll take you home" they said. I would have yelled out if I'd known.
SAMIRA: Who's that?
SALMA: A new prisoner.
SAMIRA: *(Getting up.)* Muslim or Christian?
ALIA: What a question. I haven't been asked that since I

36

was at school.

SAMIRA: You must be a Christian.

ALIA: No.

SAMIRA: Then you're a Muslim? A Jew?

ALIA: *(laughing)* No. No. No.

SAMIRA: My God. An atheist.

LABIBA: *(jumps)* What's the matter? You're not calling us to prayer?

AZZA: What is it?

SAMIRA: A new one?

AZZA: *(happy)* Alia, this can't be true!

(They hug each other. The others wake up.)

AZZA: I'm so pleased they put you with us.

BASSIMA: Pleased? How can you...

AZZA: I can't lie about it. She's my friend. I wish all my friends were here with me.

BASSIMA: How can you be so selfish?

AZZA: I mean it.

ALIA: I love her honesty.

SALMA: I like your Alia a lot but...

(She whispers in ALIA'S ear.)

ALIA: My father's a Muslim, his father was a Christian. My mother's a Muslim, her grandfather was Coptic. So what does that make me?

SALMA: The same as your father.

ALIA: If it pleases you.

SALMA: I like you, so I'm glad you're a Muslim after all.

(SALMA goes into the washroom. ALIA and AZZA sit.)

ALIA: What's all this religious stuff?

AZZA: We're not in prison; we're in a madhouse.

(ALIA looks shocked.)

AZZA: What have they done to you? And your little boy, where's he?

ALIA: He'll be six weeks old tomorrow.

AZZA: Who's looking after him?

ALIA: My neighbour's taken him until I get back.

(AZZA doesn't know what to say.) What about your daughter?

AZZA: She can look after herself.

(MADIHA lights the stove, helped by NAGAT. LABIBA goes over to the door. SAMIRA and the MUSLIM SISTERS pray or read the

Koran. *BASSIMA opens her case, takes out soap and a towel)*
LABIBA: The Warden's here!
(BASSIMA quickly shuts her case. The WARDEN enters.)
WARDEN: The Inspector's coming in later. There may be a search.
Make sure you hide that stove and anything else that shouldn't be
here. I've got a migraine already. *(She goes out.)*
AZZA: She's the same every day. Always something wrong.
BASSIMA: *(to ALIA)* You haven't brought anything with you?
ALIA: They told me I'd be gone for two hours. Then I'd be home
again.
*(BASSIMA puts her case in the corner, goes into the washroom with
soap and towel. AZZA goes to a small bag, takes out a djellaba and
a towel which she tears in half.)*
AZZA: Take it. I've two of these with me. You have one. My sister
sent them, she may send me more. We're allowed clothes, but not
food, and you can't eat what you get in here.
MADIHA: At least there's tea. *(She gives ALIA a glass.)*
AZZA: Tea and cigarettes... valium, speed...
(They laugh.)
AZZA: In the prostitutes' cell you can get anything.
ALIA: Is there any water to have a wash?
BASSIMA: *(Returns.)* They call that a washroom but the water's
freezing.
(ALIA takes the towel and djellaba and goes in.)
ALIA: I'm used to that. I'm just glad there's water here.

*(The PRISON WARDEN returns with the INSPECTOR.
NEFFISSA jumps up and runs away from the door.)*

NEFFISSA: There's a man coming.
*(The MUSLIM SISTERS put on their veils. SALMA too. The
WARDEN opens the door.)*
SALMA: It's only the Inspector. It's not a man, after all.
SAMIRA: Of course, he's come to see you, hasn't he? To get
information.
SALMA: What?
SAMIRA: *(sarcastic)* You don't understand anything, do you, poor
girl?

38

(The INSPECTOR puts on his dark glasses before entering.)

WARDEN: Ready, ladies? The Inspector's here.

(MADIHA hides the stove and the tea things. THE INSPECTOR looks around coldly, examining each of them.)

INSPECTOR: Where's Madame Alia Ibrahim Chawky?

(ALIA comes out of the washroom, wearing the djellaba, a towel slung over her shoulder, her hair wet. She goes up to the INSPECTOR, stares him in the eye.)

ALIA: I'm Alia Ibrahim Chawky.

INSPECTOR: *(overly polite)* Excuse me, Madame Alia. I'd like a few details from you, if I may. There are some omissions.

ALIA: Really? Is that possible? With all your technology and foreign experts?

INSPECTOR: You seem well up on it all.

ALIA: I know what I've seen.

INSPECTOR: Happy here?

ALIA: *(inspecting the cell)* Absolutely. It's infinitely preferable in here, away from the newspapers and the photographs.

(She stops at the sight of the portrait on the wall.)

ALIA: Can't get away from him anywhere.

INSPECTOR: Where do you live?

ALIA: In the house where you arrested me.

INSPECTOR: Ah, yes... um... and you're married?

ALIA: No.

INSPECTOR: Not married?

ALIA: No.

INSPECTOR: A widow?

ALIA: No.

INSPECTOR: Divorced?

ALIA: I divorced him.

INSPECTOR: Ah yes, his name?

ALIA: I don't remember.

INSPECTOR: But you have children?

ALIA: No.

INSPECTOR: But it's noted here that you have a child of only six weeks.

ALIA: Since you know so much, why ask me?

INSPECTOR: We need the name of the child.

ALIA: What for?

INSPECTOR: We just fill in these forms correctly. The name of your son is required.

ALIA: He's my son. It's my business.

INSPECTOR: Your attitude could get you into trouble.

ALIA: Is that a threat?

INSPECTOR: Nothing of the sort. I've got to get on, that's all. I've so many others.

ALIA: Don't forget anyone, will you?

INSPECTOR: It's not my job to say who comes or who goes - it's not my prison.

ALIA: Then whose prison is it?

INSPECTOR: How should I know? It belongs to God.

ALIA: God has prisons, does he? I didn't know that.

SAMIRA: Allah forgive you, sir. These prisons are not God's, they are his. *(She points to the portrait.)* They belong to injustice, not to God. *(She falls on the floor, crying.)*

(The MUSLIM SISTERS rally round her.)

AZZA: Everyday you come here and drive us mad. We've had enough.

INSPECTOR: What did I say?

RACHIDA: Shame on you...shame.

INSPECTOR: All I said was...everything belongs to God, even this place we're in now.

AZZA: We've had enough of your questions.

INSPECTOR: I've had all I can take, too. Why can't she just give me the name?

ALIA: Why must you have it? What do you want with a new born child anyway? *(Silence.)*

INSPECTOR: I'm sorry but I must fill out the form. I can't leave it blank. I'd lose my job. I do what I'm told, that's all. Now, let's finish this and I'll go. You won't see me again. *(ALIA says nothing.)* It's a formality. We don't want your son. What would we do with children? Or anyone else? I've a little boy myself and a new baby. I haven't seen him yet. I couldn't get home...You think I like being here all the time?

AZZA: You can phone home for news. Your wife's there looking after the children while ours are out there, somewhere, alone.

INSPECTOR: It's your own fault, you women who want to work, to be independent, to meddle in politics. Well - this is politics.

(He gestures the cell, the portrait.)

LABIBA: I have no wish to meddle in politics, I simply work in an office where they asked my opinion. So I gave it, that's it. That's why I'm here.

BASSIMA: We all spoke out. We tested their democracy and this is what we got.

MADIHA: This has gone on long enough. When's it going to end?

INSPECTOR: *(Shrugs.)* We're still waiting for new orders.

AZZA: It's not enough they've put us here? What more can they want?

INSPECTOR: Madame Alia, you have to tell me, please. *(She says nothing.)* You refuse to answer. Believe me, you will, whatever it takes.

(The INSPECTOR goes out. The WARDEN returns.)

WARDEN: What was that for? You don't know him like I do. Yesterday he saw Zouba leave here. He had her strip, then he searched her. Thank God he found nothing because if he did, I'd be the one he'd have for it and he won't stop until he gets what he wants. *(Silence.)* Tomorrow, he'll tell me to put you in solitary. I'll come and get you straight away. If he tells me to beat you - I'll beat you and if I can't get you to cough up, he'll send for others. *(She comes nearer.)* I'm on your side, but in front of them, I can't be. I can't lose my job. Once they had me hit a poor woman, worse than Sabah, the beggar who hangs around here - I knew she was innocent and I hit her. What could I do? I hit her and I asked God to forgive me. I went home, sick, went to bed for a week. We're human beings, we care more than you do.

(The WARDEN wipes her tears, looks at the women then goes out, locking the door.)

(Silence. BASSIMA smokes a cigarette.)

BASSIMA: I'm afraid for you, Alia. It's not worth it.

MADIHA: Try and be flexible.

SALMA: What's that?

LABIBA: She's always been stubborn - makes trouble for herself and those around her.

NAGAT: They won't hurt your son. They've already taken his mother from him. That's enough.

AZZA: Anything's possible. You've no idea.

NAGAT: What would they do to children?

AZZA: When they fail with us, they start on them.

BASSIMA: *(laughing)* If they fail with Alia, who will they beat?

AZZA: Somebody weaker - Nagat, Etedal or Salma.

SALMA: They'll beat me too, will they? I haven't done anything.
(She hits herself on the chest. They all laugh except SAMIRA who carries on reading the Koran.)

SAMIRA: Don't worry. Even if they beat everyone else they'll leave you be. They never hurt their own.

SALMA: *(Does not pick up on this.)* It's not fair. My dad and my mum used to hit me - even my gran' used to hit me.
(SALMA laughs. BASSIMA takes food from her case.)

MADIHA: Who wants tea?

SALMA: Me, me, me.
(BASSIMA looks astonished.)

BASSIMA: You never stop.

SALMA: Lots of sugar.
(SALMA sees BASSIMA eating biscuits.)

SALMA: Can I have some?
(BASSIMA gives her one. She crams it into her mouth.)

SALMA: Gimme, gimme.
(BASSIMA gives her another one. She eats it greedily.)

BASSIMA: What an appetite!

AZZA: It's her age, at sixteen you're ravenous. I hide the food to keep mine slim.

BASSIMA: *(Laughing with a mouthful.)* Like her mother.

AZZA: Why not? I've always been thin.

BASSIMA: I couldn't care less.
(ALIA goes to the door.)

ALIA: I need some fresh air.

AZZA: I'll just take my rollers out and join you.
(AZZA opens a box and takes out make-up, eye-liner and a mirror.)

AZZA: *(to BASSIMA)* I could write to my daughter with this - got a bit of cigarette paper?

MADIHA: They let you keep it?

AZZA: It's Zouba's.

LABIBA: You'll catch something.

AZZA: That's all I need.

LABIBA: I've forgotten what my face looks like. I wouldn't let my husband near me.

AZZA: I'll go for you then, he'll do just fine for me.

BASSIMA: *(laughs)* Then Labiba will kill you and she'll never get out.

LABIBA: I wouldn't do that. She's my friend.

AZZA: What's the matter? Too ugly? Wouldn't he fancy me?

LABIBA: Not at all, I think you're lovely. I didn't think of you that way.

AZZA: Why not?

LABIBA: My husband would go after anything - even his own mother. Now he's getting on, he's after the young ones like you.

AZZA: They're all the same. Why do you think I'm divorced? Or more to the point, I *asked* for one. I'm the one doing the divorcing, aren't I, Alia?

(ALIA walks around, not listening. AZZA laughs and BASSIMA tries to hide this from SAMIRA . Exit AZZA to join ALIA)

BASSIMA: You look very tired, Labiba.

LABIBA: Very, very tired. I can't take any more. I couldn't sleep. I actually started praying last night. It's like your period, it comes and goes.

BASSIMA: Mine went ages ago. What are we going to do? You'll be the first to go. You've had nothing to do with politics.

LABIBA: Nothing. I don't even read the newspapers.

BASSIMA: What newspapers? Come on, you have to laugh. At least you've got a family to go back to.

LABIBA: Who'd miss me? We only stay together for the kid.

BASSIMA: You'd do the divorcing, would you? *(Laughs, stops.)* Alia frightens me.

LABIBA: She is stubborn. I've known her for twenty years.

BASSIMA: She's frightened for her son.

LABIBA: She's not frightened. She's never frightened.

BASSIMA: What could they do to a baby?

43

(ZEINAB, one of the criminals, enters haughtily, carrying a tray of cigarettes and tea. The WARDEN follows.)

ALIA: Some personality!

AZZA: One criminal to another. She's almost running the place.

ALIA: Let's go in.

(ALIA and AZZA go back in. ZEINAB is sitting next to BASSIMA.)

ZEINAB: Is it all there?

BASSIMA: Perfect.

AZZA: Listen...

ZEINAB: I'm a bit down today.

AZZA: Why? That's not like you.

WARDEN: She's had some bad news. Her daughter's real sick.

AZZA: What's up?

ZEINAB: I swear to God if she dies...

WARDEN: Sorry, ladies. But she killed for that girl.

ZEINAB: Yes. Yes. I killed the son-of-a-bitch. My father said "If you leave him, I'll cut you up." Seven kids I got from him, all dead, except her, the little one. Lazy bastard, slept all day, a thief like his father, stoned out of his mind. She told me what he did to her.

MADIHA: Why did she do it?

WARDEN: She saw him with the little one.

MADIHA: With your daughter?

ZEINAB: *(Looks at her hands.)* I killed him. When I saw him do it - with my own eyes. *(She shuts her eyes.)* I hit him with the pickaxe, chopped him up, put him in a bag and threw him into the sea. *(She laughs.)* The fish finished him long ago.

(ZEINAB gets up suddenly.)

AZZA: Where are you going?

ZEINAB: Where do you want me to go? To see my daughter. She's all I've got.

WARDEN: She's not here. You can't see her. She really thinks she's going to...Where is she? In the middle of Egypt?

ZEINAB: It depends on God... if He takes her, I'll cut him out too.

WARDEN: Ssh, Madame Samira will kill you and cut you up if she hears you.

ZEINAB: *(crying)* Who will? Nobody can kill me - it's my daughter who's sick that's killing me.

WARDEN: Get up. Get up. God'll look after her. Today has been a nightmare. The Inspector's out there, looking for a cell to put the new girl in. Seen her?

ZEINAB: Which one?

WARDEN: The one out there with Azza . Called Alia Ibrahim Chawky. May God protect her.

ZEINAB: What's she done? Killed someone?

WARDEN: She's so full of herself, that one. Even braver than you - "I divorced him", says she.

ZEINAB: I should have done that. How many times did I dig and plant and carry it all on my back like a slave?

WARDEN: She's nobody's slave, her. These politicals are something else.

ZEINAB: They're soft, come off it.

WARDEN: These are ladies, not peasants.

ZEINAB: Who do you think you are? Three pips on your shoulder and you think you're so great? Peasants are better than them in God's eyes. *(ZEINAB sees the cress which is dying.)* Look at your "ladies". Can't even keep the cress alive. It's had it.

(LABIBA comes up to the WARDEN.)

ZEINAB: Is that the new one?

WARDEN: No.

LABIBA: *(Approaches ZEINAB shyly.)* I want to ask you something.

ZEINAB: At your service.

LABIBA: When you saw your husband...I mean to say when you saw...

ZEINAB: Him with her? It's not a secret, everybody knows.

LABIBA: What did you feel?

ZEINAB: Nothing. I killed him straight off.

LABIBA: Ah! And your daughter?

ZEINAB: I don't understand.

LABIBA: Were you jealous?

ZEINAB: *(tapping her chest)* Jealous of her? My daughter's my life. I'd have killed and killed again for her.

(AZZA and ALIA come out.)

AZZA: Labiba's always jealous. You know her daughter's very pretty. She's even jealous of me and I wouldn't look at a married man.

45

ZEINAB: They're not worth it. What about you, beautiful?*(To ALIA)*

WARDEN: This is Madame Alia who's just arrived. *(ZEINAB looks at ALIA admiringly.)* Such a good person. Such a pity she'll be going into solitary. Aren't you scared?

ALIA: No. Never have been and never will.

ZEINAB: Must have nine lives, like me, eh?

WARDEN: *(Cuffs her.)* Like you? She's an educated woman, Zeinab. I don't know what he'll do. The Inspector's gone mad.

ZEINAB: What can he do to her? She's not frightened. I've been there and I'm still alive.

WARDEN: You're used to it. They haven't got a clue.

SALMA: What 's so bad about solitary? I thought prison was full of ghosts and rats and snakes.

WARDEN: Prison's no joke and I can throw you in solitary any time. *(SALMA makes for the WARDEN who holds up her hand.)*

WARDEN: Keep off! You've no right to be any closer than three metres. That's the rules.

SALMA: How do we know the rules? We can't listen to what they say on the radio in here. *(Everybody laughs.)*

WARDEN: What are the rules? That prison should straighten you out.

SALMA: They want to set us right do they?

AZZA: *(laughing)* And file our nails. By the way they're long, we don't have any scissors.

ALIA: Or anything else. *(They all laugh.)*

AZZA: We could sharpen them on men.

ZEINAB: Not all of them.

AZZA: Why not?

WARDEN: Because she's in love with a guy in the men's prison. They write to each other and want to get married next year.

ZEINAB: Why not now?

WARDEN: They have to give their approval.

ZEINAB: They have to stick their nose into everything. *(She stops laughing.)* Honestly you're all wonderful - only why did you let the cress die?

ALIA: What?

ZEINAB: I can't bear to see anything die. A dose a day's all they need. I've made a vegetable garden in our yard. *(ZEINAB drags*

ALIA outside.) Come and see.

WARDEN: Don't start. She can't go out there.

ALIA: And what d'you use for gardening?

ZEINAB: A pick-axe.

WARDEN: A pick-axe!

AZZA: And you took my tweezers?

ZEINAB: I'll get you one. Everyone here can garden.

WARDEN: They won't garden. These are ladies.

ALIA: Oh no, we're not. We're going to plant things.

SALMA: Me too.

WARDEN: What do you know about growing things?

ALIA: All my aunts are peasants. In my village I was always in the fields with my cousins. If I hadn't gone to school I'd still be there.

SALMA: You remind me of someone - my aunt Tafida. She was nice and she was pretty...She's not there any more.

AZZA: Where is she?

SALMA: She went to Bahrain and she never came back.

ZEINAB: Alia's one of us. I'm going to get her a pick-axe so she can plant things.

ALIA: And some seeds. Bring me some Molokhia seeds and some cress and some parsley and some broad beans.

SALMA: I love beans!

ZEINAB: I'll steal some from the dealers. They've got everything. Colour T.V., the lot.

(Suddenly we hear a cry from inside the cell. RACHIDA has fainted. They surround her and MADIHA tries to revive her with cologne, rubbing some on her skin.)

SAMIRA: Take that away.

MADIHA: Call a doctor quick.

WARDEN: Straight away.

SAMIRA: She can't see a doctor.

WARDEN: Are you going to let her die?

MADIHA: Get a woman doctor.

WARDEN: I'll call one. *(RACHIDA signals 'no'.)*

SAMIRA: Wait, she wants to say something.

RACHIDA: I don't want anybody.

WARDEN: Why Rachida? Why? You're in prison my little one and you must look after yourself. We're lucky to have a woman doctor.

MADIHA: This is silly Rachida, let the doctor have a look at you.

SAMIRA: God will look after her.

WARDEN: But the medicine could help her.

HADIA: Believe in anyone else and you offend Him.

WARDEN: It's a crime to call a doctor now, is it? I can't take any more of this.

(ZEINAB returns with a pick-axe.)

ZEINAB: Here you are. Dig deep, it's hard to get anything to grow here but God's given it to us, so might as well use it.

WARDEN: Better off talking to them Alia, than wasting your time digging. Talk some sense into them.

(Exit WARDEN locking the gate.)

SALMA: Can I have a go?

ALIA: We'll take it in turns.

SALMA: This is my part of the yard.

ALIA: And this is mine.

AZZA: I'll do the watering.

MADIHA: I'll do the planting.

(ALIA begins digging, SALMA clears the stones, LABIBA comes out.)

LABIBA: What's all the racket?

SALMA: We're going to have beans, we're going to eat beans.

(SALMA skips around.)

LABIBA: I'm not hanging about in here till beans grow. *(To BASSIMA, who's smoking.)* Can you believe it? They think they'll be here to pick them.

BASSIMA: Probably longer. We'll never get out with Alia around.

(ALIA is joking with SALMA, AZZA, MADIHA and NAGAT.)

BASSIMA: She's forgotten all about her son. I'd go out of my mind with worry.

LABIBA: Alia's like that. She can forget anything.

BASSIMA: Anything but herself. Never lasted two minutes on a committee. Too headstrong.

LABIBA: Full of herself.

BASSIMA: She's always got to make herself felt. Nothing but trouble. She's always banging her head against a wall like a kid.

She's free to do as she likes, so long as she doesn't hurt us.
(SALMA fills a bucket of water from the washroom and carries on watering the ground.)
BASSIMA: Look at that girl. I never know how to take her. Is she sly or just naive?
LABIBA: It's a madhouse...us with them - these people who don't even believe in doctors!
(RACHIDA has dozed off. ETEDAL watches the gardening. ZEINAB returns with seed.)
ZEINAB: I've got the seeds.
(ETEDAL takes the bags, looks at her.)
ETEDAL: *(Touches her hair.)* Why don't you cover it?
ZEINAB: What is this? You going to your own funeral?
ETEDAL: I'll wear what I like.
ZEINAB: Who told you to wear it? Your dad?
ETEDAL: It's my decision. I'll pay the price.
ZEINAB: You done something wrong?
ETEDAL: It's a crime to wear the veil at school, so -
ZEINAB: Going hungry is the only crime I know.
SALMA: Is that the seeds?
(SALMA takes a bag and runs off. ALIA digs energetically. AZZA collects the stones. MADIHA smooths the ground with her hands.)
MADIHA: The seeds need sorting.
ETEDAL: I'll do it.
BASSIMA: I like Nefissa. She never upsets anyone.
LABIBA: Careful, she can hear us.
BASSIMA: I didn't say anything wrong. Rachida's nice, too. Face of an angel. Poor thing, in her condition and suffering with it. I really feel for her. What if she has it in here?
LABIBA: Let's hope we're not still here then. She's not far gone.
BASSIMA: That's all we need - a baby screaming.
LABIBA: Couple of days ago I was woken by a baby crying - new born. I don't know why, I had the strangest feeling I'd been born here and that I was going to die here. Can you believe I'd forgotten the world outside, as if I'd never known it. I forgot my husband's face, my daughter's face, what our house was like...
BASSIMA: *(Smokes.)* Stop it. Don't go on like that. Let's get some fresh air.

49

(They go to the yard. NEFFISSA takes out a pencil and paper from her cape and makes notes, then puts them away and reads the Koran. WARDEN appears followed by ZOUBA.)

WARDEN: Clean the washroom and get the laundry and be quick about it in case the Inspector comes. I'll be watching.

ZOUBA: O.K., Madame Foufou. *(Sees the prisoners busy gardening.)* My aren't we working hard! What next?

AZZA: Since Alia came things have changed.

ZOUBA: I've got something to tell you.

(She takes AZZA into a corner and takes a piece of paper from her blouse. NEFFISSA secretly watches them.)

ZOUBA: It's from your daughter.

AZZA: It's not true! How'd you get it?

ZOUBA: Keep your voice down. It fell out of the sky, that's how. Read it quick in the washroom, then burn it. You must burn it. They might search us. I'd be a gonner. Not you - me.

(AZZA goes into the washroom. ZOUBA collects the laundry. AZZA comes back and hugs ZOUBA.)

AZZA: Thank God, thank God. It's all all right. *(She kisses her.)* How can I thank you?

ZOUBA: A cup of tea?

(AZZA makes tea and gives ZOUBA a cup.)

AZZA: Mmm. The best tea I've ever tasted.

ZOUBA: Because you're happy.

AZZA: And because I've been moving around and working - I've got back some energy. I feel I can breathe again.

(ALIA enters, sweating and goes to the washroom.)

ALIA: I need to shower.

AZZA: The water's freezing.

ALIA: You go first. Take it slowly.

ZOUBA: Give me your clothes and I'll wash them for you.

ALIA: No. I'm used to washing my own.

ZOUBA: You don't have anyone to do if for you?

ALIA: No.

ZOUBA: I never do the washing at home. I've got a fantastic place - all mod-cons. But in here I'd do anything for a fag. I'm addicted.

ALIA: Me too.

ZOUBA: Oh yeh? To what? Cigarettes? Drugs or something else?

50

(They laugh.) So what are you addicted to?

ALIA: To life. You can do anything if you want to.

ZOUBA: I can't give up smoking. I hate myself. I smoke to forget.

ALIA: You're a good soul, Zouba.

ZOUBA: Am I? *(She bursts into tears.)*

ALIA: See, you're crying. That's your soul. Don't fight the despair - feel it.

ZOUBA: Feel what? I want to kill myself but I go on for my daughter.

ALIA: I'm a mother, too. I've left my son to come here. I'm prepared to stay and even die here. Why? Everyone says I should be at home looking after him, everyone from the Inspector down. What does bringing up children mean? Feeding them, clothing them, paying their school fees? Everyone's frightened of speaking out because of their children. And so it goes on. I'd rather go to prison - that's worth passing on.

ZOUBA: You could die here.

ALIA: I'd die out there if I said nothing.

(AZZA enters with wet hair.)

AZZA: That was really good. I took my time. I went right under. After a while I almost thought it was warm.

ZOUBA: That's why you're in here. Can't tell hot from cold. We know we've got bodies - we sell them.

AZZA: And we sell our opinions. When we refuse to, they send us here. That's what politics is about.

ZOUBA: What?

AZZA: About the fact you risk getting beaten for bringing a letter.

ZOUBA: The whole world's upside down. Honest people die of hunger while thieves and liars rule the world. Some of the girls on the game never have to come in here. Why? - Money, that's why. And the dealers live like kings.

ALIA: It's all a sham out there. In here we know what's what and I don't feel so uneasy...there's nothing to hide. I could see people were fed up, getting more and more worried about the country falling apart but everyone told me: "You're wrong, Alia, people are perfectly happy and everyone's better off."

AZZA: Three or four people are better off while millions go under.

(ETEDAL enters in a rush, carrying a bucket.)

51

ETEDAL: I'm going to water the beans. *(She sees ZOUBA, ALIA and AZZA drinking tea.)* Tea?

AZZA: There's some in the pot. Come and sit with us.

ETEDAL: I like you, you know, but...you'll suffer forever.

AZZA: I like you Etedal, but you'll end up like the others with no proper education.

ETEDAL: I'll marry a good man.

ZOUBA: To take charge of you.

ETEDAL: Why not?

ZOUBA: If he's honest, he'll be poor. If he goes off you, he'll remarry. If he goes abroad for work, he might not come back. If he dies, you'll end up begging.

ETEDAL: Stop it. You only think of the worst.

ZOUBA: Well, what if it happens? You gonna sit and wait for a miracle?

SAMIRA: That's all we need. Get out! Before you upset the lot.

SALMA: What's up?

(ETEDAL goes and fills the bucket with water.)

SAMIRA: Keep out of it, you, you little spy, I'll throw her out if I want to.

(All the prisoners crowd round, hearing the shouts. ALIA goes to SAMIRA.)

ALIA: No you won't. It's not your cell. Some of us want her to stay.

(ZOUBA rushes out to the yard, SALMA, ETEDAL, MADIHA and NAGAT go after her. They call for ZOUBA to come back. AZZA goes out too.)

AZZA: Come inside Zouba.

(ZOUBA refuses and remains sitting with her head on her knees, crying gently.)

ALIA: *(to SAMIRA)* What's more, you've no right to accuse Salma of being a spy. Who agrees?

(Silence. They all look at each other.)

BASSIMA: We've no proof, but she seems so naive...

ALIA: Is that a reason to accuse her? Spies are rarely naive.

NEFFISSA: She says she doesn't even know why she's here.

ALIA: I don't know why I'm here. I've never joined a political party, never been on a committee - only expressed my opinions.

AZZA: I don't know why I'm here.

MADIHA: Neither do I.

NAGAT: Neither do I.

ETEDAL: Me neither.

BASSIMA: Well I know why I'm here. Because I've a duty to stand up for human rights.

SAMIRA: I'm here because I respect God in a world of atheists.

(They all listen intently.)

ALIA: There are twelve of us in here and half of us have no idea why we're here. So don't accuse Salma without any proof.

SAMIRA: Then why did the Inspector take her aside? Whisper to her? She tells him our secrets, that's why.

ALIA: He'd hardly do that, if she was really working for him.

AZZA: Besides, she's as good as gold.

ETEDAL: Yes, she is.

NAGAT: It's true.

MADIHA: She's good, despite all this.

HADIA: I know her, we sleep next to each other. We talk a lot.

(HADIA takes SALMA'S hand and sits next to her.)

ALIA: Most of us disagree with you, Professor, so you've no right to accuse her -

SAMIRA: I know she's a spy and I'm never wrong. God speaks to the pure and the faithful.

ALIA: God speaks to us all and you're not being fair to Salma.

SAMIRA: I'm never wrong.

HADIA: You are, Samira. Where's your proof?

SAMIRA: God speaks to me, everyday.

HADIA: And God tells me every day that she's not a spy.

SAMIRA: I know God. I've seen him. You haven't.

HADIA: I have, too.

SAMIRA: You've never seen him. You Faramawia.

HADIA: You're the Khomeiniste.

*(They hear the **PRISON WARDEN** outside talking to **ZOUBA**.)*

WARDEN: What are you doing here? The Inspector's on his way. Hurry up...clear off.

(ZOUBA goes. WARDEN enters, worried.)

WARDEN: The Inspector's coming. I've never seen him like this. He's got men coming and going, bringing things in. We're all afraid of what he'll do.

(WARDEN looks at ALIA.)

WARDEN: Madame Alia, couldn't you just do what he asks? He'll destroy you.

ALIA: My father tried it. My brother tried it. My husband tried it. They tried it at work - and now this little man wants to try it. Let him. I'm not afraid.

SALMA: *(Hugs ALIA.)* I'm not afraid.

(ZOUBA and ZEINAB return.)

ZOUBA: The Inspector wants to take Madame Alia.

ZEINAB: We won't let him.

WARDEN: What are you doing here?

(SABAH comes back.)

SABAH: *(sings)* The girl gets thrown inside,
                While the son-of-a-bitch -

WARDEN: Come on, clear off, the lot of you.

ZEINAB: He won't touch her. He won't dare.

(ALIA paces up and down. SALMA and ETEDAL begin to cry. The WARDEN doesn't know what to do. After a moment she exits.)

WARDEN: *(mutters)* Wish he'd drop dead...

HADIA: *(Raises her arms.)* May God strike him dead on his way.

SAMIRA: May God take him and all men like him.

ETEDAL: May God take him.

AZZA: Who is he? He's a nobody. We should complain to his boss.

SALMA: Yeh. Why don't we?

MADIHA: We've nothing to write with.

ETEDAL: I've got something.

(She brings out a pencil and a scrap of paper from under her cape.)

AZZA: I'll write it and we'll all sign it.

SAMIRA: I'm not signing anything.

AZZA: Why not?

SAMIRA: What's the use of complaining about one tyrant to another?

NEFFISSA: That's right. They're all the same.

*(There's a din outside. The **PRISON WARDEN** returns.)*

WARDEN: Get to your places, or else. Where's Neffissa?

(NEFFISSA gets up immediately. Everyone is surprised.)

WARDEN: Come with me. The Inspector wants to see you.

NEFFISSA: I've done nothing. You can't put me in there instead of -

ALIA: You can't!

WARDEN: Why would he do that? What have you been up to?

ALIA: I won't allow you to take her in my place. Take me. I'm ready now.

WARDEN: The Inspector's not ready for you. He's got other things on his mind. This place is getting jumpy since you arrived and we're all working overtime.

(She leads NEFFISSA out.)

HADIA: What will they do to her?

SALMA: Maybe she's got a visitor.

AZZA: It's not allowed.

SALMA: Please help her.

HADIA: May God have mercy -

(Lights fade. Only the portrait remains illuminated and seems even more menacing. A strong voice calls out:'No mercy. Never.' The lights fade up on HADIA who is on her knees staring at the portrait.)

HADIA: Who spoke? Was it you?

(Lights fade down on HADIA. The portrait remains illuminated.)
(Downstage lights fade up on NEFFISSA standing in the INSPECTOR'S office next to a desk with a telephone. She raises her arms and murmurs something. The INSPECTOR arrives, wearing dark glasses and comes up behind NEFFISSA who is busy praying.)

INSPECTOR: Tell me what you tell God, Neffissa, and take off that veil, since we're alone.

(NEFFISSA removes her veil and gives her notes to the INSPECTOR. He reads them and puts them in his pocket.)

INSPECTOR: This individual's wearing me out, Neffissa. What do I do with her?

NEFFISSA: Put her in solitary as soon as possible before things spread.

INSPECTOR: And what if I do? There's nothing in the rules about this. If things change and they're relaxed, then I'll be in trouble for

55

punishing her. I've asked for a transfer back to the police. At least the rules are clear there and you know what you're doing.

NEFFISSA: Put her in solitary and get out. She's stirring things up all over the place and you're in charge.

INSPECTOR: You don't know what's happening outside. We're having a crisis. *(Gestures the portrait.)* He thinks the world's against him.

NEFFISSA: His agents tell him who these people are, don't they?

INSPECTOR: But if it's true?

NEFFISSA: Just put her away. She's dangerous.

INSPECTOR: You're right.

NEFFISSA: I'm going back.

INSPECTOR: What will you tell them?

NEFFISSA: I'll say my father died.

INSPECTOR: *(Laughs.)* Again?

NEFFISSA: *(Puts on her veil.)* Why not?

(Lights fade on them and come up in the cell. ALIA continues to pace up and down while everyone else waits. The WARDEN tries to get the prisoners to move away from the door. There is a silence and then we hear the sound of gunfire. Lights out on the portrait. The WARDEN opens the door.)

WARDEN: It's over! You're free to go! Free...
(ETEDAL, HADIA and SALMA begin to dance around. RACHIDA gets up slowly and joins them. LABIBA kneels.)
LABIBA: Thank God!
(AZZA and ALIA hug each other.)
AZZA: Congratulations.
ALIA: To you, too.
(NEFFISSA rushes out. The prisoners outside come in.)
ALL: We're free...free!

(Lights fade. Silence. Lights up on the portrait - a new picture has replaced the old one. In the cell ALIA remains, standing. The doors are locked)

(SABAH is behind the door, singing.)

56

SABAH: *(sings)* Sad times these, bending double those,
Who once lived well.
Here's the girl thrown into prison,
And the son-of-a-bitch ruling as he pleases.
The pretender's unmasked,
A real charmer but his heart's full of smoke.
Patience...patience...
Everything in it's time.

(WARDEN arrives and unlocks the door.)
WARDEN: Back again Sabah? We'll never get rid of you.
SABAH: They take her and let her go. They let her go and they take her. They've nothing else to do.
WARDEN: Clear off, love. The Inspector's on his way.
(WARDEN goes into the cell and looks around.)
WARDEN: The Inspector's coming, hide all your things. Don't want any trouble, I've got kids to think of.

(INSPECTOR enters, wearing dark glasses. It's not the same person but his gestures and movements resemble the former INSPECTOR.)

INSPECTOR: Excuse me. I'd like a little more information. *(He takes out pencil and paper.)* Your name Madame? *(ALIA says nothing, stares back at him.)* I'm waiting. *(ALIA says nothing.)* Aren't you tired of this? *(ALIA says nothing.)* Answer me. Aren't you tired? *(ALIA says nothing.)* I'm tired. I really am. I'm worn out but it seems you're not. What are you made of? Tell me? What? Steel?
ALIA: Yes.
INSPECTOR: What are you?
ALIA: Human.

(The sound of a curlew. Black-out.)

END

END OF THE DREAM SEASON

by Miriam Kainy

Translated by Helen Kaye and Miriam Kainy

The play was first produced at the Beit Lessin Theatre in Tel-Aviv on November 8, 1991, directed by Amit Gazit.

CHARACTERS *(in order of appearance)*

DR. YOSEFA AMSALEM, a physician (about 40)
NOAM ORGAD, an attorney (early 30s)
ELISHEVA AMSALEM, mother of Yosefa and Amnon (about 65)
AMNON ISH-SHALOM, Yosefa's brother (about 45)
NECHAMA ISH-SHALOM, Amnon's wife (about 30)
DR. RAMI LEVY, a physician and Yosefa's former lover (about 40)

The action takes place in the entrance-hall of an old Jerusalem house, used as the living area. There are two entrances - the yard door and the front door. Everything is old-fashioned but clean and well-kept, including the telephone which dates from the fifties, and a really old kerosene heater. The kitchen area is offstage. The sleeping area and bathroom are also offstage behind a wall.

ACT ONE, SCENE ONE

The phone rings. YOSEFA enters, holding an old carton in her hands. As she hurries to answer the phone, the bottom of the box opens and its contents tumble to the floor - old photo albums, notebooks and letters.

YOSEFA: Fuck! *(lifts receiver)* Yosefa Amsalem, good evening...yes mother...nothing...I'm fine...*(She's trying to pick up the stuff on the floor as she speaks.)* Yes, I got through...no they weren't angry - said they shared my grief...No, they won't take a substitute because by the time they find a suitable doctor and by the time they show him the ropes...right. Nothing - I'm going over some of granny's papers, and

58

then to bed... Of course in granny's bed, it's the only one here...
Because it's more comfortable in bed than in a sleeping-bag on the
floor... Why should I throw it out? I aired it and changed the
sheets...So what if granny died there - so what?...Is the bed in
shock?...No, no, it doesn't stink. Every house has its own smell and a
smell isn't a stink. *(Trying to end the conversation.)* O.K.Mom...No,
thank you...Because I like being alone, alright, I'm accustomed to being
alone...Mom...Mother...Fun? You and me? You're too much...Alright-
(Offstage from yard, noise of car crashing into gate.) Mom, I have to
go now...Because terrorists just crashed the yard and - *(Puts the phone
down, and opens the yard door.)* - the gate's gone. *(Shouts.)* Oh, shit!
What do you think you're doing?

NOAM: *(off)* Who the hell shut the gate?

YOSEFA: Get that car out of here , you hear me?- Get it *out*!

NOAM: It won't start.

YOSEFA: So push.

NOAM: You push *(Shouts.)* Mrs Amsalem!

YOSEFA: Don't you get out of the car. Get the car out of here.

NOAM: *(coming closer towards the door.)* Why is the gate shut?

YOSEFA: Because it's impossible to sleep here in the morning. Cars
driving in before the birds wake up.

NOAM: Where's Mrs Amsalem?

YOSEFA: Who the hell are you?

NOAM: *(appears at the doorway, wearing army uniform)* An
attorney, from the office upstairs.

YOSEFA: And now you're coming to work?

NOAM: I'm on reserve duty. I promised Mrs Amsalem that - you
must be Yosefa.

YOSEFA: Correct. What am I supposed to do with that gate?

NOAM: I'll get it fixed, O.K.? *(YOSEFA isn't mollified.)*
What do you want me to do, slit my wrists?

YOSEFA: *(NOAM begins to amuse her.)* Is that the latest? To slit
wrists?

NOAM: *(looks about.)* Has Mrs Amsalem gone to bed?

YOSEFA: Forever.

NOAM: I beg your pardon?

YOSEFA: She's dead.

NOAM: Impossible. We agreed to meet this evening and -

YOSEFA: What can we do? Looks like she had a more important appointment...

NOAM: Excuse me - do you mean that she's really -that -?

YOSEFA: Yes. Phone for a tow.

NOAM: *(goes to phone)* I could go upstairs to the office -

YOSEFA: You're getting everything wet.

NOAM: *(backs up and takes off his shoes)* I'm sorry, I mean, my condolences - I mean...I don't even know what to say...I'd have been here earlier but it's the rain...There was this awful traffic jam - and I had a flat too - When is the...the funeral?

YOSEFA: It was already.

NOAM: How could that be? When?

YOSEFA: This afternoon.

NOAM: *(takes off his coat)* I don't believe it.

YOSEFA: Are you going to call?

NOAM: *(takes out his address book.)* Yes...yes...I just can't believe it. What happened?

YOSEFA: It's called cardiac arrest. *(Picks up the scattered papers and returns them to carton.)*

NOAM: *(doesn't quite know how to react)* Er... did she say anything before she -?

YOSEFA: We'd been chatting, nothing special. I fixed her supper and when I brought it in, she'd fallen asleep.

NOAM: So, and...

YOSEFA: For good.

NOAM: Poor thing.

YOSEFA: Me?

NOAM: She...she...She was so longing for you. It's...it's as if she's still here.

YOSEFA: Maybe she is. You drew up granny Allegra's will, didn't you?

NOAM: Nobody drew up her will. She dictated it to me. She just

60

wanted to be sure it was all legal.

YOSEFA: That figures.

NOAM: It's already been read?

YOSEFA: Yes, after the funeral. I insisted. *(Feels a bit awkward about it.)* Your boss did say that it wasn't the thing to do, but I have to get back to work. I just picked up and left. I didn't even have time to go via the office in New York. *(Pushes the phone at NOAM.)*

NOAM: I know. *(Starts dialling.)* Mrs Amsalem told me that this time she'd pull you out of there, no matter what - that she has to see you before she bails out. I never thought she'd do it so soon. *(Replaces the receiver.)*

YOSEFA: What happened?

NOAM: Busy.

YOSEFA: So what else is new? Half the cars in Jerusalem are probably stuck.

NOAM: Did you know she'd left you the house?

YOSEFA: Don't be ridiculous - it never entered my mind. By every law of logic she should've left it to Amnon. He was the good boy, got married, had kids....

NOAM: But it was you she loved.

YOSEFA: She could've left me something else. Cut out the arse-licking.

NOAM: Boy, are you two alike.

YOSEFA: *(pushes the phone at him)* If you don't mind.

NOAM: *(dials)* Will you stay here?

YOSEFA: What on earth will I do here? Why, will that be a problem? I mean for your office?

NOAM: No, no problem, except that one of the reasons I came to work here was - *(Replaces the receiver.)* Busy.

YOSEFA: That you fell in love with the house. I don't believe it.

NOAM: Fact.

YOSEFA: How much time do you have on the lease?

NOAM: I don't exactly know. I'm new...

YOSEFA: But just the same, she went ahead and dictated the will to you, named you executor and recommended that you be -

61

NOAM: We became friends.

YOSEFA: Your boss was very offended.

NOAM: I can imagine. But, you see, she...she wanted someone who wasn't involved in the family tangles. It's a shame I wasn't here when you read the will. I could've explained.

YOSEFA: There's nothing to explain. Everything's very clear, isn't it?

NOAM: Yes, just that - if you ask me, she didn't mean you to sell it.

YOSEFA: I'm not asking you. *(Having second thoughts.)* Is that what she said?

NOAM: No, actually, I asked her...but she didn't -

YOSEFA: The very day I got here, you went off on reserve duty -

NOAM: Yes. I thought I'd catch you both together this evening.

YOSEFA: You're getting carried away. *(She pushes the phone at him again, it rings and she answers.)* Yosefa Amsalem, good evening Hello...Hello...Dead! Now your car will stay stuck in my gate until - Hello...Yes...Rami? *(Long silence.)* Yes. I'm here...Of course I recognised...How did you know I was in Israel?...Since when do you read obituaries?...I didn't think it was the kind of reading that goes with a cup of coffee - After your night rounds...Of course...Don't know - A few weeks...No, I've not been back since...No, you can't come over. Because - no, I'm not alone, but that's not the reason...Not now and not ever - Rami, really! After ten years what on earth do we have to talk about? O.K. If I change my mind, I'll call...Yes, alright, I'm writing it down. *(She writes the number on the wall in pencil.)* Thanks. Bye. *(Replaces the receiver, pulls herself together and gives phone to NOAM.)* It's all yours. *(NOAM dials. YOSEFA takes some pot out of her purse and starts to roll a joint. NOAM watches her fingers.)*

NOAM: Was that Rami Levy?

YOSEFA: Excuse me?

NOAM: On the phone?

YOSEFA: I don't recall inviting you into my private life.

NOAM: Sorry.

YOSEFA: Do you intend to spend the night?

NOAM: "So why aren't you dialling?" - I'm dialling. Did you bring the pot with you?

62

YOSEFA: No, it's local. What's so funny?

NOAM: Nothing. You're doing it just like Mrs Amsalem, just like the way she used to roll up grape leaves, except that she stuffed them with meat and rice. She too had those little fingers...like a child's.

YOSEFA: Let's not talk about my fingers, O.K.?

NOAM: They're sweet...*(Touches her hand lightly - they look at each other. Silence.)*

YOSEFA: What else did she tell you about him?

NOAM: Who told whom about what?

YOSEFA: What did granny tell you about Rami Levy?

NOAM: Ah - she said that people like that shouldn't practice medicine.

YOSEFA: *(laughs)* How about some details?

NOAM: You asked for it. She said that he'd never have graduated from medical school, not in a million years if you hadn't helped him... that he's not a mensch... that after you'd been together for eight years, he left you...

YOSEFA: That's what she said?

NOAM: That's what I understood.

YOSEFA: What exactly did she say?

NOAM: *(imitates ALLEGRA)* "Six months after Yosefa left, he up and marries a blonde kugel." *(YOSEFA laughs.)* For a minute I was scared she'd hear me.

YOSEFA: *(finished rolling the joint, takes a deep drag)* Blond kugel. She really gave you a view of the family album. Want some?

NOAM: I'd prefer rum.

YOSEFA: *(gets up to look for it in the kitchen cabinets, talking as she does so)* Rum? Why rum particularly?

NOAM: Because I like rum.

YOSEFA: Rum it is. Who am I to tell you how to screw your brain? *(NOAM goes over to where the rum is kept and gets it.)* I don't think there's anything here except sweet wine and the whisky I bought from the duty free. (*She holds the whisky in one hand and a bottle of red wine in the other.)* Take your pick.

NOAM: *(holding up the bottle of rum, the same way she does)* Do you mind if I help myself?

63

YOSEFA: Be my guest.

NOAM: *(pours the rum and lifts his glass)* To the memory of the magnificent Mrs Amsalem, and to the health of her grand-daughter the...(*YOSEFA stops him with a gesture. NOAM drains the rum as though it were water.*)

YOSEFA: That is an alcoholic beverage. I'll be accused of corrupting a minor. What else did she tell you?

NOAM: Who?

YOSEFA: Granny Allegra. You're really not on the ball. *(The telephone rings, YOSEFA answers.)*

YOSEFA: Amsalem, good evening...yes...yes, Mr Cohen... *(Her expression shows her amazement.)* No, Mr. Cohen, I'm afraid you can't talk to Mrs. Amsalem because... she passed away...yes...yes, Mr Cohen, you were at the funeral,this afternoon...yes, we do forget, it hap -pens...yes, it will be very hard without her.Thank you so very much.

NOAM: It's going to be tough on Cohen. Every day, at five o'clock, he presents himself with a red rose, they have coffee and chat. Are you alright?

YOSEFA: Fine. *(Dries her tears, and laughs, embarrassed.)* I've suddenly realised, she's really gone.

NOAM: I can't even begin to take it in. *(They look at each other.)* Do you want me to make you a cup of tea, strong and sweet, with lots of mint, the way you like it?

YOSEFA: You even know how I like my tea?

NOAM: Mrs Amsalem told me. I'm sure she told you about me.

YOSEFA: Not really.

NOAM: I can fill in the gaps, if you're interested.

YOSEFA: I don't even know what to ask.

NOAM: Is that so important?

YOSEFA: No, just a little embarrassing.

NOAM: *(Picks up the rum, fills his glass, lifts the bottle.)* Want me to put some in the tea?

YOSEFA: No. You knew what I looked like?

NOAM: Yes - no...you don't look like the photographs. *(Drains his glass in a gulp.)*

64

YOSEFA: If you go on like that, you'll never get out of here.

NOAM: So what? *(Crouches down beside her, she pushes him away)*

YOSEFA: So nothing. *(He loses his balance and falls on his arse,which amuses her.)* Dial, and don't stop until you get them.

NOAM: Do you really want me to do that?

YOSEFA: I don't know. Why? Do I sound as though I'd say one thing and mean another?

NOAM: Sort of - *(Without warning they grab each other and kiss. Just as suddenly, YOSEFA breaks away.)* What's the matter?

YOSEFA: Nothing...I don't even know your name.

NOAM: Noam...What is it?

YOSEFA: It isn't.

NOAM: And so?

YOSEFA: I have no idea who you are.

NOAM: We can start like that...or not. But I have the feeling that...that I've known you for a long time...that - Don't you?

YOSEFA: I don't know.

NOAM: You... *(Strokes her face.)*

YOSEFA: Mm. I have...aah...my period.

NOAM: So what?

YOSEFA: So...

NOAM: You don't....

YOSEFA: I do, but...

NOAM: But what?

YOSEFA: Some men, you know...

NOAM: You think I'm one of those?

YOSEFA: Don't know. *(NOAM grabs her.)* Not here.

NOAM: In Mrs Amsalem's bed?

YOSEFA: She'll never know...*(They laugh, NOAM picks her up, they exit to bedroom area.)*

SCENE TWO

About an hour later. The front door opens and ELISHEVA AMSALEM enters. She looks around the room, sees NOAM'S wet coat and shoes, walks over to the yard door, peeks outside and sees

the car stuck in the gate. She goes to the table on which lie
ALLEGRA AMSALEM'S album and will, opens the album, takes out
the will and starts reading it. The phone rings. She picks it up just as
YOSEFA, wearing a robe, enters.

YOSEFA: Yosefa Amsalem, good evening...

ELISHEVA: *(startled, drops the receiver)* You gave me a fright...

YOSEFA: *(picks up the receiver)* Hello, Vivi...Nothing, nothing -
How great that you called...No, you're not interrupting, just a family
misunderstanding...How did you know that I?... Tell me, are death
notices required reading in this country?...Listen Vivi, I have people
here...Maybe you'll come over...Tomorrow at ten? Great, we'll hop
over to the Old City. *(A shriek from the ear piece makes YOSEFA
pull the phone from her ear.)*

ELISHEVA: Have you gone crazy?

YOSEFA: *(returns phone to her ear, speaking to her mother and Vivi
at the same time)* What's the matter? What did I say?

ELISHEVA: Don't you watch TV? Or listen to the radio? To the Old
City?

YOSEFA: *(into the mouthpiece)* Alright, alright. I didn't say
anything...No, we don't have to. The fridge is full of food that Granny
cooked...Great. Bye.

ELISHEVA: *(picks up a shoe)* You're not alone?

YOSEFA: *(goes towards her)* If you'd knocked...

ELISHEVA: I did...you were - busy.

YOSEFA: And how did you get in?

ELISHEVA: *(shows a key)* I was worried. You said that terrorists
had broken into the yard...I didn't know what you meant.

YOSEFA: You could've called.

ELISHEVA: The line was busy.

YOSEFA: Not for...the last hour. Is that why you came?

ELISHEVA: I have to talk to you. *(Looks toward the bedroom)*Alone.

YOSEFA: What's so critical? Why can't it wait till tomorrow?

ELISHEVA: Tomorrow everybody's having dinner at my place. I
need to talk to you before-

YOSEFA: *(ironically)* Ah.classified material. *(The phone rings, ELISHEVA and YOSEFA both reach for it, but YOSEFA gets there first.)* Yosefa Amsalem, good evening...Excuse me? Just a minute - who told you the house was for sale?

ELISHEVA: Ask who it is.

YOSEFA: O.K. So tell that somebody that the most basic good manners demand that he wait at least until after the Shiva...No, I do not want to talk about it now. *(Replaces the receiver.)*

ELISHEVA: Who was it?

YOSEFA: I have no idea.

ELISHEVA: Why didn't you ask?

YOSEFA: Because it doesn't interest me.

ELISHEVA: Simon Karo.

YOSEFA: Oh, come on! What has he got to do with -

ELISHEVA: You'll see. He'll pop up.

NOAM: *(his entry silences ELISHEVA at once)* Good evening Elisheva.

ELISHEVA: Good evening Mr Orgad.

NOAM: *(tries to find an excuse for his presence)* The toilet float got stuck. Yosefa asked me to fix it. *(To YOSEFA.)* I think it's O.K. now.

ELISHEVA: There must've been a real flood. *(Presents NOAM with his wet shoe. To YOSEFA.)* Would this be the terrorist gang?

NOAM: What?

YOSEFA: *(the situation amuses her)* Yes. He didn't see the locked gate.

ELISHEVA: And rammed his car right into it. I see.

NOAM: I needed to call a tow. It was busy, and -

ELISHEVA: There was a leak in the bathroom.

NOAM: Yes. I fixed it for Mrs Amsalem too.

ELISHEVA: And you grabbed the opportunity to explain to Yosefa why you, and only you, are fit to administer the estate.

YOSEFA: *(to end this, she gives NOAM the phone* Try the tow again. Maybe the line's not busy anymore. *(NOAM starts dialling.)*

ELISHEVA: Maybe you should call your wife first, so she won't worry.

YOSEFA: *(a wicked grin)* Married?

ELISHEVA: With a child - The sweetest little girl, four years old. Didn't you know?

YOSEFA: We didn't get around to little details like that. Mother, stop invading my panties. Believe me, it'll be a lot more embarrassing for you than for me.

NOAM: I'll call from my office.

YOSEFA: As you like... *(NOAM turns to go.)* Your address book. *(Picks it up and crosses to him.)*

NOAM: I'll come tomorrow.

YOSEFA: Not at the crack of dawn.

NOAM: As for the will, it's not -

YOSEFA: Never mind.

NOAM: I hope I didn't embarrass you... Goodnight.

YOSEFA: That's alright *(NOAM exits. To ELISHEVA.)* What timing. Unbelievable! What would you have done if you'd caught us in the middle? Would you have waited for us to finish, or asked us to stop?

ELISHEVA: You are so crude.

YOSEFA: *(picks up the carton she dropped in Scene One and takes it offstage)* Your daughter. I know it's sometimes difficult for you to believe that.

ELISHEVA: Did you manage to ask his name?

YOSEFA: Yes.

ELISHEVA: He's using you.

YOSEFA: It's mutual.

ELISHEVA: He's using you just like he used Allegra.

YOSEFA: What? Did he and Granny?...

ELISHEVA: Yosefa! He's as hungry as a fox in a chicken run and he aims to gobble up what he can, before the farmer spots him. The second Amnon saw him, he knew exactly what we were dealing with. What is the matter with you? Do you think this is love at first sight or what? He's young, good looking, and has a young and pretty wife...

YOSEFA: So what does he need me for, huh?

ELISHEVA: Don't you understand. He wants to make sure that he administers the estate. He has long-term plans. I don't want him to hurt you.

YOSEFA: So you're hurting me instead.

ELISHEVA: How can you? - And right after your beloved grandmother's funeral.

YOSEFA: Granny would've given me her blessing.

ELISHEVA: Yes. You could get away with anything. Sefi, why won't you get some professional advice? *(Moves around, not knowing how to attack the subject she came to talk about.)* It's been years since you've had a permanent relationship.

YOSEFA: Nothing's permanent. Even if it seems super-permanent. Is that what you wanted to talk about?

ELISHEVA: *(realises it's pot she's looking at)* What's that? Sefi, that's a dangerous drug.

YOSEFA: You don't say? *(Puts it away.)*

ELISHEVA: It has a cumulative effect.

YOSEFA: So does life.

ELISHEVA: It's illegal.

YOSEFA: Anything else?

ELISHEVA: And if they catch you?

YOSEFA: You'll bail me out.

ELISHEVA: Where did you get it from?

YOSEFA: I inherited that from granny too.

ELISHEVA: *(both burst out laughing)* It was easier to bring up ten Amnons -

YOSEFA: Than one Yosefa. I've been here a whole week and you waited till tonight to say that. What self-control. You wouldn't have bothered to come over tonight just for that. *(Silence.)* The will, right? If you want something besides all that weird jewellery granny left you, just say the word...no problem, despite what you said.

ELISHEVA: I don't want anything, I don't need anything, not from her. It is simply not right that you should get everything and Amnon, with a wife and kids, should get nothing.

YOSEFA: Why nothing? Two apartment buildings in the middle of town are not exactly nothing.

ELISHEVA: Sometimes, with all your sophistication, you really are -

YOSEFA: Dumb. What to do? It happens.

ELISHEVA: Those buildings are a paper asset, they're rent-controlled. The maintenance costs more than the rent those tenants pay.

YOSEFA: Alright, but she also left him thirty thousand dollars.

ELISHEVA: How can you compare that to a house on half an acre in the centre of Jerusalem?

YOSEFA: I don't know. I surrender. Also, it doesn't interest me.

ELISHEVA: Why should it interest you? You've always had everything handed to you on a silver platter.

YOSEFA: *(ironically, mimics ELISHEVA)* And that is so unfair.

ELISHEVA: It really is unfair. You've been away for ten years. And Allegra used to say if Mohammed won't come to the mountain, the mountain must go to Mohammed. An old woman of ninety, and she'd fly over to visit.

YOSEFA: And in the end she goes and leaves me the house. And what did I actually do for her?

ELISHEVA: Nothing. Amnon has. He came over, brought the children, took her home for the holidays. And she, all she ever did was complain and criticise.

YOSEFA: But she loved me and I loved her. Tell me, do you think that I arranged for -

ELISHEVA: No, I know it's all that law-boy's doing - that Noam. He's the executor and, I just hope you have enough common sense despite all the...wooing, not to let him administer the estate.

YOSEFA: Why not? Granny wanted him to.

ELISHEVA: She was out of her mind. Would a person in her right mind, live in the entrance-hall of a six roomed house?

YOSEFA: She rented out the top floor...

ELISHEVA: And locked the entire ground floor. Everything's rotten. And I don't understand how she could say that she's keeping the house for the family and at the same time go and leave it to you. She knew that you'd sell it.

YOSEFA: Shall we dig her up and ask her?

70

ELISHEVA: I can't talk to you.

YOSEFA: Hold it. Supposing she'd left it to you, wouldn't you be selling it? And Amnon? And supposing she'd left it to all three of us?

ELISHEVA: Have you any idea what could be done with this house?

YOSEFA: Make a museum of it. What do you actually want?

ELISHEVA: I want to know what you intend to give Amnon.

YOSEFA: You want to know? Or Amnon wants to know?

ELISHEVA: I do.

YOSEFA: Aha.

ELISHEVA: And I don't want Amnon to know that I talked to you.

YOSEFA: Why? I didn't ask. Alright *(Knocking at the yard door.)*

ELISHEVA: *(as YOSEFA goes to door)* First ask who's there.

YOSEFA: *(as she opens the door)* Who's there? *(AMNON enters straight to kitchen area.)* Hi.

(ELISHEVA makes herself as small as possible; doesn't want to draw attention to herself. AMNON doesn't notice her, because he doesn't expect her to be there.)

AMNON: *(sees YOSEFA's robe)* Were you in bed already?

YOSEFA: 'Course not.

AMNON: *(searches in the kitchen cabinets according to NECHAMA'S instructions)* On the bottom shelf of the right-hand closet...*(Doesn't find it.)*

YOSEFA: Is it something Nechama left?

AMNON: *(nods)* A big black bag, umbrella and, somewhere here...

YOSEFA: And she's waiting in the car?

AMNON: *(opens another cabinet and finds what he's looking for)* Look Yosefa, about the house. I have a suggestion...*(YOSEFA draws his attention to ELISHEVA'S presence.)* Mom, what are you doing here? *(Silence.)* How did you get here?

ELISHEVA: By cab. I wanted to talk to Yosefa. Is that a crime?

AMNON: The will, right?

YOSEFA: I didn't say anything.

AMNON: I particularly asked you...

ELISHEVA: You always give up, always. And that old woman did precisely what she ought not to have done.

71

AMNON: Let's say...

ELISHEVA: I'll bet that Noam put her up to it.

AMNON: *(to YOSEFA)* Noam is Noam Orgad, the attorney who drew up the will.

ELISHEVA: She knows. She's already entertained him.

AMNON: *(to YOSEFA)* That's pushing it a bit. *(Pause.)* Is that really his car stuck in the gate? I thought he was on reserves?

YOSEFA: That too.

AMNON: In all events, the case is closed. Grandma's dead.

YOSEFA: That's what you think. While Mom's alive she can't really die. *(A knock at the door.)* If I'd decided to live on a pedestrian crossing I'd have more quiet and a whole lot more privacy. *(She opens the door, NECHAMA enters.)*

NECHAMA: You couldn't find them.

AMNON: Why? *(Holds up bag and umbrella.)*

NECHAMA: *(apologising)* The car's cold and the heat doesn't work...

YOSEFA: Who wants tea?

AMNON: No, we have to go. *(Turns to leave.)*

NECHAMA: Amnon said you plan to sell.

YOSEFA: He's right.

NECHAMA: It's a shame. This is a house, a real house. They don't build 'em like this anymore. Now it's just a stone facing. Here it's all real, the wood is wood, the stone, stone.

ELISHEVA: See, Nechama knows how to appreciate...

AMNON: Grandma left the house to Yosefa. She, and only she, will decide what she wants to do with it.

ELISHEVA: Yes, but one can talk about it, consult...

YOSEFA: *(ironically)* After all, we're a family. *(There is complicity in the silence between brother and sister.)*

NECHAMA: When they read the will, I thought, this house is nearly a hundred years old. Only the family's ever lived here. Selling it would be like selling -

AMNON: The Wailing Wall.

NECHAMA: Stop it.

ELISHEVA: *(laughs)* She's right. This place could be fantastic.

72

YOSEFA: Paradiso - and what about the ghosts that drift around here?

AMNON: That's true. *(To ELISHEVA)* You wanted to get out of here so badly you couldn't even wait till your apartment was ready.

ELISHEVA: Of course, because Allegra - she...even in our bedroom, she decided where the bed would go. She knew everything better than anybody.

AMNON: *(to ELISHEVA)* You complained that it was dark here.

NECHAMA: Well, that's no problem, if you take down this wall and replace it with glass, you'd get light nearly all day. And a view.

ELISHEVA: A lot of people have done that. I'd make a showcase of this place, if she'd given it to me. You could make a veritable palace of it.

AMNON: And who's supposed to live in this "palace"?

ELISHEVA: There's room for all of us. After all, one day Yosefa will come home ...and I could sell my apartment. *(To NECHAMA.)* And you could sell yours, we could invest...*(While she's developing this theme YOSEFA and AMNON conduct a silent dialogue.)*...you could easily get three great apartments in here, and a garden. *(Sees YOSEFA and AMNON.)* Do you think I can't see you?

NECHAMA: *(ignoring YOSEFA, talks to AMNON in response to ELISHEVA)* That's exactly what I said, and less than a quarter of what the building license allows has been used.

AMNON: May I remind you once again that Grandma left the...

ELISHEVA: It was Noam's doing, our attorney - he exploited the fact she wasn't that lucid, and appointed himself executor of the will.

AMNON: You know that's not true.

ELISHEVA: Not true? How could she write...*(finds the will on the table and reads from it)* "and the family home I bequeath to Yosefa, the only true remaining Amsalem, to her and to her children after her." *(A small silence.)*

YOSEFA: God gives nuts to the toothless.

NECHAMA: It's all because of me. I'm to blame.

AMNON: Nechama.

NECHAMA: I couldn't -

AMNON: Stop it.

73

NECHAMA: Stop telling me "stop it". I couldn't - Nechama Amsalem. It's simply not me.

ELISHEVA: How well I understand that. If only you knew how many times I asked, I begged....Your father didn't even want to hear about a name change. I told him - it's not even a Hebrew name, and it's not a pretty name. If he had taken my advice...

NECHAMA: She told us, "Do what you want".

ELISHEVA: How well I know that sentence.

AMNON: She said, "Ish-Shalom isn't Amsalem, they don't sound the same, or mean the same." What difference does it make now?

NECHAMA: At first - That's what she said at first. But in the end, she said, "Do what you want."

ELISHEVA: Which means that if you really do what you want, you'll pay for it. *(To YOSEFA.)* I want to know what you intend to give Amnon.

AMNON: I've no part in this.

YOSEFA: I know.

AMNON: *(to ELISHEVA)* Come on, I'll take you home.

ELISHEVA: And if she gives you nothing?

AMNON: Why should she? I got -

ELISHEVA: What you got? Nothing but a crumb.

AMNON: I'm not a welfare case.

ELISHEVA: You're not Rothschild either.

AMNON: I've never been better off than...

ELISHEVA: You have a family, a wife and children...

YOSEFA: And an insurance agency that's very successful. I didn't say anything.

ELISHEVA: Do you know what she'll do with all this money?

AMNON: It's none of my business and none of your business either. It's hers.

ELISHEVA: She'll give it away. Every crippled street beggar will get some, 'till there's nothing left, not for you and not for your children. *(To YOSEFA.)* Am I right or not?

YOSEFA: I don't know what you're talking about.

ELISHEVA: The day after we bought you a bicycle, you sold it and

74

used the money to take the neighbourhood children on a picnic.

YOSEFA: I quit. I want to shower and wash my hair and get into bed. I'm tired. That doesn't mean you have to take off. On the contrary, make yourselves at home. There's tea, coffee, preserves, sesame cookies that Granny made yesterday. She'd surely be delighted to know that everybody's visiting here. *(She moves to bedroom area, shifting her glance just prior to exit.)* Ah, yes. *(To ELISHEVA.)* Not to prolong your suspense, everything that Granny left me - everything, without exception goes to me and Amnon, half and half, equal shares. *(In response to her declaration AMNON retreats into himself. ELISHEVA and NECHAMA are so astounded that they react only after YOSEFA has left.)*

NECHAMA: Thank you very much. Really, thank you very much.

AMNON: *(shoves his chair back in place, speaks angrily.)* All's well that ends well. I hope you're both satisfied. *(Exits.)*

NECHAMA: Why is he angry?

ELISHEVA: *(NECHAMA goes to her and they hug each other.)* She should live and be well - exactly like Allegra - The grand gesture without blinking an eye-lid.

SCENE THREE

Six weeks later. The beginning of April. YOSEFA, in jeans and a spring shirt, comes in from kitchen with flowers, AMNON in her wake.

AMNON: Did you sign or not? I need to know.

YOSEFA: You've been avoiding me for weeks, and that's all you have to say? If it weren't for the "mysterious buyer", you wouldn't be here even now, right?

AMNON: Have you signed?

YOSEFA: No. But even if I had, there's an escape clause in every contract *(Looks for a vase.)*

AMNON: Not always. Whatever you agreed on with Roth, he'll add twenty thousand.

YOSEFA: No more games, O.K.? Who is this "he"? *(Silence.)* Well?

AMNON: Michael.

YOSEFA: Michael Karo?

AMNON: You don't want to sell him the house.

YOSEFA: Do we have to lock horns with mother over twenty thousand?

AMNON: Leave Mom to me. We're not selling to Michael directly.

YOSEFA: This is Grandma's house. You know what that is. Amsalem's House going to Karo. Even if it is Michael. It sucks.

AMNON: Why sucks? He's a friend.

YOSEFA: Alright, a friend. Is that what you came for on the night of the funeral?

AMNON: Don't be silly.

YOSEFA: You thought I wouldn't find a buyer, right? And after I'd leave, very quietly you'd have sold the house to Karo.

AMNON: Is it yes or no?

YOSEFA: Whatever you want. What's important is that you'll come over, talk to me, be Nonni again. Are you mad at me? *(AMNON looks away, but YOSEFA makes him look at her.)* You're angry.

AMNON: You don't understand what you've done.

YOSEFA: I never thought that to say "Half and half, equal shares" could be construed as criminal.

AMNON: It was always between the two of us, only the two of us.

YOSEFA: Do you think that without the agreement we made at my batmitzvah, I wouldn't share?

AMNON: It's not the same thing. Nobody knew, or needed to know.

YOSEFA: Just one question? Let's say Mom doesn't know, or Nechama. What will you do with the money? Half the house - it's not exactly peanuts...stuff it in your mattress?

AMNON: It'd be nobody's business.

YOSEFA: Something you wanted to do and now you can't?

AMNON: Not exactly, but...

YOSEFA: Secrets. Always secrets. Sometimes I am tempted to take the lid off your brain and see what's cooking there.

AMNON: What's the matter?

YOSEFA: The whole time we're talking, I have the feeling that what's going on in here *(Points to his head)* is much more interesting, than anything you have been saying.

AMNON: Not that I'm aware of.

YOSEFA: Nonni, it's me, your sister Yosefa...*(Gives up on trying to reach him.)*

AMNON: Now you're angry with me.

YOSEFA: No. I just don't understand you.

AMNON: Stay a few more weeks. We'll take a trip - We've had almost no time together.

YOSEFA: Is that my fault? I've barely managed to see you. No. You need a radical airing out because you are totally screwed up. Come over and stay with me in october. Alone! But for now, I have to get back to work. My fuses are beginning to blow.

AMNON: And I thought you were having a good time.

YOSEFA: You bet, except that fucking is not the only answer for one's life. I came for two weeks, extended it to four and now it's been nearly two months. It's not fair to the rest of the team. And in New York they'll begin to think they can manage without me. *(Picks up the phone, dials.)* Good afternoon, may I talk to Noam please?

YOSEFA. No, don't interrupt him. Ask him to come over when he's through.

AMNON: What do you need him for?

YOSEFA: To begin with, we have to tell Noam we're not selling to Roth. Then, since you're here, you can sign for him to administer the estate.

AMNON: Why him?

YOSEFA: Someone has to do it, no?

AMNON: Yes, but why him particularly?

YOSEFA: Because granny wanted him to, and because he's got one hell of a mind.

AMNON: I didn't think it was his mind that turned you on.

YOSEFA: Honey-lamb, the mind is ninety percent of it, only ten percent is...What do you have against him?

AMNON: If you could have seen the way he danced around grandma.

YOSEFA: She fascinated him.

AMNON: So much so that he'd spend whole evenings listening to the

77

same old stories over and over - give me a break. With him, it's all figured out.

YOSEFA: A psychological assessment, or just gossip?

AMNON: Simple facts. Do you know how much an administrator gets? Up to six percent of the value of the assets. Get it? And it's not just the house, there's the buildings in town.When it comes to money, you're retarded.

YOSEFA: Maybe. What difference does it make if he gets it, or somebody else? You know what? You manage the estate.

AMNON: *(ironically)* Thank you very much.

YOSEFA: Why?

AMNON: I don't need for mom to manage me, and I don't want you to come to me one day and say...

YOSEFA: Did I ever say anything?

AMNON: Yes.

YOSEFA: Remind me.

AMNON: When I sold the stamp album Uncle Joseph left you...

YOSEFA: Oh for heaven's sake, that was twenty years ago - and you really did goof.

AMNON: Sefi, please. Why are you so set on Noam? Is he hassling you?

YOSEFA: Of course not. We haven't even talked about it. Maybe once.

AMNON: I don't understand you. Why can't you see?

YOSEFA: How did granny put it? *(Imitates ALLEGRA'S way of talking.)* "Nothing like a stiff prick to keep the brain in the crotch." *(She laughs.)*

AMNON: She never said anything of the kind.

YOSEFA: You don't say.

AMNON: You're becoming a joke. You run around with him, holding hands in public.

YOSEFA: And if we stayed home, you'd say he was ashamed to be seen with me.

AMNON: Everybody knows he's married.

YOSEFA: *(ironically)* Dreadful. It has never happened before. A married man exploits an innocent girl and when his wife hears of it - What a scandal!

AMNON: Trust him, he's figured that out too. He may even have told her. Because the bottom line, and he'll demonstrate that, is a credit balance - and she'll happily pay the price.

YOSEFA: This is getting disgusting.

AMNON: Does he love you?

YOSEFA: Why don't you ask him?

AMNON: Is he going to leave his wife and move in with you?

YOSEFA: Why, did you leave Nechama when you had that thing going with Rachel?

AMNON: That was before we got married.

YOSEFA: Aha. And from the moment you put the ring on her finger you get a hard-on only for her. Human beings are not monogamous.

AMNON: He's a young man.

YOSEFA: And I'm an ageing spinster Lord, are you screwed up, are you square! As far as you're concerned, it's only the man who can be older than the woman, never mind by how much - ten, twenty years, that's fine. Like you and Nechama for example.

AMNON: No, no, I didn't mean... *(Sees that she's really hurt, tries to take his foot out of his mouth.)*

YOSEFA: What I have with Noam....oh, never mind, you wouldn't understand anyway.

AMNON: I'm sorry, Sefi...*(Grabs the vase of flowers and makes doggy noises.)* All over. Friends?

YOSEFA: Idiot! Friends. *(She gets out the fixings for a joint.)* I'm rolling. You want a drink? *(AMNON laughs.)* Now what?

AMNON: Nothing. I just remembered how you and Rami used to get stoned.

YOSEFA: Here, right here. After grandma went to bed.

AMNON: Have you seen him?

YOSEFA: What for? Actually, he called right after the funeral.

AMNON: No regrets?

YOSEFA: I never regret anything. If he'd really loved me, he'd have got something going, and come after me, and instead... *(Footsteps in*

79

the yard. YOSEFA jumps for the door.)

AMNON: You can smell him coming, huh?

YOSEFA: And is there no-one to smell you? *(She opens the yard door before NOAM has time to knock. He can't see AMNON, who's stayed where he was. NOAM has a take-away bag in one hand, a bottle of wine in the other and an envelope of photos between his teeth which YOSEFA removes.)*

NOAM: Our trip to Mount. Hermon. *(Holds out the take-away and wine.)* Put this in the oven and this in the freezer, and till that heats up and this chills, we'll have time...*(Grabs YOSEFA'S arse.)* Ah, I'm crazy about your arse...crazy, crazy, crazy. *(She giggles, AMNON clears his throat, NOAM sees him. Embarrassed he lets YOSEFA go.)*

AMNON: Hello.

NOAM: Hello Amnon.

YOSEFA: *(to NOAM)* We've decided you'll administer the estate.

NOAM: What? *(to AMNON)* Listen, you don't have to. I'd be a liar if I said I don't want to. I do - a lot, but...

AMNON: It's fine.

YOSEFA: *(to NOAM)* See?

NOAM: You don't understand. The administration of an estate is a long-term commitment, and if Amnon doesn't trust me, it's not going to work.

YOSEFA: Don't worry, you'll get to be real buddies yet. He didn't like Rami at first, right?

NOAM: I'll put in a clause that, if for any reason whatever you...

AMNON: No need to, it's fine.

YOSEFA: Noam, enough. Before I forget. There's another buyer.

NOAM: Do you want me to revoke the papers I've drawn up for the Roths?

AMNON: Precisely.

YOSEFA: You can keep the same contract, just change Roth for Karo.

NOAM: Karo? If there was one person in the whole of Jerusalem that Mrs Amsalem...

NOAM *and* YOSEFA: absolutely loathed, it was Simon Karo.

80

AMNON: Is there a clause to that effect in the will?

YOSEFA: I'm not granny - and it's not Simon but Michael. Obviously mother is not to know.

NOAM: That means that... that you're leaving soon?

YOSEFA: It means that - something like that, yes, but you can come to visit in October.

AMNON: *(ironically)* Am I supposed to bring him with me?

YOSEFA: We can work it out. October is a long month, a beautiful month. *(The phone rings.)* Yosefa Amsalem...Yes, this is the number...Speaking...Yes, I'm writing...

AMNON: *(to NOAM)* Don't use the old contract. Draft a new one. New amounts, different payment schedules. Leave the name open. Come to my office tomorrow.

YOSEFA: *(writing, her expression changes)* How much?...Are you sure?...Yes. Thank you very much. *(Replaces receiver and sits.)*

AMNON: What happened?

YOSEFA: Nothing, it'll work out. It's just a matter of money.

AMNON: If you don't want to say, don't say, but don't -

YOSEFA: I...I'm keeping quiet. It's alright, don't worry. Go home.

AMNON: I'll come over this evening.

YOSEFA: Call first.

AMNON: *(at the front door to NOAM who has gone with him)* Tomorrow at ten, in my office. *(Exits.)*

YOSEFA: You too.

NOAM: What happened?

YOSEFA: Nothing.

NOAM: Would you like to specify?

YOSEFA: Nothing to specify.

NOAM: Amnon put me down, right?

YOSEFA: Yes, but that has nothing to do with it. I want to be alone.

NOAM: I want to know what happened...Yosefa, it doesn't matter what - I'll understand.

YOSEFA: Go away.

NOAM: Was it something I did?

YOSEFA: Don't be silly.

NOAM: You said no matter what happens, we'll tell the truth. No games. If you don't want to see me any more, say so.

YOSEFA: *(kisses him)* You're a honey. No. *(Opens the yard door.)* Go on.

NOAM: I'm not budging 'till you say.

YOSEFA: O.K., O.K. I have to have an abortion.

NOAM: Why?

YOSEFA: Oh for heaven's sake Noam. Three guesses. *(Short silence.)*. I'm pregnant.

NOAM: What? And you don't want it? Haven't you ever wanted a child?

YOSEFA: What is it with you?

NOAM: I know I'm not supposed to say this, but you're not a twenty year old any more. If you want a child, then...

YOSEFA: You're right. If I took an idiot like you into my bed, then I deserve...

NOAM: *(raising his voice)* Why am I an idiot? Maybe I'm not the most sophisticated or sensitive guy on the block, and I haven't been half-way round the world, but...*(Realises that's not the way.)* Sorry...I apologise. *(He reaches out and she responds.)* I'm sorry...All that I wanted to say is that...never mind.

YOSEFA: Go ahead. Say it, then go.

NOAM: Look, that... foetus has a father, right?

YOSEFA: I don't believe this.

NOAM: Discuss it with him...At least tell him.

YOSEFA: Fine. I'm telling him.

NOAM: *(silence)* It can't be.

YOSEFA: Why? Did you have a vasectomy?

NOAM: No, but I... How can that be? How much time have we been... together?

YOSEFA: Six weeks. The first time we were "together" I had my period, and I asked you if it bothered you. Remember? *(NOAM nods.)* I was due two weeks ago. I waited and waited, till I got fed up and went to find out why.

NOAM: When did you find out?

YOSEFA: Just now. That was the telephone call.

NOAM: Tell me what to do, and I'll do it.

YOSEFA: Nothing.

NOAM: No way.*(Remembers suddenly)* I have a friend, a doctor- he...

YOSEFA: He did your wife's last abortion? No thank you. I'm set up fairly O.K. for doctors. *(Goes to the telephone, checks for the number on the wall, dials and waits.)*

NOAM: I'll come with you. *(YOSEFA shakes her head.)* I want to...

YOSEFA: No! *(Into the receiver.)* Hello. Could I talk to Dr. Rami Levy please?

NOAM: Why him? What do you need him for?

YOSEFA: *(waves at him to shut up)* Um, Rami, it's Yosefa. No, nothing happened, that's to say, I need an abortion. Rami, you still there?...Yes, second month. No, I don't want to talk about it...No, not at the hospital. What do you recommend? The only condition is that it's no-one who studied with us, or taught us...Male or female? *(Thinks.)* A woman...Tomorrow if possible because I'm leaving next week...I'll wait.

NOAM: I'll pay for it...

YOSEFA: *(puts her hand over the mouthpiece)* A minute ago you were doing figure eights to get me to keep this baby, for my benefit, for my sake... *(Back to phone.)* Yes, alright...No...because..give me the number...Yes. *(She writes on the wall.)* No, I don't want you to come with me. I'll take a cab....Thank you...Yes, I'm sure. *(Hangs up.)*

NOAM: Yosefa..

YOSEFA: I'd like to be alone.

NOAM: Aren't you on the pill?

YOSEFA: And you? Do me a favour, and leave me alone, please. Tomorrow evening I'll have to spread my legs, they'll dig around my insides with their instruments, just the thought of it...*(NOAM hugs her)*

SCENE FOUR

The next evening. The room is dark. Without any warning YOSEFA bursts in through the front door, leaving it open. She tosses her purse, turns on the light, goes to the phone, dials, waits, hangs up.

83

Dials again, waits and again hangs up. Takes out the whisky bottle, pours a hefty slug, takes a swallow that makes her shudder. Dials again. RAMI appears in the doorway, upset. As she dials, he comes up behind her very quietly.

RAMI: Have you gone completely crazy? What did you think you were doing? If she'd called the police before she called me, you'd be sitting in jail right now.

YOSEFA: What does she have to complain about, that stupid cow? Lies me down, opens my legs, puts on soothing music, syringe in hand, she chirps in my ear, "Don't worry darling, five minutes it'll all be out..."

RAMI: And so you trashed her office. She had it coming, she really had it coming.

YOSEFA: What's it to you? Why are you butting in? And what exactly are you doing here?

RAMI: You called me. You involved me. You didn't have to.

YOSEFA: I'll pay for the damage, O.K.?

RAMI: I said you would, but you'll have to call her and apologise.

YOSEFA: Oh sure. I hope I really took that place apart.

RAMI: You did - Satisfied? So pick up the phone and -

YOSEFA: I feel sick.

RAMI: *(takes the glass from her hand and sniffs)* Of course, if you will drink whisky on an empty stomach...some milk.

YOSEFA: Rami, please don't start ordering me around.

RAMI: Can I make myself some coffee?

YOSEFA: Whatever you want. You know what? - I'll have some milk. *(RAMI starts for the kitchen.)* No, I'll have coffee too.

RAMI: *(goes back to making coffee)* Two spoons?

YOSEFA: Three. Did you tell... your wife that...?

RAMI: Yes. *(Looks around.)* Nothing's changed here.

YOSEFA: It's changed, if you look at details. But that never was your scene.

RAMI: If I could find the coffee and the sugar then...*(Decides to skip it.)* You know, I've imagined meeting you a million times.

YOSEFA: But this situation you'd never imagine.

RAMI: The truth? No.

YOSEFA: I've managed to surprise you this time. *(RAMI nods.)*
Myself as well. What shall I do?

RAMI: Are you really asking?

YOSEFA: Don't know...yes.

RAMI: Don't you want the child?

YOSEFA: I...it's not that simple. For instance, right now I'm supposed
to be in Kutchabamba. *(It's obvious from the look on RAMI's face
that he doesn't know what she's talking about.)* Bolivia, to expand a
field clinic we set up a few years ago to bring local health-workers
back to New York and then off somewhere new. I can't leave my
pregnancy here or in New York and come and visit it every now and
then. And the child? - What do I do with a child?

RAMI: What everybody does. Bring it up. Look, take a few days to
calm down...think. If you want, we'll talk. You're not at the stage
where you have to decide right away.

YOSEFA: Are you in a hurry?

RAMI: No, that is, I thought I'd go home before going back to the
ward for rounds.

YOSEFA: A shower, change of clothes, something to eat. You're ready
to sacrifice all that for me?

RAMI: Even dinner. I'll make do with a sandwich from the snack bar,
how's that?

YOSEFA: Above and beyond.

RAMI: The coffee. *(Exits.)*

YOSEFA: The coffee, yes.

RAMI: *(offstage)* Is this your first pregnancy?

YOSEFA: Are you asking?

RAMI: Look, a few years have gone by since...so why...? *(Silence.)*
You don't know who the father is?

YOSEFA: That'd be just like me, right?

RAMI: *(coming back with the coffee)* My mistake. I take it all back.
Rape?

YOSEFA: *(roars with laughter shaking her head)* And the next

85

question has to be - Incest?

RAMI: You're forgetting I know Amnon. He wouldn't dare even if he were dying to. Can I say it all, no holds? *(YOSEFA nods.)* You were dying for a child.

YOSEFA: We were.

RAMI: O.K., we were.

YOSEFA: We tried. We tried for four years.

RAMI: And since then, have you been using contraceptives?

YOSEFA: Sometimes...condoms. There's A.I.D.S. after all and I can't send everyone for testing before.

RAMI: You've been trying to get pregnant for twelve or thirteen years...

YOSEFA: I stopped trying. I was sure I couldn't get pregnant.

RAMI: You just weren't careful.

YOSEFA: In Peru the Indians believe a woman can't get pregnant 'till the man puts a roof over her head.

RAMI: Maybe Allegra was descended from the Indians. How else do you account for the fact that she left the house to you?

YOSEFA: Is it common knowledge already?

RAMI: Almost.

YOSEFA: I'm selling it.

RAMI: Sure. You're a big girl, you know what you want and what you're doing. You could have a great place here, a child...

YOSEFA: My dreams look a bit different.

RAMI: *(ironically)* A lot grander. And they didn't include a child.

YOSEFA: Why are you so hot for me to have this kid?

RAMI: I'm not hot for anything. If you really didn't want this baby, you'd have opened your legs and let the doctor take it out, never mind what she says or thinks or whatever...O.K...yes, I want you to have this baby. And don't ask me why, because I don't know. *(They speak almost simultaneously.)*

YOSEFA: I'll tell you then. You want to see me house-bound. With or without you, the main thing is to fade into the woodwork. You always did try to clip my wings, that were so much bigger than yours. Every time I made it, you punished me. And the more I succeeded, the

86

greater the punishment...and of course,worst of all was when I got the scholarship and you didn't.

RAMI: I remember it a bit differently, but... hold it, hold it...I'm doing it again, apologising for crimes I never committed. That's it. I'm ready to help you, I want to help you. I'll be happy to do whatever you ask, but I won't sign up for Rami-bashing anymore. *(Turns to leave.)*

YOSEFA: What are you talking about?

RAMI: Oh come on!

YOSEFA: Are you glad you didn't marry me?

RAMI: Yes *(Backs up and only then turns to her, speaks jokingly.)* Don't misunderstand me. All you need to do is whistle, and I'll hop happily into bed with you. Oy, why did I have to say that? Oh well, alright. As if you didn't know anyway.

YOSEFA: And that despite the fact you're living on cloud nine with "the blonde kugel"? You called her that...

RAMI: I still do, sometimes. Were you offended? How could I after being with you?

YOSEFA: You were alone and she spread her legs.

RAMI: It's banal I know, but not to that extent.

YOSEFA: So.

RAMI: She said I have a beautiful prick.

YOSEFA: What?

RAMI: That's what she said. And nobody ever said that to me, ever.

YOSEFA: And that's why you married her?

RAMI: There were other reasons, but that makes the best story.

YOSEFA: And she didn't want you to go in for psychiatry. Too many years of being a resident.

RAMI: No darlin', they just turned me down. We can't all be geniuses like you. As it happens, orthopaedics really suits me better. Even your Dad said I ought to do something with my hands - metalworking, carpentry so it's in the general vicinity isn't it? A failure, but respectable. *(YOSEFA laughs, RAMI backs up to the front door.)* I'm glad I've made you laugh. Don't sell the house. Don't have an abortion. Don't leave us alone in the dark. Forget what I said. Do what you want. See you.

YOSEFA: I don't think so.

RAMI: What?

YOSEFA: That we'll meet again...

RAMI: Too bad.

YOSEFA: *(RAMI is right by the door)* Rami...Can you fix me up with another doctor?

RAMI: If you're sure that's what you really want.

YOSEFA: No. But get me a doctor.

RAMI: *(the doorbell rings)* Who is it?

YOSEFA: I've no idea.

ELISHEVA: *(ringing repeatedly)* Yosefa!

YOSEFA: It's mother, my brother and sister-in-law. No sweat...Through here. *(Steers him to the yard door.)*

AMNON: *(from the yard)* Yosefa.

YOSEFA: *(points him to bedroom area instead)* It'll take a second.

RAMI: Ten minutes - tops. *(Exits.)*

ELISHEVA: *(enters the same moment)* Why didn't you open the door? *(Walks over to the yard door and lets in AMNON and NECHAMA who are carrying folded cartons.)*

YOSEFA: I was in the bathroom. If you'd waited a minute before whipping out your key, maybe I wouldn't feel as though I was living on a pedestrian crossing. It's a good thing this house only has two entrances. You know what? Give me the key.

ELISHEVA: Allegra gave it to me, when Daddy and I got married.

YOSEFA: And as her legal heir, I want it back.

ELISHEVA: This key has been on my key-ring for forty six years. *(As she begins to detach the keys, behind her back AMNON signals to YOSEFA something like "What are you doing?")*

YOSEFA: Alright, alright. Keep it.

ELISHEVA: *(replaces key)* As far as I'm concerned there's no problem, after all...

YOSEFA: Just don't use it when I'm home.

AMNON: *(wanting to stop the discussion, turns to ELISHEVA)* Where do you want to start?

ELISHEVA: *(to YOSEFA)* I just want you to know...

AMNON: Mom, if you want us to go through everything this evening... *(ELISHEVA goes towards the bedroom area.)*

YOSEFA: *(blocks the way)* Excuse me, I can't, I mean you can't...Not today, not while I'm here. I don't want to watch you pawing through granny's things after I leave. *(She sits.)*

ELISHEVA: There's a limit to everything. I gave up my bridge game, Amnon and Nechama took a babysitter because only tonight suited you.

YOSEFA: I'm really sorry, but...*(Gets nauseous.)*

NECHAMA: Aren't you well?

AMNON: Have you been drinking?

YOSEFA: I'm fine.

ELISHEVA: You probably have an ulcer.

YOSEFA: Why an ulcer?

ELISHEVA: It started the same way with me. Go for a test, you'll see.

NECHAMA: Are you pregnant?

AMNON: Oh, come on!

ELISHEVA: Impossible.

YOSEFA: Yes.

ELISHEVA: Are you serious?

YOSEFA: Yes.

ELISHEVA: How did it happen?

YOSEFA: Like for most women, by fucking.

ELISHEVA: Why do you always have to be so crude?

YOSEFA: *(to herself)* What am I to do?

NECHAMA: Get married.

AMNON: Nechama.

NECHAMA: That is...what I meant to say was...

ELISHEVA: *(moves closer to YOSEFA)* That's all you needed... That's why you're so edgy. *(To NECHAMA.)* We'll take her to your gynaecologist.

NECHAMA: Yes.

ELISHEVA: He's a fine doctor.

NECHAMA: Yes.

ELISHEVA: It's not pleasant, but it's not that terrible either. If we have no alternative then, it's not such a catastrophe.

NECHAMA: I really had no alternative. *(To YOSEFA)* You'll come to us...afterwards. You have to rest a couple of days.

ELISHEVA: Rest? At your place? You know, sometimes I absolutely don't understand you. How can anybody rest with the two little ones running all over the place, and the parrot screeching its head off? *(To YOSEFA)* You'll come to me, that's what. I promise not to say one word to annoy you. I'll take a few days off. We'll get some videos, Chinese take-away. We'll have a great time.

AMNON: Mother!

YOSEFA: Thank you, really thank you. Maybe, instead of fixing me up with an abortion and quarrelling about who'll take care of me afterwards, you'll ask me what I want?

ELISHEVA: What do you want? *(Silence.)* Surely you're not going to go ahead with it now?

YOSEFA: Maybe...maybe I want to have someone to fight with in another twenty years or so.

ELISHEVA: By yourself? Are you thinking of bringing up a child by yourself?

YOSEFA: Millions of women do it all over the world. Actually most women bring up their kids alone, even the married ones. Isn't that so, Nechama?

NECHAMA: It's not the same. You can't compare...A family is different.

AMNON: Nechama.

YOSEFA: Interesting. That's exactly what I thought. A tight, supportive family, especially when the going gets tough.

NECHAMA: You don't understand. I know a woman like that, a single parent. Everybody's helping her, the family, friends, and even so, she barely gets by.

YOSEFA: Actually, I do understand. And I promise you that if I decide to give birth, I won't ask anybody for help.

ELISHEVA: Do you mean to tell me that you'll give up everything, all you've accomplished, just so you -

YOSEFA: Nonni, tell her to stop. *(YOSEFA kicks away the cartons and flees to the bedroom area. The conversation continues loudly enough for YOSEFA to partly hear.)*

NECHAMA: Maybe she has someone and she's not telling? Yosefa likes to play those sort of games sometimes, to see what people will say.

AMNON: Nechama, for heaven's sake!

NECHAMA: Maybe she has someone in Bolivia. A gentile...

AMNON: Where did that come from? Come on! Has she lived like a nun since she got here?

ELISHEVA: It can't be...Not him...

NECHAMA: Heaven forbid. He's married, he has a child.

AMNON: Nechama.

NECHAMA: Amnon. She's shovelling dirt over all of us, on the whole family. Why do we deserve this? Why? Why do our children deserve it? What will you tell your children when they ask you? How will you look them in the face?

ELISHEVA: She's right.

AMNON: *(to ELISHEVA)* And didn't Miss She's Right do exactly the same? Ran wild. The eldest daughter, and got married to a non-believer. *(To NECHAMA.)* Your father cut you off. Your mother said it was a blot on the whole family.

NECHAMA: No, it's not the same. They stifled me. I wanted to live my life, that's all.

AMNON: And Yosefa wants to live her life.

ELISHEVA: Who's stopping her? But this concerns the whole family.

AMNON: That's exactly what grandma said to you when you insisted on leaving this house.

NECHAMA: How can you even compare? What's she's doing is wanton, irresponsible. It really is a blot on the whole family.

AMNON: And a blot is worse than murder? When you had to have an abortion, you said it was murder?

NECHAMA: Amnon!

ELISHEVA: *(draws closer to NECHAMA, scolding AMNON)* Just one minute. Do you want her to have this child?

AMNON: No. But if that's what she wants, then...she's my sister, I love her. I want things to be good for her.

ELISHEVA: And I don't love my own daughter?

AMNON: I didn't say that.

ELISHEVA: *(ironically)* But to you she's really important, more important than me, Nechama and your children, separately and together?

AMNON: No. Important, period. Without making comparisons.

ELISHEVA: How does she always manage to wind you around her little finger?

AMNON: *(ironically)* What can I do?

ELISHEVA: And if she has this bastard, it'll be good for her?

AMNON: He won't be a bastard. Even according to Jewish Law he's legal.

ELISHEVA: Illegitimate. What difference does it make? She's destroying us, dragging us down into the sewer. Your father, God rest his soul, knew when to decamp. How many times did he tell me "Elisheva my love, you have to prune fruit trees, or you'll get mouldy fruit." How right he was. I didn't want to listen. I wanted you to be free, to do what you wanted to do. Not like me, standing under the wedding canopy at sixteen. Do you really think that I didn't want to study, to travel? I won't let her. I simply won't let her. *(Starts for bedroom.)*

AMNON: *(bringing her back)* Mother, calm down. Sit quietly and calm down. What's going on in our heads is going on in hers too. How can she bring up a child? In a South American shack, or by remote control to New York? She's leaving in a few days.

ELISHEVA: What did she have to come for anyway? When Dad died she was too busy. When you got married, she sent a cable - she couldn't make it. Only Allegra, everything because of Allegra.

AMNON: Did grandma get her pregnant? Mom. *(Comes closer to her.)* If she wants a baby, it's her last chance.

ELISHEVA: *(pushes him away)* I don't want to hear talk like that. And anyway, she never wanted children. That hurt me a lot, but she never spoke of a child. She was with Rami for eight years. He loves children. Now that I think of it, maybe that's why he left her.

AMNON: *(ironically)* Maybe.

ELISHEVA: For sure. He got married a year later, they had a son and now he's got three.

AMNON: Is that what Rami told you?

ELISHEVA: I don't even talk to him. He's brought us nothing but disgrace.

NECHAMA: If Yosefa wants the baby, I'll help her. We'll help her.

ELISHEVA: *(to AMNON)* Has she gone mad? Have you all gone mad?

AMNON: Mom,.I'm going to make coffee. Anybody want some?

NECHAMA: I'll do it. *(Crosses to kitchen.)*

AMNON: *(to ELISHEVA)* Calm down, she'll have the abortion.

ELISHEVA: How can you be so sure?

NECHAMA: Amnon really does know her better than any of us.

AMNON: Yosefa always has her toes on the red line, but she doesn't ever cross it. *(A knock at the yard door. NECHAMA, being closest, opens it. NOAM stands there with a bunch of flowers.)*

NOAM: Hi. *(Surprised by the family presence.)* Um, I didn't know you were here...Someone brought me flowers and Yosefa likes flowers.

ELISHEVA: Filth! *(Hits NOAM with the flowers he brought.)* Get...out! And don't show your face again.

AMNON: Mother!

YOSEFA: *(entering)* That'll do. I heard everything.

AMNON: *(to ELISHEVA)* Come on.

ELISHEVA: *(starts walking towards front door, then stops)* Remember what Allegra used to say: "Take a dog to bed and you get up with fleas."

YOSEFA: Get her out of here before I go crazy. *(AMNON starts to lead ELISHEVA out, NECHAMA in their wake.)* And don't leave me with the cartons. *(AMNON comes to get them.)*

ELISHEVA: Why, are we your errand crew? *(To AMNON.)* Leave it. She tells us to bring them - we bring. She tells us to take them away - we take.

AMNON: *(gets ELISHEVA and NECHAMA out)* I'll come over in the morning.

ELISHEVA: *(pushes back into the room)* One day a bluefly's son will inherit Amsalem House. *(They leave.)*

NOAM: Did you tell them? *(YOSEFA nods.)* Sit down. You're like a ghost. Was it dreadful?

YOSEFA: It didn't happen.

NOAM: You're not pregnant.

YOSEFA: I am.

NOAM: So why...? What do you intend to do?

YOSEFA: I still don't know.

NOAM: You can't ignore it.

YOSEFA: I'm not ignoring it. I...

NOAM: In the end it'll be too late.

YOSEFA: So I'll have it.

NOAM: Be serious.

YOSEFA: I am.

NOAM: And what about me?

YOSEFA: What about you?

NOAM: I can't...I can't have a child.

YOSEFA: Noam, I've been hassled enough for one night.

NOAM: You can't do something like that on your own.

YOSEFA: Stop it.

NOAM: I don't agree.

YOSEFA: I haven't asked you to agree.

NOAM: But...

YOSEFA: I need to be by myself. I need to think.

NOAM: A child is a mutual responsibility.

YOSEFA: You're released from it, alright?

NOAM: No way.

YOSEFA: There is. I'm releasing you. You know what, you draft a document, that you have no obligations towards me or to the...

NOAM: No.

YOSEFA: What else do you want? In another week I'll be gone. If you don't want to, you'll never hear from me again.

NOAM: What have I done to deserve this? I love you, I want you, but not a child. We can't have a child.

YOSEFA: Let's say you donated the sperm. Does that suit?

NOAM: No. I've never done that,.on principle. Even when I was a student and didn't have a cent to my name. Sefi, emotionally, I couldn't bear the thought of my child wandering somewhere in the world. I couldn't. Just couldn't.

YOSEFA: And I, emotionally, can't go through with an abortion.

NOAM: Yosefa, think logically. You have a fascinating job, research, people who admire you. Do you want to give it all up?

YOSEFA: For a child? It could be...I don't know. I still haven't decided.

NOAM: And what am I supposed to do meanwhile?

YOSEFA: Nothing. There's nothing you can do. You'll have to live with whatever I decide.

NOAM: What made you choose me exactly?

YOSEFA: I didn't.

NOAM: I don't believe you.

YOSEFA: Don't believe me.

NOAM: No, I won't let you.

YOSEFA: What will you do? Hit me? Kill me?

NOAM: If Allegra was alive you wouldn't dare.

YOSEFA: You think you knew Allegra? You imagine that you know what went on underneath that black scarf of hers, behind the smile, or the stories? I've been reading the will she dictated to you for two months and I still can't figure out what she was getting at. What did she really mean "...and I leave the house to Yosefa, the only Amsalem still remaining, to her and her descendants"? Maybe she haunted you so that you could impregnate me. Did you think of that?

NOAM: On purpose, you did it on purpose. You stopped taking the pill, right? You asked about my parents, my sister, my daughter. You wanted to know whether my genes were good enough for you. You're worse than a whore.

YOSEFA: Oho! Have you come a long way. You know, it's not even funny how quickly love can become a burden. *(RAMI enters from*

95

*bedroom area and crosses towards the door. **NOAM** is thunderstruck, **YOSEFA** on the verge of laughter.)*

RAMI: Ten minutes were over long ago. I got dehydrated.

YOSEFA: Let me introduce you - Doctor Rami Levy, attorney - Noam Orgad. And if you'll excuse me, I need a short break. *(She exits to bedroom area. The two men look at each other without a word. **NOAM** goes to the yard door, **RAMI** to the front door.)*

CURTAIN

ACT TWO, SCENE ONE.

*Late morning, May - some six weeks after the previous scene. There have been some changes to the room, the most significant of which is a typewriter. **YOSEFA** is typing. **AMNON** is pacing up and down.*

YOSEFA: Stop pacing. It's driving me crazy.

AMNON: If you hadn't insisted on Noam managing the estate, this wouldn't have happened.

YOSEFA: Is it Noam's fault that you decided to go with Nachmias?

AMNON: That clerk of Noam's. It's his responsibility.

YOSEFA: And how was Noam's clerk supposed to know that Nachmias was fronting for Karo? You've complicated everything.

AMNON: What kind of a lawyer lets his office leak confidential information?

YOSEFA: Alright ...What do we do now?

AMNON: I don't know. *(Silence, then there's a furious ringing and loud knocking at the front door.)* That's mother.

YOSEFA: *(shouts)* Just a minute! *(Whispers to **AMNON** as she steers him to the yard door.)* Go, I'll think of something.

AMNON: I'm not going to leave you here with all of this. *(More ringing and knocking.)*

YOSEFA: Are we going to get it? *(Exits to open the door, off.)* What's the matter with you?

ELISHEVA: *(off)* Pay the cab.

YOSEFA: *(off)* What?

ELISHEVA: *(enters)* Pay the cab-driver. I forgot my purse.

YOSEFA: *(off)* O.K., fine. *(Looks for her purse, finds it and exits.)*
ELISHEVA: *(sits down to rest a minute. Looking up, she sees AMNON and is momentarily surprised)* Aha. I knew I'd find you here. How did you get here so fast?
AMNON: By car.
ELISHEVA: Don't get smart with me. I won't allow it. I will just not allow it. How low can a person get?
AMNON: Mom, you don't understand.
ELISHEVA: I understand very well. You tried to trick me.
AMNON: No-one tried to trick you.
ELISHEVA: No. You just didn't tell me. *(Sarcastically.)* I had to hear it from Mister Administrator, Noam's clerk. *(Imitates the clerk's voice.)* "What do you mean, Roth? He backed out long ago - out of the picture - they're selling to Nachmias. Do you mean you didn't know Mrs Elisheva?" What do you think? That I don't know who Nachmias is? That I can't add two and two? How can you sell Amsalem House to Simon Karo? How can you?
YOSEFA: Simon's been in a retirement home for ages.
ELISHEVA: Michael. Is that any better? You thought I wouldn't find out.
AMNON: We didn't know. I'm not sure yet that Nachmias is buying the house for Michael.
ELISHEVA: Amnon, look at me. How could you? Your father is probably spinning in his grave. Even Allegra doesn't deserve this. *(To YOSEFA.)* I don't understand. What happened? Why? Did Karo offer a few cents more? I'll make up the difference, alright?
AMNON: It's not Karo, but Nachmias and it's not a few cents.
ELISHEVA: Don't tell me you didn't know who was behind Nachmias, and if you didn't, then you're a fool. I always said that your friendship with Michael would lead to no good.
YOSEFA: You always said that Michael was a darling.
ELISHEVA: He's a Karo!
YOSEFA: That's not exactly a crime.
ELISHEVA: Don't try to be funny. Simon was with us in the resistance...

AMNON: We know the story - both sides of it.

ELISHEVA: There aren't two sides. He sold out the best we had. Your own father sat in jail for months because of him. And he...it paid him - Oh boy, did it pay him. How do you suppose they managed so very nicely? Simon snitched to the British. And you go and sell him the house. I won't let you, I absolutely will not let you.

AMNON: That was nearly fifty years ago.

ELISHEVA: There's no forgetting that. I won't let you.

YOSEFA: Mom, you're getting upset for nothing. We haven't signed anything yet. We're negotiating, and we're not selling.

ELISHEVA: Stop it.

YOSEFA: Honest, we've decided not to sell.

ELISHEVA: I don't want to hear about it.

YOSEFA: Look, ask Amnon. We talked about it last night. Noam also says it's not a good time to sell.

ELISHEVA: That's enough. I've heard enough lies for one day. Go and sign with Roth. And that's it.

YOSEFA: But they don't want to any more.

ELISHEVA: I don't care. You will not sell to Nachmias. *(To AMNON)* Please get me a glass of water. *(AMNON exits to fetch it and YOSEFA shows signs of nausea.)* You're having such a hard time with this...this pregnancy, and in the end, I don't understand why it's so hard for you to decide.

YOSEFA: When you say decide you mean an abortion. *(AMNON comes in with the water.)*

ELISHEVA: What I mean is that you can't put it off indefinitely.

AMNON: Stop it.

ELISHEVA: *(to YOSEFA)* And your health...if you do it too late, you'll endanger your health.

YOSEFA: "Professor Elisheva Amsalem" if the foetus is abnormal they do it even in the fifth and sixth month.

ELISHEVA: That's true.

AMNON: After all, mom, we agreed that she'd decide once the answer came from New York.

YOSEFA: There aren't that many alternatives. Without twenty-four hour a day help, I won't be able to work.

ELISHEVA: And they don't want to give it to you.

YOSEFA: They haven't answered yet.

ELISHEVA: That's no way for them to act. You've worked like a dog for them for ten years, and when you tell them you're pregnant, they... the World Health Organisation - it's a disgrace.

AMNON: Don't worry, either way, it'll work out.

ELISHEVA: The question is - when? Pretty soon she'll start showing.

YOSEFA: I'm only in the third month.

ELISHEVA: The fourth.

YOSEFA: You know the exact date of fertilisation?

ELISHEVA: *(dismisses what she says with a wave)* I started showing in the second month. It happens suddenly - You wake up one morning and there's the tummy. And then...

YOSEFA: A scandal. Even worse than selling the house to Karo. *(The phone rings. YOSEFA answers.)* Yosefa Amsalem, good morning. Yes, yes, Mr Cohen. No, Mr Cohen you can't talk to granny because...because she died. You were at the funeral... Yes, people do forget. Yes, it's very hard without her. Thank you so much.

ELISHEVA: I'll die of pure shame if you start running around with a big belly. What'll happen if those people over there in New York don't give you what you want?

YOSEFA: I don't know. I'll find something else. I'll have an abortion. I haven't decided yet.

ELISHEVA: Think, decide. *(To AMNON.)* One never knows with you. *(Moves towards front door.)*

AMNON: Where are you going?

ELISHEVA: Back to work. I left a library full of people to come here.

YOSEFA: Amnon will take you.

ELISHEVA: You and Amnon still have some talking to do. I'll catch a cab. *(Leaves.)*

YOSEFA: How did Dad manage to live with her for so many years?

AMNON: Why did you have to tell her "We're not selling to Karo"?

YOSEFA: You were standing there like a golem. What did you want me to do? Don't worry, it'll work out.

AMNON: How?

YOSEFA: Why should we sell to Karo particularly?

AMNON: Because I say so.

YOSEFA: And I say, maybe we won't sell at all. What can happen? We'll keep the house for ourselves.

AMNON: Yosefa!

YOSEFA: I just thought that...

AMNON: Don't even think about it.

YOSEFA: Alright, alright. Lighten up. You'll have to find somebody else to act for Karo.

AMNON: Yes, and that's the problem. *(Someone rings and knocks at the front door. YOSEFA hurries to answer.)* What does she want now?

YOSEFA: She doesn't have money for a cab, she forgot her purse. *(Grabs her purse and runs out.)*

AMNON: *(dials)* Michael Karo please. No, it's personal. Please tell him that Amnon called. He knows which Amnon. It's urgent, very urgent. Yes.

SCENE TWO

A morning in June, a month after the previous scene. ELISHEVA and NECHAMA are dragging a wooden chest to centre. Until now it has been in a corner of the stage. NECHAMA is doing the work, with ELISHEVA trailing behind her.

ELISHEVA: It's so stuffy in here. *(Sits as NECHAMA opens the chest.)* We should have hired someone to get rid of all this junk, pack the books and that'd be that. Today, with door to door service....

NECHAMA: Yosefa wants to go over everything herself.

ELISHEVA: And who does the dirty work in the end? You and I. *(ELISHEVA gives the orders while NECHAMA does the work.)*

NECHAMA: *(taking a wedding dress out of the chest)* We'd have missed Allegra's wedding dress.

(NOAM knocks at the door and comes in with an envelope.)

NOAM: Is somebody getting married Nechama?

100

NECHAMA: You're not invited.

NOAM: That's it. Moving day?

ELISHEVA: *(as if it's choking her to talk)* It's being sent.

NOAM: What a coincidence! *(Waves the fat, sealed envelope.)* The mailman brought a registered letter to the office. I saw the envelope and decided to be the messenger.

ELISHEVA: Mazel Tov.

NOAM: Where's Yosefa?

NECHAMA: She ran to the store for a few things.

NOAM: I asked her not to go out so much, you can already see...

ELISHEVA: So did I.

NECHAMA: You can't see it unless you know.

ELISHEVA: That's what you think.

NECHAMA: She can't sit around the house all day. *(ELISHEVA gives her a look.)*. You were the one that said it was stuffy.

ELISHEVA: Oh well, the main thing is that things have worked out. At least she's leaving. Is the sales contract signed?

NOAM: No. Yosefa didn't want to commit to a definite date to vacate and without that...

ELISHEVA: Today. You'll make her sign today.

NOAM: Alright. *(Takes a book from the pile.)* What does she need all this stuff for? *(YOSEFA comes in through the open yard door with a bag of groceries in one hand and a bunch of wild flowers in the other. She's a little rounded, but the pregnancy isn't really showing yet. Only her continual light touches to breast and belly give away her condition.)*

YOSEFA: That's what I keep asking myself the whole time. I live out of boxes and suitcases, in rented apartments or shacks. I've never had a home in my whole life, and I'll never have one.

ELISHEVA: The letter arrived.

(NOAM leaps for the letter and holds it out to her, realises her hands are full, takes the things from her, and YOSEFA grabs the letter and kisses it)

YOSEFA: Have I been waiting for you. *(Tears open the envelope.)* I told you so, all you need is patience - the first to take a step - loses.

101

(Runs her eyes over the letter.) What's this? What are they doing?

ELISHEVA: What's wrong?

YOSEFA: *(continues reading)* They've gone mad, this isn't happening... *(Goes to the phone, dials.)*

NOAM: Who are you calling?

YOSEFA: New York.

NOAM: It's night. It's night in New York now.

YOSEFA: So it is. *(Replaces the receiver.)* I don't understand this. After all, they agreed I'd go back into the field with live-in help and a fifty percent airfare discount. All they had to do was make it official, and now - do you see? *(She shows the paper to ELISHEVA.)* My contract says "The employee is not entitled to any facilitating services for the raising of a child".

ELISHEVA: *(takes the papers from her)* What will you do?

YOSEFA: I don't know. *(Pulls the papers back.)* I don't get it. This letter's from an attorney... What's going on here? *(NOAM and ELISHEVA exchange a look. The phone rings.)*

NECHAMA: There, they've changed their minds.

YOSEFA: In the middle of the night? It's probably Mr. Cohen. *(Even so, she picks up the phone as for an overseas call.)* Doctor Yosefa Amsalem...Yes...yes...yes. Right, I'm not alone. No. I'm fine - it's just your timing...I'm writing...obstetrics...yes I know where the ward is - next to the ultrasound. Tomorrow at 10.30. Fine, yes... just a minute. *(To NECHAMA)* Can you come with me?

NECHAMA: What?

YOSEFA: Amniocentesis.

NECHAMA: Sure.

YOSEFA: *(into the mouthpiece)* Thanks. Bye. *(Replaces the receiver.)* Not that I understand why I need to have this test now - In the end it'll turn out that I'm growing a four-legged chicken.

NECHAMA: Wait for the results.

NOAM: She can't. It takes a few weeks.

YOSEFA: Don't interfere - Do you mind? *(Returns to the papers.)* There's something not right here...I don't know what - but...all these clauses and sub-clauses, it's as if...They've never been this petty.

102

NOAM: You've never been pregnant.

YOSEFA: You are so right. This wouldn't happen to a man.

ELISHEVA: Maybe you ought to leave. Once you're there you'll figure out what to do.

YOSEFA: That might be the best...*(Considers the idea favourably for a moment.)* No.

NOAM: You said that if they didn't return you to the field, you'd have...

YOSEFA: So I did.

NOAM: Yosefa, we made an agreement.

YOSEFA: They made one with me too.

NOAM: You promised.

YOSEFA: Why did I have to tell you it was yours? - If I'd told you that the Holy Spirit made me pregnant, you'd've believed me, and at least I might have some peace and quiet.

NOAM: Yes. Sure. And in another fifteen to twenty years or so you'd dump the file on me. One fine day a young Amsalem would appear on my doorstep and say "Noam Orgad? - I'm your son."

YOSEFA: Oh boy! Life isn't a Victorian melodrama. Hold it...hold it...that's what I didn't understand.. *(Points at the first line of the first page.)* "In answer to your letter..." I never wrote, not even once. It was all done by phone - Noam....

NOAM: You sent a fax.

YOSEFA: I faxed them before I was pregnant. *(Silence.)* What did you write them? What exactly did you write them - you know I can find out?

NOAM: You don't understand. You've got a lousy contract. I was protecting your interests.

YOSEFA: Did I ask you to?

NOAM: I told you - all those transatlantic calls weren't worth a plugged nickel till you had something in writing. At least now you have a start. *(Gestures at the papers in her hand.)*

YOSEFA: You're nuts. Totally nuts.

NOAM: Possibly. I only want you to know that under the circumstances I've gotten you the best opening deal there is. That was the proper way to start negotiating.

YOSEFA: You went through my drawers, into my private papers?

NOAM: You showed me the contract yourself.

YOSEFA: And you remembered all the clauses.

NOAM: You consulted me.

YOSEFA: How can you look me in the face? You make love to me, laugh with me, tell me you love me, that you can't live without me - and when I fall asleep, you get up and paw through my papers.

NOAM: Don't you talk about love.

YOSEFA: So how did you get the address?

ELISHEVA: *(pulls YOSEFA to her)* What difference does it make?

YOSEFA: I want to know.

ELISHEVA: The address isn't a problem.

YOSEFA: *(to ELISHEVA)* He poked through my papers, into what's most privately mine. I've never felt so humiliated in my life, so exposed. *(To NOAM)* How dare you! *(To ELISHEVA)* D'you know what he did to me? *(To NOAM)* Do you understand what you've done? The minute they got a letter full of demands from a lawyer who's supposedly representing me - they won't talk to me, and hell can freeze over before they meet me even part way.

NOAM: Yosefa, calm down.

YOSEFA: *(quietly)* Get out.

NOAM: Think logically for a minute. Let me help you. I can help you. Nothing's lost. The process has just begun. I'll come with you, we'll find a way to get you back into the field with all the help you'll need.

YOSEFA: I don't want or need anything from you.

NOAM: You have to.

YOSEFA: I don't have to do anything.

NOAM: You put it off and put it off so that it'd be too late, so that you couldn't do anything anymore. You did it on purpose - you want people to know. Because the second people see that stomach...

YOSEFA: They'll what?

NOAM: What can I tell my wife? - "Ilanit, I'm about to have a baby."

ELISHEVA: You don't have to tell her anything.

104

NOAM: Someone will. Some concerned soul will whisper it in her ear.

NECHAMA: Fact. Till now, nobody did?

NOAM: A fuck's different. Nechama, even if someone would tell her, she could deal with it somehow. But a child?

YOSEFA: A fuck. Is that what I mean to you? A fuck.

NOAM: You know what? - Not just a fuck - a screw. But I didn't screw you - you screwed me. You used me like a prize bull.

YOSEFA: Because that's what you are - a prize bull. (*Suddenly changes her tone.*) Listen sweetheart, you think that my pregnancy is your problem? You committed a felony. No-one asked you to represent me.

NOAM: What are you talking about? I'm administrator of the estate. I represent your interests.

YOSEFA: Only for the estate - nothing else. I don't know how to say it in lawyerese, but I do know that you had no right to write in my name. Did you forge my signature as well?

NOAM: I didn't forge any signature. I didn't poke through your drawers. I want you to leave - that's true. But she organised this botch - your mama. (*Imitates ELISHEVA'S voice.*) "Don't worry - it'll be alright, you have my word - Sefi will never know." (*To ELISHEVA, who's trying to disappear.*) You really did a job on me.

YOSEFA: (*to ELISHEVA, using her phrases*) After all, we're a family - a family.

NOAM: You, you the old Jerusalem aristocracy - the elite of the elite, salt of the earth. (*Sizes up the situation and exits.*)

YOSEFA: You went through my drawers.

ELISHEVA: Everything was on the table.

YOSEFA: That's why you didn't want to give the key back. You invaded my space - Everything's kosher - to get rid of me. (*Silence.*)

ELISHEVA: I just want you to know one thing -

ELISHEVA and YOSEFA: It was for your own good.

ELISHEVA: Nechama, are you coming? (*NECHAMA hangs her head and shakes it. To YOSEFA*) You won't be satisfied until you see us all covered in blood, buried under this ruin. (*Exits.*)

YOSEFA: We have only one mother. (*Sits and retreats into herself.*)

NECHAMA: D'you want me to get you something to drink? *(YOSEFA shakes her head.)* D'you want me to leave? *(She shakes her head again.)* Shall we go on? *(Indicating the scattered objects.)*

YOSEFA: No, not now. I need to think. When Noam comes back, we'll see what can be done.

NECHAMA: Noam will come back?

YOSEFA: Wait and see.

NECHAMA: Are you O.K?

YOSEFA: I've never had it better. Can you imagine what sort of a mother I'll be? Just like mine.

NECHAMA: No. You have to decide... how you want -

YOSEFA: Nechama, please, what's it mean, decide? There are things inside a person, from the minute we're born, even before we're born - we are conditioned. I should have let that stupid doctor "get it out" and it'd be over.

NECHAMA: Don't talk like that. *(Footsteps approach the door.)*

YOSEFA: What did I tell you? *(NECHAMA opens the door before NOAM has time to knock.)* That was fast.

NECHAMA: What do you want?

NOAM: *(crosses to YOSEFA, holding out a paper. NECHAMA bars his way)* I only want her to sign.

NECHAMA: You keep away from her.

NOAM: Take it easy. *(He gives the paper to NECHAMA, speaking to YOSEFA.)* You said - "Draw up a waiver and I'll sign." I wrote it exactly as you wanted.

YOSEFA: D'you recall what you've done since then?

NOAM: I protected your interests. The fact you don't understand, that's something else.

YOSEFA: *(to NECHAMA)* Let me have that. *(She looks through the paper.)*

NOAM: I suggest you sign.

YOSEFA: And if I don't?

NOAM: I can sue you for fraud and theft of sperm.

YOSEFA: I put my hand into your balls and stole me a bit of sperm?

NOAM: For your sake, I hope you have a better understanding of

106

medicine than you do law. You broke an agreement. And the
agreement stands, even if it's not in writing.

YOSEFA: *(she's scrolled the paper)* You were executor of the will.
You were nominated as administrator of the estate. *(Holds out the
scroll.)* Now you can take the whole lot and shove it up your arse.
(Tosses it at him.)

NECHAMA: That's enough, go away, leave her alone. Get out of
here.

NOAM: *(to NECHAMA)* Go ahead, protect her. Why not? You and
Amnon are counting on the money you'll get from the sale of the house.
Forget it - it's hers. She'll never sell.

NECHAMA: Fine.

NOAM: Dr Yosefa Amsalem, I'll sue you for so much that this house
and all yours and Amnon's inheritance won't be enough to cover the
damages.

YOSEFA: Counsellor Orgad, I'll be delighted to see you in court, for a
public laundering.

NOAM: You think you're done with me? Don't you believe it! This is
just the beginning. *(Exit.)*

YOSEFA: That's it. Now it's over.

NECHAMA: Do you love him?

YOSEFA: I like going to bed with him, specially now. This
pregnancy's giving me nightmares.

NECHAMA: How can you?

YOSEFA: *(mischievously)* In bed, it just got better.

NECHAMA: With all the...

YOSEFA: With all the...when you and Amnon fight, then...

NECHAMA: Then we don't. *(They both laugh. AMNON enters
from yard door.)*

AMNON: Didn't you start packing yet? Where's Mom?

NECHAMA: *(takes the letter to AMNON)* This came today.

AMNON: Great.

NECHAMA: Read it. Noam wrote a letter to the World Health
Organisation.

YOSEFA: Mother and Noam. They were so eager to get rid of me that they messed up everything, and now I'll have to start over. Good thing I didn't sign the contract.

AMNON: Serious damage? *(YOSEFA nods.)* Final?

YOSEFA: Only death is final.

AMNON: *(looks over letter)* Nechama, the kids have to be picked up from nursery school.

NECHAMA: Oops, right.

AMNON: D'you need the car?

NECHAMA: I have mine. *(Takes her purse and turns to leave. To YOSEFA.)* Come over later.

AMNON: Look, despite everything, they suggest you concentrate on research in New York.

YOSEFA: A medical secretary that finished college last week can do that. You don't have to be a doctor for that. If they don't return me to the field, what's left? What's left....five people left out of hundreds. Five - who've been with me all these years. We dreamed together and together we lost the dream. Forty thousand children die in the world every day, and we tell ourselves, that if it wasn't for us there'd be forty one thousand deaths. People die of syphilis when one factory in the United States could supply the needs of the entire world, if it only wanted to...What keeps me there? What keeps all of us there is the togetherness. Without that, what else is there? Everything's falling apart, so you scramble your brain - with whisky, or pot. Believe me, the missionaries with their God and bandages did more than us. At least they gave them Jesus and the hope of heaven ...I thought, if I have a child, there'll be someone for me to take care of as well, at least for a few years...And even if we fight, it's not...I thought that if I'm lucky, he'll love me too - I started to get used to the idea - another little vanished dream. What does it matter? It's just petty cash.

AMNON: Sefi, what's the matter?

YOSEFA: I have to get an abortion.

AMNON: Is there no alternative?

YOSEFA: Is there?

AMNON: If you want a child, this may be your last chance.

YOSEFA: What do you suggest?

AMNON: Ignore them all. Don't go back to New York. We'll sell the house. Buy an apartment. Find work. Stay.

YOSEFA: Nonni. You have to know when to admit defeat.

AMNON: You're scared.

YOSEFA: Very good Amnon! D'you have your car here? *(He nods.)* Take me into town. I'll book my flight, call New York tonight, and in the morning, God willing, I'll "get it out of here"...

AMNON: D'you want Nechama to come with you?

YOSEFA: No. I'll ask Rami. Come on, help me tidy up some of this mess. *(They start tidying the stuff from the chest.)* Now go and call our mother and tell her I'm having an abortion tomorrow. She'll be delighted.

SCENE THREE

Early next morning. YOSEFA is tidying up. Closes up the typewriter, stuffs her papers into a large envelope. A ring at the front door.

YOSEFA: Coming! *(Hurries to open the door and comes back, RAMI behind her.)*

RAMI: Ready?

YOSEFA: One second. *(Exits to bedroom area and returns with a small bag.)*

RAMI: It's alright. *(Checks time.)* We still have a few minutes. Calm down.

YOSEFA: Do I have to have a general anaesthetic?

RAMI: It's preferable.

YOSEFA: I've never had one. Don't worry, I can't trash a hospital. *(Freezes.)*

RAMI: What's up?

YOSEFA: Dizzy. Nothing - it's because of fasting.

RAMI: And your low blood pressure.

YOSEFA: So what's new? - It'll pass.

RAMI: Are you sure about this abortion?

YOSEFA: A hundred percent. Give me my bag.

RAMI: Do you want to rest a while?

YOSEFA: No.

RAMI: There's time. I'll make myself some coffee meanwhile.

YOSEFA: Go ahead.

ELISHEVA: *(off)* Yosefa...Sefi... *(The two listen. RAMI asks with his hands what he should do. YOSEFA pushes him to kitchen area and joins him. The stage is empty. ELISHEVA comes in through the front door carrying flowers. As she looks for a vase, she just happens to see the envelope with YOSEFA'S papers on top of her desk. She puts down flowers, takes out the papers and begins to look through them. YOSEFA enters from kitchen area, her shoes in her hand.)*

YOSEFA: "Everything was on the table."

ELISHEVA: *(unsuccessfully tries to stuff the papers back. YOSEFA takes and replaces them in the envelope)* Amnon said you were going out very, very early and wouldn't be back till evening.

YOSEFA: Which is to say you'd have plenty of time to go over all the -

ELISHIVA: I wanted to -

YOSEFA: Throw a surprise party in honour of the abortion.

ELISHEVA: No. I wanted to make up... to make it up with you...

YOSEFA: "With a bouquet", like for a birth. How touching. After yesterday's business I need a good long break from you.

ELISHEVA: If you'd listen just once...if, just for once, you'd take my advice...

YOSEFA: I'd now be a bank-teller - married with two kids, peeking into their notebooks and diaries.

ELISHEVA: I shouldn't have touched your papers. I apologise. I'm sorry.

YOSEFA: You're not sorry - you've won. And that's all that mattered to you. You were seething from the day I got here. You even tried to come between me and Amnon - "How does Sefi always manage to wind you around her little finger?" - Divide and rule - I've tried to get away from you for ten years - as remote and as far away as possible. You called me "whorish" - a "fool", "vulgar", "repulsive". I tried to please you for years. It never worked. So I did the "I'll show her" bit. Instead of living my own life, "I showed you". I'm warped - because of you.

ELISHEVA: When you open that mouth of yours sometimes, it's enough to make one curl up and die. I'll take it all though, whatever comes out. We'll talk. We'll make peace.

YOSEFA: Because you want to. Why? For what? - I'm not the daughter you dreamed of.

ELISHEVA: I thought you'd be my best friend - a sister.

YOSEFA: I wanted you to be my mother - a mother! (*To RAMI, who is coming out of the kitchen.*) Come on, we have to go.

RAMI: Hello, Mrs Elisheva.

ELISHEVA: You! What are you doing here?

YOSEFA: He's come to take me to the...

ELISHEVA: Has he been here all this time? Why didn't you tell me? He had no business hearing this - it's a family matter.

RAMI: *(picks up her bag)* Is this your bag?

YOSEFA: Just a minute, I have to rearrange...*(Empties the bag and starts replacing the contents.)*

ELISHEVA: *(to RAMI)* Stirring things up again. For years you've been spitting into the well you drank from.

RAMI: Let's go, we're wasting time.

ELISHEVA: I'll take you.

YOSEFA: You'll take me. You'll bring me back - videos, Chinese take-away...

ELISHEVA: Tell him to go. Don't you understand? He used you. If you hadn't helped him, he never would have graduated from medical school.

RAMI: That's true.

ELISHEVA: Who asked you? Garbage - we picked you out of the garbage. *(To YOSEFA.)* The day you left, he had someone else. Six months later he was married.

YOSEFA: I thought you were delighted. You'd tried to separate us for eight years.

ELISHEVA: *(talks over YOSEFA)* We took you out of a stinking hole. Took you into our home, the family...

RAMI: Who asked you to?

111

ELISHEVA: You were a little foreign kid...

RAMI: Primitive.

ELISHEVA: Afraid of your own shadow. We made a human being of you.

RAMI: Your own private welfare case.

ELISHEVA: We bought you new clothes.

RAMI: Because you burnt the old ones - you said I had lice.

ELISHEVA: You had lice, you had...

RAMI: In your eyes I was a nothing. *(To YOSEFA.)* That's it. D'you have everything? *(She nods.)*

ELISHEVA: You really are a nothing. And I don't talk to a nothing.

YOSEFA: And who are you talking to now?

ELISHEVA: Get out of here. Out. Get out I said.

YOSEFA: Come on. I could have a child, but I won't. If you hadn't interfered, if only you hadn't interfered...

ELISHEVA: You never wanted children.

YOSEFA: I never wanted? I never wanted? *(Points at RAMI.)* He tried to get me pregnant for four years. I could have been a mother long ago. I can still be a mother. I have a child in my womb. I can be its mother - And always the constant fear - to be a mother like you. I'm different. I can be different. It's not written anywhere that I have to be a mother like you. *(Puts the bag down and sits.)*

ELISHEVA: I'm to blame for everything. What now? You don't have time to...

YOSEFA: I'm dizzy.

ELISHEVA: You can't put it off any more.

YOSEFA: Mother, wait...

ELISHEVA: Come on Sefi, come along. I'll take you.

YOSEFA: I can't. Not now.

ELISHEVA: Not now. And not ever. You'll destroy us all. You always were that way. You did whatever you wanted and presented the bill to others for payment. Let me tell you this - that thing in there will never be my grandchild - never.

YOSEFA: You are a horrible woman. You are simply a horrible woman.

112

ELISHEVA: You'll be as solitary as a stray dog. I hope that Allegra is spinning in her grave, repenting everything she's done to this family. May her soul never know a moment's peace. *(Exits, and slams the door behind her.)*

YOSEFA: *(a long silence)* I won't have an abortion.

SCENE FOUR

One month later. Summer, morning. RAMI enters from kitchen with a bottle of champagne and two glasses.

RAMI: Champagne.

YOSEFA: *(offstage)* In the morning?

RAMI: *(gets glasses)* In all the novels the aristocracy drinks champagne in the morning, so I thought, why shouldn't we celebrate for once?

YOSEFA: *(off)* I was just trying to call you.

RAMI: What?

YOSEFA: I called the ward.

RAMI: And..?

YOSEFA: *(RAMI pours the champagne)* They said you'd left. Were you on your way here?

RAMI: Yes. How's the research coming?

YOSEFA: So-so.

RAMI: *(steps over to the tape-deck. Sees a butt in the ashtray)* What's this? Pot again?

YOSEFA: *(yells from the bedroom)* Just a minute. I can't talk and dress at the same time. *(Enters, obviously pregnant, and she enjoys displaying it to him.)*

RAMI: *(indicating the butt)* At least not now.

YOSEFA: *(hurls the butt through the yard door)* O.K?

RAMI: Just kidding you. Pregnancy suits you. *(Turns on tape, hands her a glass of champagne, takes her hand and they start to dance.)* Cheers!

YOSEFA: You enjoy seeing my wings getting shorter.

RAMI: D'you think I've nothing better to do than to measure your wings?

113

YOSEFA: So why are you spoiling me like this? Is all this celebration in honour of my new son? *(RAMI stops dancing.)* Didn't you know?
RAMI: No.
YOSEFA: The results of the amniocentesis arrived this morning. It's a boy. I thought they'd told you.
RAMI: *(stops the tape)* No. Honey, we're not at the same party. *(Holds out a sheet of paper)* In one week, in exactly one week, I take office.
YOSEFA: And what's that?
RAMI: Head of Orthopaedics. I wanted you to be the first to know.
YOSEFA: Congratulations. Up the ladder, one rung at a time. What's the next step?
RAMI: I knew you'd say something like that.
YOSEFA: I stole your thunder, didn't I?
RAMI: I'm always happy to share it with you.
YOSEFA: You planned this from the start. From the beginning - the sweetest little revenge.
RAMI: What a pal.
YOSEFA: Didn't you?
RAMI: Once you helped me, now I'm helping you. It's simple, so simple.
YOSEFA: Nothing was ever simple between us.
RAMI: That's true.
YOSEFA: Stop agreeing with me all the time.
RAMI: Alright. Enough, don't be angry, it's not good for you or for him.
YOSEFA: Don't bug me Dr. Levy *(Puts her hand on her stomach.)*
RAMI: You have to start working. Sitting at home is driving you crazy.
YOSEFA: And where would I work?
RAMI: In your condition, you'll have to accept whatever you're offered.
YOSEFA: Whatever you offer me.
RAMI: I've tried to help you.
YOSEFA: Of course you have. And you got me a job at a well-baby

clinic.

RAMI: The fact that you graduated with honours ten years ago, is irrelevant.

YOSEFA: You'll run a department and I'll work at a well-baby clinic. Doesn't that seem a bit off-balance to you? *(A knock at the yard door.)*

RAMI: I'm not walking into that trap again.

YOSEFA: Do what you want. *(Goes to open door.)*

NECHAMA: *(as they hug)* Boy or girl?

YOSEFA: Boy.

NECHAMA: I've brought some cheese. Get out the wine in the freezer. Amnon's just coming, and we'll celebrate.

YOSEFA: Don't you congratulate me?

NECHAMA: That's for after you've had the baby. Why did the results take so long?

RAMI: Because the amniotic fluids weren't clear. *(NECHAMA, who hasn't noticed RAMI, feels awkward.)* Hi, Nechama.

NECHAMA: Hello Rami. It's been a long time.

RAMI: Yes, and it's a pity. When you started to go out with Amnon, you were a bud about to blossom. Now, you're a sight for sore eyes - you're a beauty, really. Nechama, say something nice to me too, you always had a good word for me.

NECHAMA: You haven't changed a bit.

RAMI: What a shame, and I've tried so hard. *(NECHAMA laughs in embarrassment, and retreats a little.)*

YOSEFA: Not enough, I guess. Why don't you read her the whole Song of Songs?

RAMI: Don't mind her. A little healthy jealousy never hurt anybody.

YOSEFA: Up yours. *(NECHAMA, wanting to get out of this situation, sticks the plans on the wall.)*

RAMI: For shame! What language. *(Looks at the plans.)* What are these?

NECHAMA: *(laughs)* I made some plans. In order to live here, the place has to be renovated.

RAMI: Ah. *(To YOSEFA.)* Aren't you selling?

YOSEFA: No.

115

RAMI: Life is full of surprises.

YOSEFA: That's not to say I'll be caged. I'll learn to fly with my fledgling on my back.

RAMI: And you'll tow the house too - the flying turtle.

YOSEFA: You've forgotten that my wings don't interest you - right? You're in for a few more surprises.

RAMI: I believe it. And all because of Allegra. *(Pours himself more champagne.)* She was a good Jewish lady. I hope that she's sitting among the righteous feasting off the fatted calf.

YOSEFA: You bet.

RAMI: *(to NECHAMA)* Did you study architecture?

YOSEFA: Drafting.

RAMI: *(to NECHAMA)* Does Amnon let you work? *(She looks at YOSEFA, not understanding.)*

YOSEFA: Are you aware you've started talking nonsense?

RAMI: Why? Your father wouldn't let your mother go out to work until you were at Medical School.

YOSEFA: What has that got to do with anything?

RAMI: I dunno. *(To NECHAMA.)* Will you show me what you've done?

NECHAMA: That wall will go *(Indicates bedroom area.)* I'll extend that one by one or two metres, close it off with glass...a little conservatory - you'll be able to see the Old City and the Wall, even from here...

RAMI: *(exchanges a look with YOSEFA)* I always said you were talented.

NECHAMA: *(very embarrassed)* Yes, you did.

RAMI: What does Amnon say about it?

NECHAMA: Amnon doesn't know yet. It's a surprise. They're just sketches really, because...Yosefa hasn't said what she wants.

RAMI: Don't worry. Now she won't stop talking.

NECHAMA: Were you that scared?

RAMI: She was dead certain she had a monster in there. And where will Yosefa's office be?

NECHAMA: *(indicates the stage)* Here, right here. *(Unprepared for*

116

it, she doesn't quite know what to do with all of RAMI's friendliness, so she keeps talking to keep silence at bay.) I won't remove this wall... it's so well-built that it's a pity to...

YOSEFA: Save your breath. He doesn't understand a thing about it.

RAMI: Two kitchens, two bathrooms, two residential units...

YOSEFA: Two points.

NECHAMA: Yes, we'll live together. *(Quick steps from the yard. NECHAMA goes to the door.)* Here's Amnon.

AMNON: What happened? What's the emergency?

NECHAMA: Yosefa has a boy. *(Apprehensive of the meeting between RAMI and AMNON.)*

AMNON: *(kissing YOSEFA)* And you were driving everybody up the wall.

RAMI: Hello Uncle Amnon.

AMNON: Hello. *(The men shake hands very formally.)* Give me a minute to get used to it.

RAMI: It happens very fast. Human beings are strange creatures.

AMNON: It's good to see you...It's been many years...I've been wanting to call, and thank you for all you've done for Yosefa.

RAMI: You're welcome. It's my pleasure. It's nice to pay off debts, especially old ones.

AMNON: Yes.

NECHAMA: There's wine.

RAMI: I brought champagne.

AMNON: What do you say we leave the party for tonight? I'm in the middle of stuff at the office right now.

YOSEFA: So we'll celebrate twice.

RAMI: *(to AMNON)* She's right. You really do have a good reason to celebrate. The family's together once more. A new Amsalem is on the way, you'll all be together, one might say, in the family mansion.

AMNON: *(doesn't quite get it)* Yes.

YOSEFA: Rami, shut up.

RAMI: Nechama's made some really great plans.

NECHAMA: *(who has poured wine for RAMI and YOSEFA, handing to AMNON.)* Let's celebrate, the four of us. To the way we

117

were - like then, like -

YOSEFA: Cheers.

AMNON: What drawing?

RAMI: Haven't you seen it?

YOSEFA: Rami, watch it.

RAMI: What for? *(To AMNON.)* In order to live here, the place has to be renovated. *(To YOSEFA.)* Am I right?

YOSEFA: You're sticking your nose into things that are none of your concern.

AMNON: What about these plans?

RAMI: *(to YOSEFA)* Am I restricted to solving occupational problems?

YOSEFA: You're restricted - period.

AMNON: I asked - what about these plans?

RAMI: *(to AMNON)* Two kitchens, two bathrooms, two residential units.

AMNON: Nechama!

YOSEFA: *(plants herself in front of RAMI)* Out!

RAMI: If I go now, I won't be back.

YOSEFA: Don't threaten me!

RAMI: You've pushed a bit too hard this time. I'm not your errand boy - you want me to leave? - I'll leave. *(Finishes his champagne and sets down his glass.)* My best to all of you. *(Exits through the front door.)*

NECHAMA: What happened to him?

YOSEFA: Nothing. Let it be.

AMNON: I'm still waiting for an answer. What is this thing?

NECHAMA: Yosefa and I decided that if the baby's alright, we'd live here - all of us. I wanted to surprise you.

AMNON: You did. *(Pointing at the drawings.)* Whose idea was it?

YOSEFA *and* **NECHAMA**: *(NECHAMA smiling, YOSEFA trying to disappear.)* Mine.

AMNON: Have you gone mad? *(To YOSEFA.)* I don't understand you.

NECHAMA: It'll be a palace. Have you any idea how marvellous it'll be to have a garden? Do you realise how happy the kids will be here?

AMNON: *(to NECHAMA)* I will not live here.

NECHAMA: But why?

AMNON: Sefi - you said half and half - I've made plans.

NECHAMA: But she's giving us half - more than half.

AMNON: Not really.

NECHAMA: *(to YOSEFA)* You said we could have the basement. We can make a games room.

AMNON: Nechama, do me a favour. *(Goes towards the door. To YOSEFA.)* I'll talk to you tonight.

NECHAMA: No, I want to know. I want to know too. I'm entitled.

AMNON: There's nothing to know. I'm...I have to get back to work.

NECHAMA: I'm not a child any more. Yosefa, what is going on here?

YOSEFA: *(absently)* Silliness, childhood secrets...

NECHAMA: What?

YOSEFA: We always celebrated our birthdays together. Amnon got the big gifts because he was a boy, while I -

AMNON: Sefi, that's unnecessary.

YOSEFA: *(to AMNON)* Go ahead, Nechama came in her own car. *(to NECHAMA)* He always used to say to me - "Wait 'till your batmitzva, then you'll get it all." And then it came, together with his army enlistment party - and it was the same. I cried buckets and buckets. And Amnon - he can't bear to see me cry - he said "half and half - share and share alike" - not just the presents we got then, but for all the gifts and inheritances to come for ever.

NECHAMA: Why did you never tell me? That's a beautiful story.

AMNON: Marvellous.

YOSEFA: Amnon thinks that if we didn't have that absurd agreement, I wouldn't share with him.

AMNON: So, what now?

YOSEFA: You know what? Go with him, or I'll be accused of home-wrecking. We'll discuss the plans tomorrow.

AMNON: *(shouts suddenly at YOSEFA)* What do you take me for?

YOSEFA: My brother. But this is my house - mine - and I want it. Grandpa built it for granny, took her out of the walled city and settled

119

her in a garden, with a view of the Old City. You'd need a very good reason to sell.

AMNON: There is. I won't live here.

YOSEFA: And I won't sell.

AMNON: You have to.

YOSEFA: Really?

AMNON: Sefi, we've never agreed, not on anything, but at least it was live and let live. I want to live.

YOSEFA: Who's stopping you?

AMNON: You - fuck it!

YOSEFA: What are you talking about?

AMNON: *(invents an excuse)* Dad left me the most respected insurance firm in Jerusalem but also the most old-fashioned. I've computerised everything, branched out in ways Dad never dreamed of.

YOSEFA: Great, I just don't see how that connects...

AMNON: The company's mortgaged.

NECHAMA: Our company?

AMNON: Our company - yes. What does that matter?

NECHAMA: What do you mean what does that matter?

YOSEFA: Cash problems?

AMNON: No.

YOSEFA: So why?

AMNON: Why? - Why? *(It bursts out despite himself.)* Because of you.

YOSEFA: Because of me?

AMNON: Let it go.

YOSEFA: I'll come with you this very minute and sign the contract, if you'll tell me why.

AMNON: Because - because Dad left you nothing.

YOSEFA: Not true. Did mother see to that?

AMNON: No. He...he...after he got back that time from visiting you, he changed his will.

YOSEFA: Didn't he even mention my name?

AMNON: He left you one shekel. You can see for yourself.

YOSEFA: I believe you. And so that I wouldn't be hurt, you wrote me

120

"this is your share of the inheritance", and mortgaged the firm.

AMNON: We had a pact, and I honoured it.

YOSEFA: Dad left me a shekel? One shekel?

AMNON: Yes.

YOSEFA: And you mortgaged the firm to keep a pact we made at my batmitzva?

AMNON: Yes.

NECHAMA: Why didn't you tell me? *(No response.)* Why didn't you tell me?

AMNON: I told no-one.

NECHAMA: But...but, I'm your wife.

AMNON: It's not your concern.

NECHAMA: Not my concern? What is my concern? Well? - Since you do everything behind my back.

AMNON: Will you stop talking rubbish?

NECHAMA: How can you talk to me that way? How can you say that?

AMNON: We had a pact.

NECHAMA: You had a pact with me too.

AMNON: Stop it.

NECHAMA: Don't you tell me anymore to stop it. Enough. I've had it up to here with "stop it"... I wanted someone to love me, to understand me. You said you loved me, that you understand. You said that everything would be up front between us. You've kept more secrets from me than my Dad kept from my Mom.

AMNON: A person has a right to his own corner, even if he's married.

NECHAMA: A corner? I have no corner, not with you. They're all taken.

AMNON: Maybe you should consider therapy.

NECHAMA: *(controls herself)* I have not gone round the bend and I won't let you drive me there. I may be a fool, a fool for believing you. A fool for responding "Amen" to everything you said. You said "get an abortion", and I got one. Maybe I needn't have? - Maybe another doctor might have known what to do? - But you said, and I murdered a child. My child. It's over. *(She takes the plans off the wall, folding*

121

them carefully.)

AMNON: What are you doing?

NECHAMA: Here they are, all my dreams - my life's partner, the children, a home, a garden - family. I don't even have a family...I...

AMNON: The dream season has ended - how symbolic.

NECHAMA: *(to YOSEFA)* You said that Amnon can't bear to see you cry. Do you know what he does when I cry? He laughs. He stands there and laughs. Maybe you're not to blame...No, you knew - you kept your hand on the tether from a distance. But you kept hold and loved it. I've been living in a dream for twelve years...like in a bubble...*(AMNON touches her.)* Don't touch me. You're sick people. Disturbed. Even grandma Allegra said you're a disturbed family, that you infect everybody you touch...I'm not like that, and I don't want my children to be like that - twisted. I want them to grow up...I want them to grow up...*(Exits.)*

YOSEFA: Does she mean that? *(No response.)* Go after her, make up with her. *(No response.)* What do people get married for?

AMNON: You have to sell.

YOSEFA: The money you sent me - "Daddy's bequest" - I didn't touch it, it's yours.

AMNON: No.

YOSEFA: I have some savings...Take them.

AMNON: It's not that...

YOSEFA: There's a secret behind the secret.

AMNON: If Michael doesn't get the house now, he won't release his half of the company. That was the condition.

YOSEFA: How could I have missed it? Karo holds the mortgage?

AMNON: I had no alternative. When Dad died I tried to get the money together to send you.

YOSEFA: You needn't have.

AMNON: I decide what I need, or need not, do. A loan from the family - they laughed at me. Michael was the only one who came across with the money. - And we agreed, that after granny...you know...that the house would be his. And if that didn't work out for some reason, he'd keep half the firm. *(YOSEFA goes to the phone,*

122

dials.) Who are you calling?

YOSEFA: Michael.

AMNON: Sefi, it won't work, believe me. He's adamant.

YOSEFA: What is it with him and this house?

AMNON: A Karo will live in Amsalem's house.

YOSEFA: Michael? Michael was never involved in the family feuds.

AMNON: And you? - Or me? It seemed so trivial when we were young. Sefi. I've paid him fifty percent of the profits every single month for five years. I say to myself - let's say I took a loan. If Michael Karo doesn't get the house, he'll collect fifty percent from me for the rest of my life, and when I'm gone, from my children - and from their children - without investing a penny.

YOSEFA: Bastard.

AMNON: Come, let's go to the lawyer, sign the contract. Buy an apartment, or a little house - whatever you want. We'll be a family. I'm glad you stayed...I missed you...Come, let's close the deal.

YOSEFA: *(almost begging)* Nonni, please, I can't. "To her and her children after her." That's what granny wrote. I want it. It's mine. It's the only place in the world I can say "I'm home". I want to raise my son here. Here - not just in four walls with a roof on top. A house that was built a hundred years ago with a four thousand year old view.

AMNON: And I have to pay the price?

YOSEFA: No. No.

AMNON: I did it for you, because of you.

YOSEFA: No. You did it because you're dumb. Because of your perverted sense of honour... nobody'll know, nobody'll get hurt...Nonni, please, don't make me do it. *(Suddenly diverted.)* Just a minute, I know. I had a friend once, and he had a partner who cheated him. Do you know what he did? He created a new company and transferred everything to it - simply stripped the partnership...something like that...That's what he said. Did you know - did you know that you can do that?

AMNON: Not everyone does that sort of thing.

YOSEFA: If you have to, you do. It's not a crime or something?

AMNON: No. But, do you want me to strip Amsalem and Sons?

YOSEFA: So what? What difference does it make? It all stays the same, except that...

AMNON: There's no Amsalem and Sons - the end?

YOSEFA: Amsalem is just a name.

AMNON: I'm an Amsalem just like you. What are you thinking of? That if I change the name on my I.D. something's different? Every place I go, whether it's the bank, a restaurant - even for the clients - I'm Mr. Amsalem. I was born Amsalem that's how I'll die. Sefi, you have to sell this house.

YOSEFA: And the name Amsalem and Sons is more important than this house? I won't sell.

AMNON: I've nothing more to say. I'm finished. *(Sits.)*

YOSEFA: No you're not. You're conning me. You always do the helpless "what-shall-I-do-now" bit whenever you can't convince me of something. *(Crouches beside him. AMNON gets up.)* Don't leave...please...don't leave...let's talk...we'll talk it over...Come this evening...or in the morning. *(AMNON exits.)* Nonni...Nonni *(She seems totally lost, sits at the table, takes out ALLEGRA'S will.)* "Today, Tuesday the sixth of November 1990, I Allegra Amsalem, daughter to Moshe and Rachel - being of sound mind and after much deliberation, do here write my last will and testament..." *(She goes on reading the document half mumbling until she gets to the part that mentions herself.)* "And to my grand-daughter, who knew how to give love for love, whose sharp tongue was a source of life to me, whose heart and tongue are one..." *(She goes on reading the document half mumbling again.)* "...And the family home I bequeath to Yosefa, the only true remaining Amsalem, to her and to her children after her."

END

LIBRATION

by Lluisa Cunillé
Translated by Lola Lopez Ruiz

The play was first performed on the 9th March 1994 at the Sala Beckett in Barcelona, and was chosen as one of the best plays shown at the Barcelona *"Grec Festival"*.

DIRECTOR: Xavier Alberti
MUSIC: Gorecki
DESIGNER: Susana Urquia

CHARACTERS: **CAST:**

WOMAN 1   Lina Lambert
WOMAN 2   Lola Lopez Ruiz

ACT ONE, SCENE ONE

In the darkness we can hear metal creaking. It starts slowly and then speeds up, finishing with a sharp stroke. Lights up. WOMAN 1 is reading a book, sitting at the bottom of a slide in a park. Downstage, on one side is a bin. After a moment, we hear a telephone ringing close up. WOMAN 2 enters quietly from one side and stops near the steps of the slide.

WOMAN 2: *(timidly)* Hello..doesn't take her eyes off the book.) Hello... What are you reading? *(WOMAN 1 keeps looking at the book. WOMAN 2 takes a few steps closer. When she stops, WOMAN 1 closes the book suddenly.)*
WOMAN 1: You're late.
WOMAN 2: *(confused)* Only ten minutes.I had to...
WOMAN 1: *(standing)* Have you seen a dog?
WOMAN 2: A dog? *(Pause.)* No.
(WOMAN 1 looks off, puts the book in her coat pocket, takes out a chain lead from the other pocket. She exits, whistles.)

WOMAN 2: *(speaking louder)* I arrived late because of the kid.

WOMAN 1: *(off)* What kid? *(Pause.)* Do you have a kid?

WOMAN 2: Yes. Do you want to see him? *(Pause.)*

WOMAN 1: *(entering)* Is he here?

WOMAN 2: No. Look. *(Takes out a picture. They both look for a second.)*

WOMAN 1: What about the legs? *(WOMAN 2 offended, puts the picture away.)*

WOMAN 1: Sorry...it was a joke...honestly...*(Pause.)* Can I see it again please?

WOMAN 2: What for?

WOMAN 1: To get a better look at it.

WOMAN 2: You've seen it already.

WOMAN 1: Well if you don't want to. *(Walks away.)*

WOMAN 2: Don't think I always carry the photograph with me.

WOMAN 1: *(stops walking)* Uh-uh.

WOMAN 2: That I show it to everybody.

WOMAN 1: Of course not. *(Pause. They smile at each other.)*

WOMAN 1: How are you?

WOMAN 2: Fine. And you?

WOMAN 1: Come here, sit down. *(She offers a place on the slide. Takes a good look at her.)* Yes, you look very well.

WOMAN 2: Thanks. You too. *(Pause.)*

WOMAN 1: Are you comfortable?

WOMAN 2: Yes.

WOMAN 1: Would you prefer to sit on a bench?

WOMAN 2: No. I'm fine. But if you'd rather...

WOMAN 1: No. I'll sit here. *(She sits on the ground facing her)*

WOMAN 1: Are you cold?

WOMAN 2: No...well, a bit.

WOMAN 1: Do you want a scarf?

WOMAN 2: No, no. Thank you. *(Pause.)*

WOMAN 1: And how do you find me?

WOMAN 2: Fine. I've already told you.

WOMAN 1: No, you said -"You too".

WOMAN 2: I meant that you looked fine.

WOMAN 1: I looked?

WOMAN 2: You look.

WOMAN 1: Really? Well never mind...*(Takes the book from her pocket.)* A present. *(She hands it to her.)* It was wrapped but it looked like you weren't coming. I thought you wouldn't so I started to read it. *(She looks in her pockets. She stands and looks in the bin.)* The paper. *(Picks it out of the bin.)* It's dirty now. *(She lets it fall into the bin.)*

WOMAN 2: If you like, I'll lend it to you...

WOMAN 1: Have you read it?

WOMAN 2: No. But you've already started...

WOMAN 1: No...I'll borrow it later.

WOMAN 2: No, take it...And when you've finished give it back to me. *(WOMAN 1 picks up the book and sits in the same place as before.)*

WOMAN 1 I'll read it at once.

WOMAN 2: There's no rush.

WOMAN 1: I'll give it you back tomorrow..

WOMAN 2: Tomorrow?

WOMAN 1: Yes. It's not very long. *(Looks off.)* Did you hear anything? *(She stands, leaves the book on the slide and climbs the steps to the top.)* I can see it now. *(Pause.)* I have to make sure it doesn't get into the bins. *(She sits looking all around. Pause.)* Where is it going? *(Whistles.)* No response.*(Whistles again.)*

WOMAN 2: Why don't you call it by name?

WOMAN 1: Do you know anything about dogs?

WOMAN 2: No but-

WOMAN 1: *(interrupting)* It's got a ridiculous name. I don't like shouting such a ridiculous name. *(Long pause.)* I don't know why they have to make holes in the bins. Where's it going? *(Whistles.)* I bet it's eating some rubbish.

WOMAN 2: Is it a breed?

WOMAN 1: What?

127

WOMAN 2: I asked if it was a breed.

WOMAN 1: I don't know. *(Long pause. WOMAN 1 looking off, stiff, at the top of the slide. WOMAN 2 starts looking at the book.)*

WOMAN 2: *(softly)* They left the price.

WOMAN 1: What?

WOMAN 2: In the book...They didn't take the price off.

WOMAN 1: How much was it?

WOMAN 2: Don't you know?

WOMAN 1: No, I took it, when everybody's back was turned. I put it in my pocket. There were mirrors everywhere...No, that isn't true. The bookshop was empty and there was only one mirror. It was very easy. All I needed to do was take it and put it inside my pocket.

WOMAN 2: Did you honestly steal it?

WOMAN 1: Of course, otherwise it's no good giving presents. A present requires an effort, some risk. If you don't like it I can go back again and take another one.

WOMAN 2: No, this is fine. *(Pause.)* I didn't bring anything for you.

WOMAN 1: It doesn't matter. *(Whistles. Stops whistling. Pause.)*

WOMAN 2: Do you live nearby?

WOMAN 1: No, I live some distance away.

WOMAN 2: Why do you walk the dog around here then?

WOMAN 1: It isn't mine.

WOMAN 2: Whose dog is it?

WOMAN 1: It belongs to a man...a foreigner who always has trouble with roads. *(Pause.)* Listen...Why don't you go and see what it's doing?

WOMAN 2: Me?

WOMAN 1: I think it's there.

WOMAN 2: Where?

WOMAN I: *(pointing)* There, over there. *(WOMAN 2 stands, looks off, exits.)*

WOMAN 1: Wait...Don't go...It doesn't matter! *(Long pause. WOMAN 1 slides down and sits at the bottom of the slide. Pause.)*

WOMAN 1: What's it doing? *(WOMAN 2 enters looking backwards)*

128

WOMAN 2: It's very beautiful.

WOMAN 1: What's it doing?

WOMAN 2: It's a breed.

WOMAN 1: But what is it doing?

WOMAN 2: Nothing...It's biting a piece of wood.

WOMAN 1: *(stands)* What wood?

WOMAN 2: I don't know. *(Pause.)* Don't worry, it won't do it any harm. *(WOMAN 1 walks to one side.)*

WOMAN 1: I don't know where it found a piece of wood. Everything's iron here.

WOMAN 2: I stroked it. It's very placid.

WOMAN 1: Sure it was a piece of wood?

WOMAN 2: Yes.

WOMAN 1: It must have taken it from a bin. *(Pause.)*

WOMAN 2: Doesn't it belong to a friend of yours?

WOMAN 1: The dog? No...an acquaintance.

WOMAN 2: Do you have a dog?

WOMAN 1: No.

WOMAN 2: Me neither. *(Pause.)* Perhaps later...

WOMAN 1: What...

WOMAN 2: When the kid grows a bit, I might buy one for him.

WOMAN 1: I'll be back in a second.

WOMAN 2: *(leaving the book on the slide)* I'll leave it here...You can give it back to me when you finish.

WOMAN 1: Are you leaving?

WOMAN 2: Well...it's a bit late...if you like we can see each other another day.

WOMAN 1: How about tomorrow?

WOMAN 2: Tomorrow?

WOMAN 1: Yes, same time. But you've got to be on time.

WOMAN 2: Here?

WOMAN 1: Yes, I'll show you something.

WOMAN 2: What is it?

WOMAN 1: You'll see.

WOMAN 2: Can't you show it to me now?

WOMAN 1: No, it's too late now.

WOMAN 2: Can we meet earlier? In the afternoon.

WOMAN 1: No. It's got to be in the evening.

WOMAN 2: I can't make it tomorrow night. I haven't got anybody to leave the kid with. *(WOMAN 1 picks up the book.)* But we can choose some other night that will be good for both of us.

WOMAN 1: *(approaching the steps)* Yes...We'll make a date. *(Pause.)*

WOMAN 2: What's your number?

WOMAN 1: *(climbing)* What?

WOMAN 2: What's your telephone number?

WOMAN 1: I haven't got a telephone. *(Sits at the top and opens the book.)*

WOMAN 2: If you want we can decide now - which day.

WOMAN 1: No. I'll give you a call.

WOMAN 2: Yes, call me. *(Pause.)* Goodbye. *(Going off, turns before exiting.)* Will you honestly call me?

WOMAN 1: *(looks at her)* Yes. *(Goes back to the book.)*

(WOMAN 2 exits. Pause. WOMAN 1 takes her eyes off the book.)

WOMAN 1: *(speaking a little louder)* Listen...are you really sure you can't come tomorrow?

(Pause. Blackout.)

ACT TWO, SCENE ONE

In the darkness we can hear metal creaking. It starts slowly and then speeds up, finishing with a sharp stroke. Lights up. WOMAN 1 is reading a book, sitting on a metal horse with a spring base. Nearby is another little horse, exactly the same. Downstage there is a little fountain with a thin spurt of water. After a moment we hear a telephone ringing close-up and the voice of an ELDERLY WOMAN on an answering-machine.

ELDERLY WOMAN'S VOICE: Hello. I'm not here at the moment. You can leave your message after the tone. *(Pause. Tone. Silence, then sound of someone hanging up. Silence. WOMAN 2 enters quietly from the side. She carries a large rolled black umbrella.)*

WOMAN 2: *(timidly)* Hello...*(WOMAN 1 doesn't take her eyes off the book. Pause.)* It's going to rain. I saw lightning when I was coming over there. *(Pause.)* Don't you have an umbrella? *(Pause.)* This isn't mine...They lent me this one, in case it rained...It's quite big. *(Long pause.)* Look, more lightning...

WOMAN 1: *(closes the book)* Here - I've finished it.

(WOMAN 2 takes a little box from her coat pocket.)

WOMAN 2: A present. *(Gives the little box to **WOMAN 1**.)*

WOMAN 1: What is it?

WOMAN 2: Look at it. *(Pause.)* I didn't know if you'd like it. I didn't know what to give you and finally...well, I like it...

(WOMAN 1 takes a ring from the box and tries it on.)

WOMAN 2: It's too big, isn't it?...I knew it - I should have taken something else. Do you have a watch?

WOMAN 1: Did you take it?

WOMAN 2: Yes. Do you like it?

WOMAN 1: Where did you take it from?

WOMAN 2: A place.

WOMAN 1: Which place?

WOMAN 2: Just a place.*(Pause)*

WOMAN 1: Were there any mirrors?

WOMAN 2: No.

WOMAN 1: There were no mirrors?

WOMAN 2: No. There were cameras. *(Pause)*

WOMAN 1: They saw you didn't they?

WOMAN 2: No.

WOMAN 1: Yes, they saw you...they saw you...

WOMAN 2: No...no, they didn't see me. *(Pause)* Do you like it or not? *(Pause)* It was right at the end...I was about to go...well, I was nearly out...at the door, then somebody saw me.

131

WOMAN 1: And what happened?

WOMAN 2: Nothing...It was the first time, so they said it'd be alright if I paid.

WOMAN 1: *(taking the ring off)* Take it back *(Gives her the ring.)*

WOMAN 2: Don't you like it?

WOMAN 1: Yes, but it must've been very expensive.

WOMAN 2: No, it wasn't expensive - honestly. But if you don't like it...It's a bit too big, isn't it?

WOMAN 1: Can I have it back? I'll have it altered. *(Puts the ring in the box, the box in her pocket.)* Thank you.

WOMAN 2: You're welcome. *(Pause. WOMAN 2 goes to drink at the fountain.)*

WOMAN 1: What are you doing?

WOMAN 2: I'm going to drink. *(Pause.)* What's the matter?

WOMAN 1: Nothing. *(WOMAN 2 drinks and then looks at the set.)*

WOMAN 2: I thought they turned the fountains off at night.

WOMAN 1: It's always the same water.

WOMAN 2: What do you mean?

WOMAN 1: It's always the same water that comes up.

WOMAN 2: It can't be.

WOMAN 1: If somebody drinks, then they replace the amount that's lost.

WOMAN 2: I don't believe you.

WOMAN 1: It's so there isn't too much wasted.

WOMAN 2: *(looks for a moment at the jet of water)* The water is always different.

WOMAN 1: Did you think it'd be on all day and all night then?

WOMAN 2: Why not?

WOMAN 1: Because there isn't any water - it hasn't rained for months. And it won't rain tonight either.

WOMAN 2: It's clean. Come here, look - it's clean.

WOMAN 1: *(looking at the sky)* The storm is very far off.

WOMAN 2: They wouldn't let people drink if it wasn't clean.

WOMAN 1: You can't hear the thunder.

WOMAN 2: They wouldn't let anybody drink. They wouldn't even turn it on. *(She laughs.)* Stupid of me, you're kidding again and I...I took everything seriously. How silly. *(She goes to the other horse.)* And it's not going to rain either...silly of me to take an umbrella...a big one. The storm's a hundred kilometres away and I borrowed an umbrella. You see how silly I am? You see? *(Both laugh.)* What do you want to show me?

WOMAN 1: *(still laughing)* You were late.

WOMAN 2: I had to leave the kid with a neighbour - the one who lent me the umbrella - I waited for her more than half an hour at the door because she wasn't in, and when she finally arrived, she didn't want to let me go because she said it was bad luck to leave kids alone on stormy nights. I said I wasn't leaving him alone, I was leaving him with her. She went on and on - I shouldn't go, I had to stay - I don't know...And when I finally could leave it was striking twelve - I don't know where. *(She laughs for a second, then stops.)* You could show it to me now, even though it's a bit late.

WOMAN 1: No, I can't.

WOMAN 2: Why not?

WOMAN 1: Because it's already happened.

WOMAN 2: What's happened?

WOMAN 1: What I wanted to show you. You got here late. What's more I have to look after the dog. *(Stands, goes to the side. Pause.)*

WOMAN 2: Has it escaped again?

WOMAN 1: No, it hasn't escaped.

WOMAN 2: Where is it?

WOMAN 1: Over there. *(Pause.)* Didn't you hear it before? *(Pause.)*

WOMAN 2: You should have it on a lead, so it can't run off.

WOMAN 1: I told you it hasn't escaped. *(Long pause.)*

WOMAN 2: Would you like me to go and see what it's doing?

WOMAN 1: *(goes and sits where she was)* No, there's no need. As long as it doesn't leave the park.

WOMAN 2: I wouldn't mind going, and it knows me already. *(She stands.)*

WOMAN 1: Wait - it's not the same dog as yesterday. It's ...different.

133

WOMAN 2: A different dog?

WOMAN 1: Yes. *(WOMAN 2 sits. Pause.)*

WOMAN 2: Who does it belong to?

WOMAN 1: To a woman.

WOMAN 2: A foreign woman?

WOMAN 1: No. It belongs to a woman - a woman who can hardly cope with the stairs.

WOMAN 2: Which stairs?

WOMAN 1: And there isn't a lift.

WOMAN 2: Where?

WOMAN 1: Where she lives. *(Pause.)* I walk her dog every night. It's a very easy job.

WOMAN 2: A job?

WOMAN 1: Yes. And if it rains, I just walk it to the front door, the street and back again. *(WOMAN 2 moves slightly on the horse so every now and then the spring makes noises.)*

WOMAN 2: And do you always come here?

WOMAN 1: Yes.

WOMAN 2: Aren't you scared?

WOMAN 1: No. If you have a dog nobody comes too close. *(Pause.)*

WOMAN 2: What about yesterday's dog?

WOMAN 1: I've already taken it out. You can't have them together. You've got to take one at a time. That way you avoid fighting problems. *(Pause.)* It's very easy. You only need to see what they are doing every now and then and that's all.

WOMAN 2: What if they escape?

WOMAN 1: They don't escape. *(Pause.)* But if they do escape you have to get to the houses before they do.

WOMAN 2: They?

WOMAN 1: The dogs. *(Pause.)*

WOMAN 2: Do you walk lots of them?

WOMAN 1: No, not many. And I never let them drink from the fountains. This one is quite big and on his hind legs it can reach the spout. So I sit here all the time and make sure it doesn't drink.

134

(Pause.) I haven't heard it for a while. *(Pause.)* If you don't stop making noises we won't hear it. (**WOMAN 2** *stops moving. Long pause.)*

WOMAN 1: I'm going to see where it is. *(Stands, moves to one side.)*

WOMAN 2: *(standing)* I've got to go. I promised to be back before one.

WOMAN 1: Well, see you tomorrow. *(Exits.)*

WOMAN 2: Listen...

WOMAN 1: *(off)* But you've got to be on time.

WOMAN 2: I'm not sure that tomorrow-

WOMAN 1: *(off)* I'll show you something that nobody's seen.

WOMAN 2: What?

WOMAN 1: *(off)* I'm the only one who's seen it.

WOMAN 2: Show it to me now.

WOMAN 1: It's not possible...you won't be able to see anything.

WOMAN 2: Well, tell me what it is. *(Pause.)*

WOMAN 1: *(enters)* It's...a discovery.

WOMAN 2: Here?

WOMAN 1: Yes, here.

WOMAN 2: Right here?

WOMAN 1: In the park. *(Exits from opposite side.)*

WOMAN 2: What...what is it? (**WOMAN 2** *does not know whether to stay or go. She is about to leave when* **WOMAN 1** *enters.)*

WOMAN 1: *(looking back)* It's there...*(Takes something from her pocket)* Normally, I give it this and then it comes back straight away, then we can go. *(She puts it away.)*

WOMAN 2: I don't think I can come tomorrow.

WOMAN 1: Why?

WOMAN 2: I work in the mornings...very early.

WOMAN 1: So what?

WOMAN 2: And I don't have anyone to leave the kid with...

WOMAN 1: Leave it with your neighbour.

WOMAN 2: I did that today. I can't ask her again - tomorrow.

WOMAN 1: Bring him.

135

WOMAN 2: Here?

WOMAN 1: Yes.

WOMAN 2: It's so late.

WOMAN 1: Never mind - forget it. *(Sits on one of the horses, then takes the book from her pocket.)* Here... *(WOMAN 2 does not take it.)*

WOMAN 2: I can come another night. You always come here, don't you?

WOMAN 1: Forget it.

WOMAN 2: You come every night, don't you?

WOMAN 1: No. Not every night. *(Pause.)*

WOMAN 2: Do you come on saturdays? Saturdays-

WOMAN 1: I don't know.

WOMAN 2: You don't know if you come on saturdays?

WOMAN 1: On saturdays there's always someone who comes to vomit in the bins. *(Pause.)*

WOMAN 2: What about in the afternoon? A sunday afternoon?

WOMAN 1: It's got to be at night.

WOMAN 2: Why?

WOMAN 1: Because it only happens at night.

WOMAN 2: In the park?

WOMAN 1: Yes, in the park.

WOMAN 2: And nobody else has seen it?

WOMAN 1: No, nobody. It's a discovery. *(Pause.)*

WOMAN 2: I don't understand. I don't know what you mean - a discovery.

WOMAN 1: Don't you know what a discovery is?

WOMAN 2: Yes...no...I don't know...I don't understand why you'd show it to me...I don't know what to do.

WOMAN 1: You don't have to do anything. It happens without anybody doing anything.

WOMAN 2: There! I don't understand a thing, you see.

WOMAN 1: There isn't anything to understand...Look, never mind, don't come. *(WOMAN 1 stands. Moves to one side. Pause.)*

WOMAN 2: *(moving closer)* Maybe the day after tomorrow...well no, the day after tomorrow is saturday.

WOMAN 1: Doesn't matter, honestly.

WOMAN 2: If I ask her next week she's bound to say yes.

WOMAN 1: Who?

WOMAN 2: My neighbour - to look after the kid. The umbrella's hers. She lent it to me.

WOMAN 1: It's got a broken spoke.

WOMAN 2: I know.

WOMAN 1: And the colour's fading.

WOMAN 2: Fading? *(Opens the umbrella and looks at it. It is discoloured. She tries to close it.)* It's ruined. *(Pause.)*

WOMAN 1: Let me try. *(She tries.)* No, it's not possible. *(Gives WOMAN 2 the umbrella.)*

WOMAN 2: *(tries again)* What am I going to do now?

WOMAN 1: Leave it open.

WOMAN 2: I can't give it back like this.

WOMAN 1: Don't give it back then. I don't think she'll miss it. *(WOMAN 2 tries again.)*

WOMAN 1: If you want, I'll tell her it was my fault. *(Pause.)* I can ring her.

WOMAN 2: What for?

WOMAN 1: I'll tell her I broke it.

WOMAN 2: No. I'll have it fixed. *(Pause.)* I'm sure it can be fixed .*(Pause.)* Well...I'm going.

WOMAN 1: The book... *(Gives it to her. WOMAN 2 starts to go.)* Do you want me to walk you?

WOMAN 2: No, I'll take a taxi.

WOMAN 1: With the umbrella like that? *(WOMAN 2 stops.)* I can walk with you, with the dog.

WOMAN 2: No, there's no need. I'll leave the umbrella somewhere...yes it's quite bad really. *(Looking at it.)* This can't be fixed - the spoke...yes, I'll leave it somewhere...

WOMAN 1: You can leave it here.

WOMAN 2: Where?

WOMAN 1: In the bin. *(WOMAN 2 doubts this can be done, moves closer to the bin. She tries to close the umbrella without success. With difficulty she puts it in the bin, then moves to the fountain.)*

WOMAN 2 *:(moves to wash her hands, stops)* Is the discovery here?

WOMAN 1: In the fountain? No. *(Pause.)*

WOMAN 2: Listen - how do you know it's a discovery?

WOMAN 1: Because it is. Anybody could see it is. *(Pause. Suddenly, WOMAN 2 starts laughing)*

WOMAN 1: What is it?

WOMAN 2: I'm stupid - honestly. I believe everything.Somebody says something and I - a discovery, isn't it? And I believe it. *(She carries on laughing, then stops when she realizes WOMAN 1 isn't laughing.)*

WOMAN 1: It isn't a joke.

WOMAN 2: You think you can say anything and I'll believe it...so, why can't you show it to me now? Come on - why?

WOMAN 1: Because you were late.

WOMAN 2: So what? I don't see what that's got to do with it. Come on, show it to me. *(Goes upstage.)* Where is it? Come on. *(Turns her back to the audience.)* Where? *(She stops as she hears her last word echoed.)* Ah...is that...*(Echo repeats the word. She looks at WOMAN 1.)* Is that it?

WOMAN 1: What?

WOMAN 2: *(looks upstage again)* The discovery... *(Echo repeats the word.)*

WOMAN 1: The echo? No.

WOMAN 2: No? *(Echo.)*

WOMAN 1: That's the back wall.

WOMAN 2: Which wall? *(Echo repeats.)*

WOMAN 1: The voice bounces on the wall and sounds again. *(WOMAN 2 keeps looking upstage.)*

WOMAN 1: Sometimes it seems as if there are two dogs.

WOMAN 2: *(turns around)* It's very far away, the wall.

WOMAN 1: That one answers the other, but it's just an echo. *(Pause.*

WOMAN 2 moves closer to WOMAN 1.)

WOMAN 2: Well tell me what it is - go on...and you can show it to me another night.

WOMAN 1: No.

WOMAN 2: Why not?

WOMAN 1: Because you wouldn't believe it.

WOMAN 2: I would believe it.

WOMAN 1: So it's true that you believe anything anybody tells you, that you are really stupid?

WOMAN 2: I'm not stupid. Do you think I believe what you said about the book? That you stole it? Well I didn't. Because if you had taken it, they would have seen you like they saw me. *(Moves apart. Long pause. She blows her nose.)* I think I'm getting a cold. And if I get a cold, can you imagine what will happen? *(Pause.)* You can't? I'll give the cold to the kid. If I get a cold, he'll definitely get a cold as well. *(Pause.)*

WOMAN 1: If you want the scarf?

WOMAN 2: No thanks. I have to go. *(Takes the umbrella.)* I'll throw it away somewhere else - in a bigger bin. And then I'll take a taxi. *(Pause.)* Will you stay long?

WOMAN 1: A while.

WOMAN 2: Well...see you. *(Doubts, then exits.)* *(WOMAN 1 goes upstage and looks after WOMAN 2.)*

WOMAN 1: *(louder)* Listen - if you can't come tomorrow it doesn't matter! *(Pause.)* Did you hear me? *(Echo repeats the words)*

(Pause.Blackout.)

ACT THREE, SCENE ONE

In the darkness a telephone rings several times close-up. Lights up as the ELDERLY WOMAN'S VOICE on the answer-phone is heard. WOMAN 1 and WOMAN 2 are sitting at opposite ends of an iron bench, staring at a see-saw in front of them.

ELDERLY WOMAN'S VOICE: Hello. I'm not here at the moment.

139

You can leave your message after the tone. *(Pause. We hear the tone.)*
WOMAN 2'S VOICE: *(clearing her throat)* I thought you'd be at
home. You didn't say you were going out. The thing is, well, I never
know what to say to these gadgets. *(Clears throat.)* I don't know
whether to hang up and call again later on... no, it's done now, never
mind. *(Clears throat.)* Well, let's see...yes, well, it depends what time
you'll be back, because if it's too late I won't need - well if I hear you
coming, I'll go, but if it's too late, don't bother...I'll explain
tomorrow...What a mess - well, surely this must be nearly...I don't
know how these things work. *(Pause.)* Listen, do you know what I'm
thinking? It doesn't matter. Yes, maybe I can arrange it another way
so you don't do me a favour. And if you arrive very late it won't matter.
Right...see you, and thank you anyway. Good bye, good bye.
(Hangs up. Long pause. WOMAN 2 looks at WOMAN 1.)
WOMAN 2: I didn't get here late, did I?
*(Suddenly the see-saw slowly jerks, to one side with the same creaking
sound heard earlier, then stops with a sharp bump. Pause.)*
WOMAN 1: *(without altering her gaze)* It's twelve. *(Looks at
WOMAN 2.)* It's twelve o'clock now.
WOMAN 2: Do you mean that at twelve o'clock...?
WOMAN 1: Yes, every night at twelve o'clock exactly... *(Pause.
WOMAN 2 stands, moves closer to the see-saw and watches it
without touching it.)*
WOMAN 2: And there's no wind?
WOMAN 1: No. *(Long pause.)*
WOMAN 2: And does it stay like this? I mean, does anything else
happen?
WOMAN 1. No. Not 'till tomorrow at twelve o'clock.
WOMAN 2: At night?
WOMAN 1: Yes. At twelve o'clock at night. *(Long pause.)*
WOMAN 2: What if it's the other way round?
WOMAN 1: What?
WOMAN 2: Does it happen?
WOMAN 1: It doesn't matter which side the see-saw leans. At twelve
o'clock it always rocks to the other side.

WOMAN 2: Always?

WOMAN 1: Yes, always. *(Pause.)*

WOMAN 2: Maybe there's something underneath.

WOMAN 1: What...?

WOMAN 2: I don't know...How can I know? *(Pause.)* I think you should tell somebody.

WOMAN 1: Tell somebody?

WOMAN 2: Well...show it. Because you haven't shown it to anybody, have you?

WOMAN 1: To you.

WOMAN 2: Wait...I'm thinking...maybe I know who you can show it to.

WOMAN 1: Who?

WOMAN 2: *(sits on the bench)* Look - I've got a friend at work that has a friend who is a policeman...She doesn't tell anybody she's got a boyfriend who's a policeman - well she told me but she doesn't want anybody to know because-

WOMAN 1: *(interrupting)* D'you want to show it to a policeman?

WOMAN 2: No, well, I can tell her so she can tell him, and maybe he- *(WOMAN 1 starts laughing.)*

WOMAN 2: What are you laughing at? *(Pause.)* What's the matter? *(Pause.)* You're laughing at me aren't you?

WOMAN 1: *(laughing)* No...no. *(Pause.)* I was thinking...

WOMAN 2: What? *(WOMAN 1 carries on laughing, then she stops, seeing WOMAN 2 is very serious.)*

WOMAN 2: *(Stands)* You were laughing at me.

WOMAN 1: No, I wasn't laughing at you. Really, I wasn't. Maybe you're right - somebody should be told, because something's going to happen.

WOMAN 2: What?

WOMAN 1: I don't know...something.

WOMAN 2: So call the police yourself.

WOMAN 1: It might not be necessary...sometimes they patrol around here in cars.

141

WOMAN 2: I didn't mean a policeman, to show a policeman only this friend of...the thing is, I don't know anybody else...honestly, I can't think of anybody. Don't you know anybody? Of course, if you don't want to tell...well, I don't think I'd tell, and I wouldn't come back either.

WOMAN 1: You wouldn't come back again?

WOMAN 2: Well, perhaps one day - or every now and then...but of course if you bring the dogs...

WOMAN 1: At twelve o'clock I've always got to watch that none of them put their heads underneath.

WOMAN 2: Underneath? Oh, I see...

WOMAN 1: That they don't put their head at twelve o'clock in the exact place because it's a dead cert...

WOMAN 2: And where is he?

WOMAN 1: What...?

WOMAN 2: The dog.

WOMAN 1: I brought them earlier today.

WOMAN 2: Well then, you needn't worry. *(Pause.)* Do you know, I nearly didn't come. I couldn't find anybody to leave the kid with, in the end, to be on time, I left him alone. I shouldn't leave him alone. He might wake up before I get back.

WOMAN 1: You should have brought him.

WOMAN 2: No...it's too cold, and so late - but I can bring him another day. Earlier...if you like. *(Stands.)* Well...

WOMAN 1: I show you a discovery and the only thing that comes to mind is calling the police and then leaving?

WOMAN 2: What do you want me to do? I've told you I don't know what to do... I've told you. *(Pause.)* What do you expect me to do? Tell mc...what? *(Pause.)*

WOMAN 1: I shouldn't have shown it to you.

WOMAN 2: Oh, but I liked it...I mean it's something strange and good. Honestly, it was something I wouldn't have expected...well, I don't know what you want me to say...

WOMAN 1: Nothing, it doesn't matter. You don't need to say anything, really. *(Pause)*

WOMAN 2: If you want - I won't say anything at work.

WOMAN 1: No, you'd better not. *(Pause. WOMAN 2 moves closer to WOMAN 1.)*

WOMAN 2: Right...goodbye *(She offers her hand. Pause. WOMAN 1 takes her right hand from her coat. It is bandaged with a handkerchief.)* What happened?

WOMAN 1: Nothing...a dog bit me.

WOMAN 2: Which dog?

WOMAN 1: A dog.

WOMAN 2: One of yours?

WOMAN 1: They aren't mine.

WOMAN 2: Why did it bite you?

WOMAN 1: I trod on it. *(Pause.)*

WOMAN 2: Does it hurt?

WOMAN 1: No.

WOMAN 2: It must hurt.

WOMAN 1: No, not much. *(Pause.)*

WOMAN 2: Will you walk it again?

WOMAN 1: Yes, of course.

WOMAN 2: I'd be scared. If dogs know you're scared...

WOMAN 1: What?

WOMAN 2: It might bite you again.

WOMAN 1: I thought you didn't know anything about dogs. *(She stands and moves closer to the see-saw.)*

WOMAN 2: You know it's not allowed to have dogs off a lead? There are posters all over the place...and playing with balls isn't allowed either...*(WOMAN 1 touches the end of the see-saw.)* I'm only telling you because they might tell you off.

WOMAN 1: It's also forbidden to take them in a telephone box. When I rang you, I actually took the dog inside - I thought about it, and did it, and a policeman appeared, or somebody with a policeman's face because he wasn't wearing a uniform or anything and he told me...he told me it was forbidden. One day somebody will teach their dog to make a telephone call, and then it won't be forbidden anymore. Maybe he just said that because he was in a hurry and he wanted to make a call. So I went to a different telephone box and rang you with the dog inside. *(She looks up)* Full moon...a dog bites you on a full moon and it seems more normal. You see? Now you pull that face, the face you didn't pull before, when I showed you the discovery.

WOMAN 2: It's not true.

WOMAN 1: The discovery? Come tomorrow and you'll see.

WOMAN 2: No, I meant-

WOMAN 1: Never mind, don't come if you can't...because if you have to leave the kid alone or with the neighbour...

WOMAN 2: Well, I didn't leave him totally alone. She's nearby, and if he starts crying she'll hear him. When she goes out I listen to see if hers is crying too.

WOMAN 1: Oh, she's got one as well?

WOMAN 2: *(interrupting)* No, he's her son's. The son doesn't get along with his wife and when they quarrel they leave the boy with her 'till they get back together again. They always say it's the last time they'll bring the kid, but they always come back for the same reason.

WOMAN 1: I don't understand.

WOMAN 2: What is it you don't understand?

WOMAN 1: That we always end up talking about your neighbour.

WOMAN 2: Well, you asked if -

WOMAN 1: *(interrupting)* Yes, it was my fault, you're right. *(She sits on the end of the see-saw. Long pause.)*

WOMAN 2: Has the dog been vaccinated?

WOMAN 1: What?

WOMAN 2: The dog that bit you...

WOMAN 1: *(interrupting)* I don't know...I suppose so.

WOMAN 2: Didn't it have a badge?

WOMAN 1: I didn't notice.

WOMAN 2: It should have one.

WOMAN 1: Maybe...I don't know.

WOMAN 2: Well, it might have something that -

WOMAN 1: All that happened was I trod on it, that's all.*(Pause.)*

WOMAN 2: I don't know if I can find a taxi at this time - one that would take me to my place...where I live they've been building for more than a year, and no-one wants to go there this late. *(She takes a look at her watch.)* What time do you make it? This one runs fast, at least five minutes a day. *(Pause.)* D'you know, there are people that make watches work just by looking at them? I don't know how they do it.

WOMAN 1: Do you want me to fix it?

WOMAN 2: What?

WOMAN 1: The watch...

WOMAN 2: It's working.

WOMAN 1: Didn't you say it runs fast?

WOMAN 2: Only five minutes...but it's alright. *(Pause)* What do you want to do?

WOMAN 1: Do you want it fixed or not?

WOMAN 2: Yes.

WOMAN 1: Put it there.

WOMAN 2: Where?

WOMAN 1: Down there.

WOMAN 2: Here?

WOMAN 1: Yes.

WOMAN 2: What for?

WOMAN 1: Go on. *(WOMAN 2 puts the watch at the other end of the see-saw.)*

WOMAN 2: Now what?

WOMAN 1: Nothing.

WOMAN 2: Is it fixed now?

WOMAN 1: No, not yet.

(WOMAN 1 stands and balances the see-saw. It is rusty and stays still for a while. After a moment of doubt, WOMAN 2 picks up the watch before WOMAN 1 makes for it, then the see-saw rocks down on the side where the watch was before.)

WOMAN 1: For a second I thought you wouldn't pick it up.

WOMAN 2: *(seriously)* It was a joke, wasn't it? *(Pause.)* It was funny.

WOMAN 1: It was stupid.

WOMAN 2: No, it wasn't.

WOMAN 1: Sorry.

WOMAN 2: *(looking at the watch)* It's alright, no harm done.

WOMAN 1: You...you haven't hurt your hand, have you?

WOMAN 2: No.

WOMAN 1: *(coming closer)* Really?

WOMAN 2: *(moving away)* I'm fine. *(Pause)*

WOMAN 1: Now you won't come again.

WOMAN 2: What do you want me to come back for? I've seen the discovery already, haven't I? What I don't understand is why you showed it to me.

WOMAN 1: Because you came.

WOMAN 2: Have you shown anybody else? *(Pause.)* Am I the only one who's come? *(Pause.)* I even thought about bringing the kid. Can you imagine?

WOMAN 1: When he grows...

WOMAN 2: What?

WOMAN 1: You can bring him to play.

WOMAN 2: Here? I won't bring him here, never, ever. And I won't tell him anything about your...discovery either. You see, I've got the feeling that it isn't a discovery or anything - that it's something...well, like the fountain - we don't know how the water comes out It comes out but we don't know how. Do you know? *(Pause.)* You see? You don't know either. *(Pause.)* You think it's a discovery, but you see, a discovery is something different. And if I were you, I wouldn't go around telling everybody you've made a...discovery because they're going to laugh at you. I'm only warning you. I see, you thought if I believed anybody would...but I didn't believe it. And I didn't believe you about the moon either - that a dog bit you because there was a full moon. Look, I'm not ever going to tell any stories to kids. I can't bear those people who tell stories to kids and then have to explain to them they aren't true. Look, I only tell him things that are true - things that actually happen, 'though he doesn't understand. Well, he wouldn't understand stories now, either. But I talk to him anyway, even though he's asleep... He still sleeps most of the time. More than likely, he can't

146

hear me but I talk to him anyway. I even told him about the ring - when I took it, well, when I stole it and was caught. *(She smiles.)* I was lucky because I thought the police might come, but they didn't. They took me to a dark room and it was messy - Can you imagine? They left me there for quite a while, alone. Well I thought I was alone until I saw somebody in the corner. I thought the same thing might have happened to her that happened to me - that she'd been caught like me. And I started talking to her about the ring and about you having taken a book, and many other things because I was nervous. Well, she didn't say a thing, so finally I moved closer and realized there was nobody - it was a mannequin, naked. I'd been talking all the time to a nude dummy of a woman, can you imagine? Well I laughed, honestly I did. And then as they didn't call the police, I only had to pay for the ring. They told me if I paid for it, nothing would happen to me.

WOMAN 1: You shouldn't have paid.

WOMAN 2: I know. *(She stares at WOMAN 1.)*

WOMAN 1: This scarf isn't mine.Found it in the park, a while ago. It's far too small for me and I don't like the colour either. Do you like it?

WOMAN 2: No, I don't like it either. *(Pause.)*

WOMAN 2: How's the hand?

WOMAN 1: What?

WOMAN 2: Does it hurt?

WOMAN 1: No.

WOMAN 2: Honestly, you should know if the dog's been vaccinated or not.

WOMAN 1: It hardly touched me, and it's gone.

WOMAN 2: Has it got away?

WOMAN 1: Yes. *(She sits on the bench.)*

WOMAN 2: Didn't you go to its home?

WOMAN 1: No, I didn't feel like running, and anyway, you were going to come. *(She takes off the handkerchief and shows her hand to WOMAN 2)* It's nothing. *(Pause.)*

WOMAN 2: Do this. *(Opens and closes her hand.)*

WOMAN 1: *(doing it)* It hurts if I do that.

WOMAN 2: Can you open it properly?

147

WOMAN 1: Yes. *(She opens and closes her hand several times, then puts on the handkerchief again.)*

WOMAN 2: Can you do this? *(She brings together the fingers of her left hand in two's and three's in different combinations.)*

WOMAN 1: You mean this hand? *(Shows the bandaged hand.)*

WOMAN 2: No, I mean the other.

WOMAN 1: *(without trying)* No, I can't do it.

WOMAN 2: There are very few people who can do it. Even fewer can do it with both hands. I can't do it with this one...I can only do it with my left hand. I don't know why. *(Pause.)* I'll teach the kid to do it with both hands. *(Pause.)*

WOMAN 1: What's he called?

WOMAN 2: Who?

WOMAN 1: The kid.

WOMAN 2: Kid.

WOMAN 1: Didn't you give him a name?

WOMAN 2: His name's Kid.

WOMAN 1: Kid?

WOMAN 2: Yes.

WOMAN 1: Oh, it's a joke.

WOMAN 2: No, it isn't a joke. *(Pause.)*

WOMAN 1: Why did you call him Kid?

WOMAN 2: Because I like Kid. It's nice.

WOMAN 1: What about when he grows up?

WOMAN 2: What?

WOMAN 1: He'll be called Kid...

WOMAN 2: So what?

WOMAN 1: Nothing. *(Pause.)*

WOMAN 2: It's the first time I left him alone at night. Well, when one sleeps one leaves them alone as well and nobody cares about that. And in fact, he isn't alone because the neighbour's nearby. She stays up till very late watching television. I don't complain when she has it very loud because she looks after the kid so often. It's not me who asks - she wants to do it. Well, when it's too loud - the television - then I tell her

148

because otherwise the kid can't sleep.

WOMAN 1: Kid.

WOMAN 2: What?

WOMAN 1: You should say 'Kid' not 'the kid'.

WOMAN 2: Same thing, isn't it?

WOMAN 1: No it isn't.

WOMAN 2: Yes it is. *(She stands, moves closer to the see-saw. After a while she dares to touch it Pause. Suddenly a blue light flashes for a time, on one side, then disappears on the other side. Both women remain still for a time.)*

WOMAN 1: They 'll come back again later on to see if we're still here.

WOMAN 2: Well...Shall we go?

WOMAN 1: Where?

WOMAN 2: To get a taxi.

WOMAN 1: No, you go.

WOMAN 2: Are you staying?

WOMAN 1: I'll leave soon.

WOMAN 2: I'll wait.

WOMAN 1: No...it's very late.

WOMAN 2: Well, come on then. We can share a cab.

WOMAN 1: No. Never mind.

WOMAN 2: Where do you live?

WOMAN 1: Never mind. Go by yourself.

WOMAN 2: What are you going to do here?

WOMAN 1: I'll wait for the police to tell them about the dog - that it's escaped.

WOMAN 2: Will you tell the police?

WOMAN 1: Yes.

WOMAN 2: Why are you going to tell them?

WOMAN 1: Because you've got to tell them when a dog escapes, especially if it's bitten you.

WOMAN 2: Do it tomorrow.

WOMAN 1: The dog isn't mine.

WOMAN 2: What if they don't come back?

149

WOMAN 1: Well I'll tell them tomorrow. But I'm sure they'll come back. *(Pause.)*

WOMAN 2: Do you want me to stay till they come back?

WOMAN 1: No...what for?

WOMAN 2: Well, being alone here...

WOMAN 1: If anybody comes... (*She takes the chain lead from her coat.*)

WOMAN 2: You think so?

WOMAN 1: Yes, you've got to have it in your hand, like this. *(Pause.)* You can see it, can't you?

WOMAN 2: Yes. *(Pause.)* If it wasn't for the kid, I'd wait with you for the police.

WOMAN 1: It's not necessary, really.

WOMAN 2: Well...(*Moves to the side, then stops.*) I won't find a taxi now and I'll have to walk. At least tomorrow's saturday and I don't go to work.

WOMAN 1: You can take the bus.

WOMAN 2: *(absent-mindedly)* What?

WOMAN 1: The bus.

WOMAN 2: I don't know where to catch one around here, and it's so late...I'd rather take a taxi.

WOMAN 1: Yes, you'd better.

WOMAN 2: Yes...well...goodbye. *(Pause.)*

WOMAN 1: See you tomorrow. *(WOMAN 2 turns.)* It was a joke *(Pause.)* What's the matter?

WOMAN 2: Will you come tomorrow? *(Pause.)* I don't think you should come back. You could walk the dogs somewhere else...and this (*Looks at the see-saw.*) Well, you can come back some time to see how it's going.

WOMAN 1: To see how it's going?

WOMAN 2: Well-

WOMAN 1: *(interrupting)* Yes, I understand.

WOMAN 2: If you want we can come together one day. And I won't tell anybody if you don't want me to. Don't you believe me? *(Pause.)*

150

If you like I promise...
WOMAN 1: No, never mind.
WOMAN 2: I'll promise anyway. *(Pause.)* Goodbye.
WOMAN 1: Goodbye.
(WOMAN 2 exits.)
WOMAN 2: *(off)* Call me...*(Further off fading.)* Goodbye.

(WOMAN 1 looks off after WOMAN 2 for a while, puts the chain back in her pocket, then sits on the bench. She looks around and then examines the bandaged hand without removing the handkerchief. The blue light flashes. It stops. WOMAN 1 stands and exits. Pause. A telephone rings, then a conversation is heard.)

ELDERLY WOMAN'S VOICE: Yes.
WOMAN 2'S VOICE: Hello, it's me...I saw the light...I didn't know whether you'd forgotten to turn off the light and as there wasn't a sound...I might have woken you up but as I saw the light...I'm speaking softly so as not to wake the kid...*(Pause.)* No, he hasn't woken up...Well I'm going to sleep now. I might read a little bit before...No, I think I'm going straight to bed because it's quite late...Well, good night.
ELDERLY WOMAN'S VOICE: Goodnight.

(Sound of telephone being hung up, beeps for a few seconds, while the blue light appears on one side. Sound of the other telephone being hung up. Silence. WOMAN 1 enters looking in the direction of the light, takes the scarf, folds it and puts it underneath the raised end of the see-saw. She lies on the floor on her side, puts her head on the folded scarf and closes her eyes. Blackout.)

END

MEPHISTO

by Klaus Mann
Adapted by Ariane Mnouchkine
Translated from the French by Timberlake Wertenbaker

'Mephisto' was premiered by the Théâtre du Soleil on May 15th, 1979
at the Cartoucherie of Vincennes

CHARACTERS	CAST
Klaus Mann / Sebastien Brückner	Christian Colin
Hendrik Höfgen	Gérard Hardy
Carola Martin	Lucia Bensasson
Hans Miklas	Jonathan Sutton
Theresa von Herzfeld	Marie-Françoise Audollent
Otto Ulrich	Jean Claude Bourbault
Magnus Gottchalk	Yves Gourvil
Madame Efeu	Louba Guertchikoff
Knurr	Roland Amstutz
Juliette	Myrrha Donzenac
Myriam Horowitz	Anne Demeyer
Alex	Norbert Journo
Erika Brückner	Joséphine Derenne
Nicoletta van Niebuhr	Nicole Félix
Theophile Sarder	René Patrignani
Lorenz	Julien Maurel / Pierre Fatus
The Waiter	John Arnold
Thomas Brückner	Jean Dupont
Emelyne	Odile Cointepas
Ludwig	Claude Forget
Hans Josthinkel	Georges Bonnaud

At the Peppermill:

Hitler	Christian Colin
General Fonnesique	Jonathan Sutton

At the restaurant:

The Maître d'hôtel	Georges Bonnaud
The Officer	Jean Dupond

PROLOGUE
(Voice on tape.)

THE VOICE OF THE PUBLISHER: May the 5th, 1949. Dear Sir,
Thank you for sending us your manuscript of "*Mephisto*".
Unfortunately, we are unable at the moment to fit your novel into our
budget. You cannot be ignorant of the leading part Mr Höfgen is once
again playing in German affairs, and your book could be construed as a
personal attack. Had we been in East Berlin, we wouldn't have
hesitated to launch such an operation, but West Berlin presents too
many difficulties. It is with great regret that we've relinquished
publishing "*Mephisto*", but we cannot risk a ban which we fear would
be unavoidable in the present political climate. Yours sincerely, etc.
(Another voice rises. This one is alive, indignant, furious.) Sir, Your
letter of May the 5th boggles the imagination. Publishing a book in
your house is now called "launching an operation". And when this
"operation" presents certain difficulties, you abandon it. Why?
Because Mr. Höfgen is once again playing a leading part in Germany.
And you call that "reasonable" - "responsible citizenship" - "honouring
a contract". I don't know which amazed me more - the baseness of
your thinking or the artlessness with which you've confessed your
baseness. Höfgen is successful: - why then publish a book "which
might be construed as a personal attack"? Indeed. Why? We musn't
take risks. We side with power. We swim with the current. You know
as well as I do where that leads - straight to the camps, those camps no-
one is supposed to have known even existed. I am taking the liberty of
asking you to send "*Mephisto*" back by return of post. And please
refrain from ever writing to me again. Yours, - Klaus Mann.

THE ACTOR: *(to the audience)* For Klaus Mann, the story of this novel began on a November evening of 1923, in the city of Hamburg. The stage will begin by representing the Hamburg Theatre. The members of this company will play all the people Klaus Mann met and who became caught up in his story, as well as those people Klaus Mann chose to invent.

SCENE ONE

The Hamburg Theatre. Thunderous applause. The curtain goes up as an entire company comes onstage for the call. The officer, a worker, a priest, a whore, a minister, all of Germany are taking the call. The star of the evening is **CAROLA MARTIN**. *She takes several bows with her two leading actors in full evening dress. A news item has been travelling back-stage and is adding to the usual emotion of a first night. One of the actors,* **HENDRIK HÖFGEN**, *decides to make an announcement. He steps forward, to cheers and applause.*

HENDRIK HÖFGEN: *(at the microphone)* Friends -dear friends ...something has happened to put this applause, these actors' vanities, into more sober perspective. Listen to me this morning, November the 9th, 1923, a coup took place in Munich. The coup was led by Hitler and his storm troopers. *(The audience goes silent. HENDRIK continues solemnly.)* It gives me the greatest pleasure to be able to tell you that...it failed. The police remained loyal to our young republic and opened fire. The rats have fled. Hitler has been arrested. Goering is on the run. The Nationalist Socialist party has been outlawed. That's all I wanted to say. Goodnight,...thank you...thank you...goodbye...thank you...*(He bows again and again. Little by little, the applause dies down and the theatre empties.)*
HENDRIK: *(to OTTO)* Friend. Brother. Comrade. What a victory! Hitler's done for. *(Congratulations all round, kisses, embraces. CAROLA is made much of, petted. She sits at the make-up table. KNURR, the caretaker, brings a bottle of champagne and glasses.)*
HENDRIK: Champagne! Carola is offering us all Champagne.
CAROLA: I'm afraid there's only one bottle, but it did cost a fortune. And you can't expect more from a Jew.

154

THERESA: Champagne! To drink a glass of Champagne in times like these. Hold me back, someone, or I'll misbehave. No one loves Champagne more than I do.

CAROLA: *(to HANS MIKLAS)* And here's my handsome little soldier. I must tell you how much I admire you, Miklas. You're quite an actor. You were simply marvellous in that border scene. I wasn't at my best there, but you managed to save both of us from mediocrity.

MIKLAS: I did my best, Miss Martin, but you didn't help. You were supposed to let go of my hand after saying, "Remember me."

CAROLA: Yes, and you tore your hand away as if I'd set fire to it.

MIKLAS: You ought to have let go of my hand, Miss Martin, and when you didn't, I pulled my hand away.

CAROLA: I ought to have let go...yes, yes. Instead of which I held onto that hand a little too long. And it's such a stiff little hand, too -

MIKLAS: If you don't like the contact of my hand...If you find the contact of my hand displeasing - *(He stops.)*

CAROLA: I never suggested such a thing, Hans Miklas, you know that very well. I simply felt that such a brutal gesture was unnecessary.

MIKLAS: That's for the director to decide and no-one else. Especially not you, Miss Martin - you only came for the last week of rehearsals.

CAROLA: Do have a taste of my Champagne, Miklas, and let's put an end to this silly quarrel.

MIKLAS: I refuse to drink French Champagne worth its weight in gold when the rest of Germany is starving.

CAROLA: That's enough now. I'm a patient woman, but this is really too much. *(SEBASTIEN BRÜCKNER comes in. He is played by the same actor who was KLAUS MANN in the Prologue.)*

SEBASTIEN: Carola. You were wonderful. What a success! *(He stops, thrown by the tension in the air.)*

CAROLA: Sebastien, my dear. What a pleasure to see you! I completely forgot you were coming - Let me introduce you to the actors of the Hamburg Theatre - Miss Theresa von Herzfeld. Miss von Herzfeld is also an excellent stage designer - Hans Miklas...

SEBASTIEN: I found you very moving, Mr Miklas.

CAROLA: Wasn't he? Wasn't he just. Otto Ulrich. I fear Mr. Ulrich is one of those dangerous communists. Hendrik Höfgen, the greatest actor in Hamburg and soon, no doubt, in all of Germany. Magnus

Gottchalk, our director, the artistic director of the theatre, in a word, God. And his wife Miriam.

MAGNUS: Delighted. I believe we're seeing each other tomorrow. You're reading me one of your plays, aren't you? I'm looking forward to it with much pleasure. And curiosity. I'm a great admirer of your father.

SEBASTIEN: Ah yes...my tremendous Papa...

HENDRIK: (*to OTTO*) I think there were quite a few communists in the audience tonight. They were overjoyed.

CAROLA: You triumphed, my dear...It was as if you'd routed Mr. Hitler and his storm troopers all by yourself. That's an art...Yes, they'll like you in Berlin, you see. And now, please forgive me, all of you. We're invited to a dreadful reception and I have to put in an appearance. Those people are paid in dollars and it'll be lavish...I'll steal some Champagne. (*to MIKLAS*) Don't make such a face, little soldier. Your Mr. Hitler will soon be out of prison. (*She leaves, followed by SEBASTIEN.*)

MIKLAS: Champagne. Dollars. There's a kike for you.

MAGNUS: No. I do not allow that kind of thing in my theatre.

MIKLAS: What's wrong? Isn't she a Jew?

HENDRIK: Yes. Carola Martin is a Jew. Everyone knows that. Just as everyone knows that Hans Miklas is a National Socialist. And he's not the only one, either. Mr. Knurr, who's making himself look very small over there, is also a great admirer of Adolf Hitler. Don't hide, Mr. Knurr, we all know you have a swastika sewn on the inside of your jacket.

MR. KNURR: I'm not hiding, Mr. Höfgen. I'm sweeping your corner.

HENDRIK: You don't like me very much, do you, Knurr? You hoped filthy reds like me would be the first to hang when Adolf came to power, but you've been unlucky, Mr. Knurr. It's your Hitler who almost got himself hanged this afternoon. (*to MIKLAS*) And you, my lad, if you want to stay here, let me advise you to -

OTTO: That's enough from you, Hendrik. (*to MIKLAS*) As for you, why don't you try to think with your own brains? Because believe me, all these friends of yours ever do is trumpet through their arseholes. (*MIKLAS goes. HENDRIK sits and takes his make-up off. OTTO is about to leave.*)

OTTO: Are you coming? We're rehearsing tonight. I can wait for

156

you.

HENDRIK: No - you go. You can start without me.

MAGNUS: Listen, Otto, you and my wife are getting me into trouble with this revolutionary cabaret of yours. I want to talk to you. *(to HENDRIK)* Do me a favour and sit in for me tomorrow morning. Frankly, the minor essays of this century's spoiled children get on my nerves.

HENDRIK: What spoiled children?

MAGNUS: Brückner junior.

HENDRIK: Was that him? Brückner's son? *(MAGNUS follows OTTO out. HENDRIK contemplates himself in the mirror and enjoys what he sees. Of the actors, THERESA alone remains.)*

THERESA: What are you thinking about?

HENDRIK: Carola Martin."They'll like you in Berlin," she said. Berlin, will I ever get to Berlin, Theresa? I'm a provincial actor. I'll never be anything more than an obscure actor from the provinces. It'll kill me. Can you understand how much that hurts, Theresa?

THERESA: There's always a price to be paid for hurting others. And you're hurting so many people around you, you're bound to have to atone for it, one way or another. *(As she is about to leave, she throws off.)* Goodnight, Comrade. *(THERESA leaves. MRS. EFEU, the dresser and prompter is also getting ready to leave. HENDRIK calls her back.)*

HENDRIK: Darling Mrs. Efeu. Help me. Don't abandon me now. I'm exhausted. *(MRS. EFEU helps him dress and puts away the clothes he drops on the floor. He puts his cap on carefully, studying himself in the mirror, combs his hair, and leaves.)*

HENDRIK: Heil...what was his name?

MRS EFEU: He's made me miss my last tram again.

KNURR: There's no hurry, then...A little something? *(MIKLAS plays the violin. MRS. EFEU sits down.)*

MRS. EFEU: So the Nazis made a mess of it, did they? Shame. They might've brought down the price of swedes. *(She drinks.)* What's in here?

KNURR: Shit. A Jew's discovered how to distil shit. He's a millionaire now. *(MRS. EFEU laughs.)*

MRS. EFEU: And how much does he pay for it, that's what I want to know. I've got something to sell and I'm sure you do to, Mr. Knurr.

157

The one thing Germany isn't short of these days is shit. Ha ha. Well, give us another glass, then. I need a good treat.

MIKLAS: *(playing)* Armchair communists. Höfgen, that Martin woman and their little clique. But the Jews haven't won yet; no, the German people will recognise its true saviour. It won't succumb to the lies of the Jewish Marxists nor to the lies of the middle classes who suck out its blood. Hitler isn't hanging at the end of a rope yet. The Germans have lost their honour, but Hitler will give it back to them. He'll wipe his arse with the treaty of Versailles. Our movement will win. Our revolution is nigh.

MRS. EFEU: Well, you tell this revolution of yours to get a move on, because tomorrow I'm selling myself for a slice of bread.

SCENE TWO

The dressing room of a dingy night-club. HENDRIK watches JULIETTE shave her legs.

HENDRIK: Can't you hold yourself straight?

JULIETTE: Ppph. I'm exhausted. I had to do that number three times tonight - twice in a row for just five drunks. Well at least I had a full house for my entrance.

HENDRIK: Did you do the "woman with a lasso"?

JULIETTE: No, thank you. Thank you very much. Not that one. You made me sweat over it for weeks and weeks and when I did it, they pissed themselves laughing. That lasso, let me tell you -

HENDRIK: That's because you didn't feel confident enough with it.

JULIETTE: Not confident? Not confident?

HENDRIK: I choreographed you a very good number. I know what I'm talking about.

JULIETTE: You should've seen me. There was my arse pointing straight up at the ceiling, my lasso twirling and twirling round my head, while I rolled my great big ferocious African eyes and yelped a lot. And all they said was, "Just show us your bush, doll, cut the monkey business."

HENDRIK: What did you expect? They laughed because they found it disturbing. It *is* disturbing.

JULIETTE: Yeh, well. Maybe it's disturbing for you, all that stuff,

158

the lasso, getting slapped around...But them, they prefer the rumba, it's more advanced. You know, the blokes who come here, they wouldn't mind giving you a good thrashing, but they'd never think of taking one.

HENDRIK: Do hurry up. I missed the revolutionary cabaret to come and get you.

JULIETTE: Yeh. Well. It's not the first time you've missed your revolutionary cabaret. *(She drinks straight from a bottle.)* What piss. Want some? What is it you do exactly in this revolutionary cabaret of yours?

HENDRIK: Nothing to interest little girls. I'll tell you about it when you grow up.

JULIETTE: Bollocks. I've seen revolutionary theatre before, let me tell you, in the street. I know exactly what happens. They bring out a big loudspeaker and someone shouts: "Down with the bourgeoisie. Long live communism." And then the police come and arrest everybody. But what exactly is it, communism?

HENDRIK: Look at my hands...how ugly they look next to your legs. I shouldn't even be allowed to touch you.

JULIETTE: Yeh. Hands, feet, everything of yours is ugly. Your soul, everything. Why don't you let me come to the theatre when you're acting? I know what I'm going to do. One night, you'll come out on-stage and you'll see me, right there, in the middle of the stalls. Yes. And I'll be laughing very, very loud.

HENDRIK: That's not funny! I forbid you to come to the theatre - do you hear!

JULIETTE: Every time you're on-stage, I'll point my finger at you. I'll twirl my lasso and roll my great big beautiful eyes and I'll shout: "Look at the handsome monkey, ladies and gentlemen, look at dat monkey dere. Dat's me own little monkey and me be his she-monkey."

HENDRIK: *(taking her in his arms)* Ah. I love you. You're smooth, you're hard, you're strong. You're the love of my life. Do you know that?

JULIETTE: Yeh. But seriously, Hendrik, teach me communism. I want to learn something that's good.

HENDRIK: "You walk on the dead. Beauty, with mockery. Horror glitters brightly among your ornaments, and mingling casually with your expensive baubles, murder dances lovingly on your belly's proud curve, murder dances lovingly on the proud curve of your belly."

JULIETTE: Dancing in a dockland night-club doesn't do much for your brain, let me tell you. Doesn't do much for your heart either. Hendrik, teach me something. *(He takes her hand and slowly makes her slap him harder and harder.)*
HENDRIK: You don't need to know anything; it's all in your blood. My Beauty, my Africa, my Torment, my Savage.
JULIETTE: No...Hendrik...let me go. I don't feel like it. Hendrik, I like you. Stop. Please. You're hurting me.

SCENE THREE

The Peppermill, a revolutionary cabaret. **OTTO**, **ALEX**, *and* **MYRIAM** *are rehearsing. An exhausted MAGNUS, who's been waiting hours for his wife to finish, watches them. A short musical overture.*

THE M.C. *(ALEX)*: Dear Audience. Thanks to the exquisite courtesy of the official censorship which has condescended to be amongst us tonight and has had the exceptional graciousness of allowing us to act before you, the Peppermill is proud to present its great modern epic-lyrical verse drama in the form of a mystery play in seventy-five scenes. Scene the first: Myriam at the Department of Social Security. *(He lowers a drop.)*
THE WOMAN *(MYRIAM)*: It's now six times I've been here, and every time I have a form missing. Could you please tell me, Mister the Employee, Sir, if this time I have everything you need?
THE EMPLOYEE *(OTTO)*: What I need. What I need? Wait. Why are you asking me what I need? You're the one who has to have everything you need. I don't need anything.
THE WOMAN: I was told I'd find the information I need at the Department of Social Security.
THE EMPLOYEE: Yes.
THE WOMAN: Yes what?
THE EMPLOYEE: That's probable. The Department of Social Security will give you the necessary information.
THE WOMAN: I've been sitting here an hour and you still haven't given me any information.
THE EMPLOYEE: You didn't ask for information. You kept asking

160

me what I needed.

THE WOMAN: Now I'm asking you for some information.

THE EMPLOYEE: The office is closed.

THE WOMAN: What are you doing here, then?

THE EMPLOYEE: I'm waiting for it to open.

THE WOMAN: When does it open?

THE EMPLOYEE: When I open it.

THE WOMAN: When do you open?

THE EMPLOYEE: When it s time.

THE WOMAN: Will that be a long lime?

THE EMPLOYEE: Ah. Time is relative. Let us suppose I'm lounging on the soft cushions of a velvet sofa eating a bowl of chicken consommé with little balls of chopped liver in it, then a minute will pass as quickly as lightning. But if you're shivering by a coal-less stove, then that same minute will last more than a century. So you see, my dear lady, knowing nothing about the circumstances of your life, I'm in no position to give you any answers. *(He takes off his hat and puts on a cap.)*

THE WOMAN: Why are you putting on a cap?

THE EMPLOYEE: I wear a cap when I work.

THE WOMAN: Are you working now?

THE EMPLOYEE: Surely that's obvious.

THE WOMAN: Right. Now can I have some information please?

THE EMPLOYEE: Stop. Halt there. This is the Department of Social Security, not the Department of Information. If you're looking for the Department of Information, you'll find it at number 17 The Treaty of Versailles Is a Filthy Insult Avenue. Whereas this department is at number 20 The German Army Never Lost the War, It Was Stabbed in the Back by the Bolsheviks Square.

THE WOMAN: But it's social security I need.

THE EMPLOYEE: Any special kind of social security?

THE WOMAN: Yes.

THE EMPLOYEE: Stop. Halt there. Special cases are at number 12 If Germany's on the Shitheap It's Because Wages Are Too High Street.

THE WOMAN: How the hell do I know if I'm a special case or not?

THE EMPLOYEE: You mean you don't even know what kind of a case you are? You're not by any chance trying to cheat the system are you?

THE WOMAN: I'm expecting twins, my husband was badly wounded in the war, I can't find work and I don't have anywhere to live.

THE EMPLOYEE: Sounds like you need some social security. Let's begin at the beginning. What's your address?

THE WOMAN: I told you I'm on the street.

THE EMPLOYEE: Where's your permit?

THE WOMAN: What permit?

THE EMPLOYEE: Your street permit. Where do you expect me to send you the forms?

THE WOMAN: Send them to my sister at number 14 Everything Was Better under the Emperor Lane.

THE EMPLOYEE: When did you lose your housing?

THE WOMAN: On November the 20th.

THE EMPLOYEE: Now that's a shame.

THE WOMAN: Of course it's a shame.

THE EMPLOYEE: If you'd lost it on the 21st, you'd be entitled to special benefits because of the legislation passed on the 31st, which took effect retrospectively on the 21st but not on the 19th.

THE WOMAN: What about my twins? I've been told I'm entitled to a swede allowance.

THE EMPLOYEE: Certainly. Everybody's entitled to a swede allowance. But stop. Halt there. It's not here. It's at 127 Everybody's Ganging Up against Germany but That's Because They're Jealous Alley.

THE WOMAN: What kind of help can you give me here then? *(The employee looks at his watch. He takes off his cap and puts on his hat. Then he goes to sit next to **THE WOMAN**.)*

THE EMPLOYEE: Listen to me, little lady. You'd better hurry up and decide what it is you want. I've been listening to the three of you for more than an hour now.

THE WOMAN: What are you doing?

THE EMPLOYEE: That was my last day of work. Now I'm unemployed, so I'm joining the queue at the Department of Social Security. Do you think they'll be able to give me some information?

THE WOMAN: What's your address?

THE EMPLOYEE: Number 7 Fuck German Bureaucracy Circus.

MYRIAM: *(taking off her false nose)* And now: beddybye.

OTTO: *(stubbornly)* What about the next scene, the scene about

162

inflation? It isn't ready yet. We haven't found an end for it. We have
to find an end.

MYRIAM: What's wrong with my idea?

OTTO: What idea?

MYRIAM: You have the capitalist here and he holds up one gold coin.
The worker comes on with a big shopping bag full of notes, then he
brings on a wheelbarrow, but it's still not enough to buy his kipper.
(She stops and looks at the others questioningly.)

OTTO: So?

MYRIAM: So there's your scene about inflation.

OTTO: And what has it explained?

MYRIAM: That you need three million marks to buy a kipper.

OTTO: Everybody already knows that. It's something everyone
experiences every day. What we need to show is the why, the how,
who's making this happen and in whose interest.

MYRIAM: So how should I know? I don't understand the first thing
about it. It's too complicated.

OTTO: In that case everything we do here is too complicated. Is that
what you're saying?

MYRIAM: Yes. For a piece of theatre, it's too complicated.

OTTO: You're saying theatre is incapable of portraying our society.

MYRIAM: Well, sometimes I have my doubts, yes.

OTTO: That is something we must never accept. Never.*(Silence.)*

MAGNUS: *(condescendingly)* Look. There's nothing in the least
complicated about inflation. Inflation is simply a huge legalised fraud,
which allows big business to pay off its debts in devalued marks.
You're a big businessman: the state offers you big loans in good money.
You buy nice new machines. Then inflation spirals and you pay back
the state with peanuts. Wages drop, the price of exports drops. You
start dumping on the market and you get yourself paid in foreign
currency, which you stash safely...somewhere abroad. Old-age
pensioners are ruined - so are the small proprietors, tenants. Heavy
industry gets fat and the working class pays. There. Simple.

MYRIAM: Simple it may be, but I didn't understand a word of it.

MAGNUS: What didn't you understand?

MYRIAM: I told you: anything. Why is it good for heavy industry?
What about light industry? Why are exports cheap when everything
here is so expensive?

MAGNUS: Because exports are paid for in foreign currency. You'd think 700 generations of unadulterated Jewish blood would make you able to understand something as simple as that.

MYRIAM: Here we go. The Jews and money. So I'm the Jewish bank, am I? I'm married to him for fifteen years and now he tells me he's anti-Semitic.

MAGNUS: You don't want to understand, that's all. If you owe somebody one thousand marks and ten years later one thousand marks is worth one mark, then when you pay back that thousand marks, you're in fact only paying back one mark. Your net profit is nine hundred and ninety-nine marks. Do you understand now, my little Mymichik?

MYRIAM: You're getting on my nerves. (*She leaves, followed by MAGNUS. CAROLA MARTIN has come in and watched some of this. She's silent. OTTO has remained alone. He sees her.*)

OTTO: The great star from Berlin in our little Peppermill. To what do we owe such an honour?

CAROLA: I can't find my way around Hamburg at night. I only know the way to the theatre and back. I came to ask you if you'd walk me to the hotel.

OTTO: How was the reception?

CAROLA: Rotten. I brought you some canapés.

OTTO: No, thank you. It's daylight now; you'll be able to find your way back alone.

CAROLA: Come with me anyway. On the way, you can tell me what it is about me you so dislike. Rehearsing with you was...painful, to say the least.

OTTO: Please accept my apologies.

CAROLA: No. I don't accept your apologies. You're a wonderful actor, Otto - what are your plans?

OTTO: Plans?

CAROLA: For your career.

OTTO: I don't have any plans for my career and I don't want any, either.

CAROLA: What about the theatre?

OTTO: (*provocatively*) I'm not interested in the theatre.

CAROLA: Liar!

OTTO: I'm a communist. Communism is my profession and my vocation. The theatre is nothing more than a roof over my head and a hot meal on the table. Now I've told you everything there is to know about me.

CAROLA: A roof over our heads, yes. A meal on the table, yes. And a light in our darkness? Isn't it? Your theatre is beautiful.

OTTO: Come. Let me offer you a cup of coffee.

CAROLA: A big one?

OTTO: A big one.

CAROLA: And a slice of poppy-seed cake?

OTTO: And a slice of poppy-seed cake.

SCENE FOUR

*The Hamburg Theatre. **HENDRIK** is ready to listen to the "reading" of **SEBASTIEN'S** play. **SEBASTIEN** gives the last stage directions. **MRS. EFEU** and **KNURR** hover, intrigued.*

SEBASTIEN: So. Now. The children of the boarding school can be heard singing in the distance. The scene is a large hall of dark wood. Stage right, there's a majestic door which leads to the Western dormitories. Stage left, the door leading to the Eastern dormitories. Through the windows can be seen statues on the lawn. On the wall, a large crucifix, or possibly a palm branch. Anja and Esther come on. No, one moment. *(He runs to the wings, stage right, then stage left, and comes back.)* Anja and Esther come on.
*(He sits next to **HENDRIK** as **NICOLETTA** and **ERIKA** appear. They're barefoot and dressed in little girls' night-gowns. Each holds a candle.)*

ESTHER *(NICOLETTA)*: Anja, Anja, where are you?

ANJA *(ERIKA)*: Esther?

ESTHER: I've been waiting for you. I jumped out of the lavatory window. And you? How did you get out?

ANJA: It was difficult. The housemistress was lying across my door. I leapt over her body.

ESTHER: Oh. You're so brave. I wouldn't have dared do such a thing. That housemistress is frightful.

ANJA: She's ugly; she's old.

ESTHER: She's mean.

165

ANJA: She's bearded.

ESTHER: She prickles.

ANJA: She has hair on her bottom.

ESTHER/ANJA: *(laughing)* She has a hairy bottom.

ESTHER: You're so funny, Anja. You make me laugh.

ANJA: It's hot. My nightie's clinging to my body.

ESTHER: What a dreadful August! I'm boiling.

ANJA: The moon burns like a sun. It's hot.

(ERIKA lifts up her nightdress and shows herself to be naked underneath, as is NICOLETTA.)

ESTHER: Yes. I'm hot. *(They improvise a little game to see who can shock the two men most.)*

ANJA: Listen. I hear it.

ESTHER: Oh God.

ANJA: It could be the ghost.

ESTHER: No. Don't say that. I'm afraid of ghosts. Don't play games.

ANJA: I'm not playing games. There is a ghost. A ghost there is. It's the ghost of the former headmistress. They say she used to bite her favourite pupils on the throat. Here. *(She shows her neck.)*

ESTHER: I'm frightened. You always frighten me. You're wicked.

ANJA: Oh. I feel ill. Suddenly. Something...someone...bit me. Oh my god. What if the poison's deadly?

ESTHER: I'll suck it out. It's what you're supposed to do.

(NICOLETTA slides herself under ERIKA'S night-gown.)

HENDRIK: Drop the curtain, Knurr; someone might come in.

(MRS. EFEU leaves, outraged.)

ESTHER: Do you feel better now? Much better?

ANJA: Yes. Thank you.

ESTHER: Sometimes I feel afraid for you. It's as if you might die, quite suddenly. And if you died, what would become of me? I have a feeling I'm capable of horrors.

ANJA: You have a little crease. Did you know that? And your skin is shining. *(She looks into NICOLETTA's night-gown.)*

ESTHER: What cold hands you have! Have you looked at the stars? *(During this exchange, a man walks onto the stage - THEOPHILE SARDER. He walks towards the two actresses, who see him and jump.)*

SARDER: Please don't stop.

NICOLETTA: Who is that?

ERIKA: Théophile Sarder. He calls himself the greatest living German playwright. My father thinks he's right.

NICOLETTA: Oh. If your father thinks so. (*SEBASTIEN signals for them to continue. He wants to prompt them, but the two women ignore him and continue their acting.*)

ANJA: I must go now.

ESTHER: (*running after her and holding onto her*) Wait. Wait. One more little moment. I believe you are a saint. You are so gentle. You are more gentle than any other human being. Even when you say no, you do it gently. You are a saint, a dark and silvery saint. Everything you touch, you purify. Everything you do is sanctified. Everything we do together is sanctified. Anja, Saint Anja, my saint, my Anja.

ANJA: Let's not go and join the others. Come. Come with me. Come into the garden. Come into the night.

(*They kiss. The kiss lasts and lasts. SEBASTIEN becomes embarrassed and tries to interrupt them but meets with no success. He insists. The two women pull him to the floor and tease him.*)

SEBASTIEN: No. No. Please forgive me, Mr. Höfgen, they make me laugh. They're always making me laugh.

SARDER: Erika. How is your father?

ERIKA: Well.

SARDER: And your grandmother?

ERIKA: Well.

SEBASTIEN: The whole tribe's well.

SARDER: I'm afraid there isn't much skill in what you've shown us there, my boy.

SEBASTIEN: Thank you. I was thinking the same thing.

ERIKA: Don't listen to him. He can't bear anything he hasn't written himself. There are only three writers he admires: Shakespeare, Schiller, Sarder. The immortal S's.

SARDER: What are you doing for lunch?

ERIKA: I'm having it with them.

SARDER: I'll come, too, if that's all right.

ERIKA: Yes, but you'll have to take us.

SARDER: Of course.

ERIKA: It'll have to be an expensive restaurant where you pay in

167

dollars.

SARDER: Why dollars?

ERIKA: Your American royalties. Don't they pay you in dollars?

SARDER: As they do your father.

ERIKA: Leave my father out of this. You're not fit to -

SARDER: All right. All right. I'll pay in dollars. *(He goes, dragging a surprised NICOLETTA after him. SEBASTIEN follows.)*

ERIKA: *(to HENDRIK)* Aren't you coming?

(They go. MRS. EFEU, KNURR, and MIKLAS appear suddenly from the darkness of the wings.)

MIKLAS: It won't be long before we can throw all that into the sewers, Mr. Knurr. *(They're about to eat when a young boy comes in. He's dirty, thin, and very hard.)*

MRS. EFEU: Who's that?

MIKLAS: He was hanging about near the theatre. He's hungry.

MRS. EFEU: I'll get you a slice of bread...I've hidden some in the...I'll be right back. *(She goes out, leaving the two men with the boy. He looks at them defiantly. KNURR feels uneasy.)*

KNURR: How old are you?

THE CHILD: Fifteen.

KNURR: What's your name?

THE CHILD: Lorenz.

KNURR: Lorenz what?

LORENZ: Lorenz Lorenz.

KNURR: Lorenz Lorenz what?

LORENZ: Prattface.

KNURR: Listen to me, boy. If that's the way you talk, you won't get any bread and butter here, is that clear?

LORENZ: Why? I don't have the right to be called Lorenz Lorenz Prattface?

KNURR: If you think I don't know what your game is, young man...

LORENZ: If you think I don't know what your game is, you old turd burglar. The woman's off. Leaves the men. Time to set out my stall. You want to see my arse you tell me. I drop my trousers, you do your business, I get my bread and butter. *(He takes down his trousers.)*

KNURR: What's he doing? What the hell is he doing? Get him out of here. Quickly. *(KNURR slaps LORENZ, who picks up his trousers.)*

LORENZ: I want my bread and butter.

168

MIKLAS: Look. You can eat bread and butter here without having to-
(MRS. EFEU comes back with two slices of bread and butter in a greasy paper. LORENZ and MIKLAS start to eat greedily.)
LORENZ: The other day two French tourists gave me a whole meal. For just two blow jobs. They were nice. They took me rowing on the lake. Seems there's deprivation here. That's what they said.
MIKLAS: Yes, there's a lot of deprivation here, Lorenz, but it's all going to change. And we're the ones who will change it: you...me...Mr. Knurr...Mrs. Efeu. We'll make it change, you'll see. The time has come for the German people to stop dropping their trousers. The time has come for the German people to make others drop their trousers. *(LORENZ laughs.)* Yes, but in order to do that we all have to unite around a strong leader. Do you understand, Lorenz? If you want, I'll introduce you to some other boys like you tomorrow. They'll make you feel welcome, you'll see, and you'll eat a bowl of soup every day.
LORENZ: *(incredulously)* Every day?
MIKLAS: Every day. What about it?
LORENZ: Why not? *(The four of them drink.)*
MIKLAS: To our Germany!
KNURR: To the future!
MRS. EFEU: To peace!
LORENZ: What time is it, Knurr? *(KNURR looks for his watch.)*
KNURR: Where's my watch!
(With a malicious little smile, LORENZ finds the watch in MRS. EFEU's cleavage. They all laugh and a party begins, during which LORENZ demonstrates his conjuring tricks and MRS. EFEU plays the piano.)

SCENE FIVE

The restaurant. SARDER, SEBASTIEN, NICOLETTA, HENDRIK. A large and glittering table. There is another small table next to it. The MAITRE D' HOTEL places an immense menu in SARDER'S hands. The orchestra plays discreetly. A little waiter brings the lobsters which SARDER chooses with infinite care.

SARDER: The lobsters. Let us study the lobsters. We'll have this one, that one, and that little rogue over there and that naughty one over

169

there. And the one there - not that one, the one with the plump thighs. Vulgar it might be, but I detect a promise of sensuality. *(to NICOLETTA)* And I presume the little friend of the family won't refuse a glass of Hock. What do you think of this place, Höfgen? It's the only restaurant in Hamburg where you can still find a decent meal.

ERIKA: Hendrik feels ill at ease in a place like this. He's angry with me for having brought him here.

HENDRIK: I'm not angry with you.

SARDER: Oh, dear. I have a feeling we're about to embark on the subject of Revolution. It can't be helped. Höfgen, let us hear about your Revolution. But first, the lobsters. Waiter: the lobsters. *(They drink heavily.)*

NICOLETTA: I believe it is already a revolutionary act to eat lobsters which are being paid for by an old reactionary for whom one feels nothing but contempt.

SARDER: Wrong. Wrong again. It was the reactionaries who first invented contempt. It is an item of which they have a surplus. Believe me when I tell you, my dear girl, that you'll never feel as much contempt for them as they already feel for you.

(The orchestra begins a slow dance. SARDER gets up and drags NICOLETTA onto the dance floor. HENDRIK musters up the courage to invite ERIKA. SEBASTIEN, left alone at the table, watches them and drinks. Suddenly NICOLETTA leaves the dumbfounded SARDER in the middle of the floor and takes ERIKA in her arms. The two women dance together. No-one has noticed the MAITRE D'HOTEL slapping the little waiter.)

SARDER: What a shame! Freaks. We long for real women and we have to make do with freaks. Look at them. Half creatures. And they're doing it on purpose, to taunt us. I'd like to pay one of those waiters to take down their pants and give them the lesson they deserve. And look at this little runt here *(He indicates SEBASTIEN)* - the flotsam spawned by genius. He's part of it all. Do you know it's for him those two save themselves? It's for him they keep their full and beautiful mouths, their silky limbs, their ravishing little white breasts. You must have been aware of that, Mr. Höfgen; everyone is talking about it, so it must be true. Sebastien and Erika, the beautiful Brückner twins, and the family friend. The shocking little galaxy. It's disgusting. *(SEBASTIEN laughs at his indignation and leaves the*

170

table to join the two women. They welcome him with great
tenderness. He's pleasantly drunk.)
HENDRIK: I'm surprised by what you've just said, Mr. Sarder. Aren't there scenes in your own plays which are as shocking...and possibly less tender?
SARDER: Art can never be shocking. The poet purifies his most demonic creations. But what is daring on the stage becomes crude and disgusting in real life.
HENDRIK: Yes, but what about the scene in Sodom and Gomorrah, with the man and the two children?
SARDER: Chastity! That scene is about chastity! The crudeness of all that's said and done in that scene only serves to highlight its fundamental chastity. It is because that man is so different that he becomes worthy of our love. *(SEBASTIEN comes back.)*
SEBASTIEN: Blah, blah, blah.
HENDRIK: But why does it irritate you when life itself offers something different, and equally chaste?
SEBASTIEN: Yes, Sarder, why?
SARDER: Real life does not come into my plays, Mr. Höfgen. I don't have such vulgar ambitions; no - my plays have absolutely nothing to do with real life. Theatre floats in the realm of the impossible.
SEBASTIEN: I want my plays to be real life, nothing but life, inner life, exterior life, art, politics, love, this wine ...
SARDER: How banal you are, Sebastien! And I suppose you agree with him, Höfgen?
HENDRIK: Yes, I do. It is the duty of the theatre to portray life. And it becomes a political force when it deals with human progress. That's what we're looking for at the Peppermill.
SARDER: The Peppermill?
HENDRIK: It's the name of a cabaret I manage with some friends. We practice a very different kind of theatre from yours, Mr. Sarder. It's a theatre of the future, which will belong to the working class.
SARDER: The working class.
SEBASTIEN: Yes, Sarder. The working class.
SARDER: And so Anja and Esther is a play for the working class?
SEBASTIEN: Yes. Why not? Just because it isn't good enough for you, doesn't mean -
SARDER: If it isn't good enough for me, it's not good enough for the

working class.

HENDRIK: The working class doesn't need a bourgeois theatre.

SEBASTIEN: Did you hear that, Sarder? The working class doesn't need you.

SARDER: While the working class is waiting for you with bated breath? The working class doesn't need Shakespeare; it doesn't need Goëthe, Chekhov, Molière; it doesn't need Sophocles; but it needs you, and him.

HENDRIK: *(solemnly)* The working class needs a revolutionary theatre.

SARDER: The working class needs the truth. We all need the truth, and God knows that's a rare enough commodity these days.

(THE OFFICER comes on.)

SEBASTIEN: There's a man. Look at that. Isn't he handsome? What an air! How he carries himself! There's civilisation for you. Alas, alas, alas.

SARDER: Alas what? Have we produced anything better than that recently? Are your physical abilities greater than those of that soldier? Are your moral qualities superior to his? Isn't our age infinitely more drab and despairing than his ever was?

ERIKA: Eat your lobster, Theo, and stop drinking. You're being silly. You're all being silly.

SARDER: *(drunk)* I am the only one sitting at this table who has the right to judge our times. And I tell you that this vulgar, this superficial age can't begin to compare with the age in which I grew up. And yet, I reviled it. I poured on it all the poison I could dredge from my being. We we're a nation of soldiers and poets. That's bad enough, I admit, but we're now becoming a nation of shopkeepers. It makes me sick. And that silly old man who sits there so stiffly, at least he has a spine. You - Mister Höfgen, did you fight in the war? *(HÖFGEN hesitates.)*

HENDRIK: No. Obviously not. Thank God.

SARDER: There you are. No discipline and hence no personality. No breaking-in.

SEBASTIEN: *(sarcastically)* Sarder, I'm crushed. I'm crushed by all you've said. We're all crushed.

SARDER: And I'm crushed by what I see around me. Look at him. A relic, yes, but the relic of an eagle. He and I are eagles in a population of rats. We're ridiculous, yes, we're the rats' jesters but you want a

Germany populated with mice. *(He begins to cry.)*
ERIKA: Theo, shut up and eat your lobster.
SARDER: We're heading for the abyss. Our age is rotting away
before us. It's already stinking and I'm the only one who notices the
stench. I can see the catastrophe that's looming; it will be unbelievable.
All that is, will collapse, and we'll lie buried in tombs of excrement. I
feel so sorry for you, my children. You won't live out your lives.
You're already decomposing on the spot, like flowers in a sunless
spring. *(He bursts into sobs. He's about to break down completely.*
SEBASTIEN and HENDRIK take him out. NICOLETTA is
obviously upset. She begins to follow them.)
ERIKA: Where are you going?
NICOLETTA: I love that man. Passionately.
ERIKA: You've gone mad.
NICOLETTA: Yes. Just now.
ERIKA: Let me tell you something.
NICOLETTA: About the stars?
ERIKA: About that man. He's dangerous.
NICOLETTA: Why?
ERIKA: He's desperate.
NICOLETTA: Then I'm lost. Let me go, Erika.
(She goes out. ERIKA is alone. She's beat. HENDRIK comes back.)
HENDRIK: Nicoletta von Niebuhr asked me to give you a message.
ERIKA: What are you waiting for?
HENDRIK: She asks you to remain her friend. She threw herself into
the car and took the wheel. The poor chauffeur was left standing on
the pavement. He kept saying, "But it's a kidnapping, she's kidnapping
him." I thought the same. Was she your best friend?
ERIKA: She is my best friend.
HENDRIK: Of course. *(Silence. THE OFFICER leaves. The*
MAITRE D'HOTEL salutes him.)
HENDRIK: Yesterday...since yesterday...what a life! The first night's
a resounding success. I meet the son of Germany's greatest living
author. Then I meet Germany's greatest living playwright. The dollar
is worth 50 billion marks. I'm invited to an exclusive restaurant where
my meal costs 500 billion marks. I watch the inexorable power of love
at first sight. I'm still young, I'm full of promise. I think I'll ask
Gottchalk for a raise and after that, I might fall in love. At the thought

173

of falling in love I can feel my heart beat faster. I'm not used to the thought of being happy.

ERIKA: Our evening is making you think of happiness, is it?

HENDRIK: I know you're unhappy tonight, Erika, and yet you're the one who's making me think of happiness. You've dazzled me. I've been waiting for this meeting since I was a little boy. I used to watch my mother and father in their slovenly dress, drinking beer in a sitting-room that hadn't one book in it. And I swore then that one day I'd be elegant, frail, seductive and I'd mix in the company of delicate and learned people. Someone will come, I used to say to myself, Saint Nicholas, or a gangster, a woman, an angel someone will come and take me away from this sad dark and stupid Dresden backstreet. Your unhappiness tonight is making me hope for prodigious things...What have they put in this bottle? It's not wine we've all been drinking, it's a love potion. Erika, I saw you drink out of that glass. Look at me quickly or you'll fall in love with the Maitre d'. who's coming our way, or maybe even with that lobster. Erika Brückner, why don't you fall in love with me? Do you have anything more interesting to do tonight? *(He's on his knees, in front of her.)*

ERIKA: What's happening to us? Sarder is right; the world's turning too fast, it's upside down. *(SEBASTIEN comes in and watches them.)*

HENDRIK: I need you, Erika. I'm bad. Take what's good in me and make it grow. I'm lost if you don't. Save me, Erika. You're an angel. You're a witch. You're all-powerful. If you don't love me, it'll be the end of me. I'll never come to anything.

ERIKA: Let's try. Yes, let's try since you want it so much. What else is there for us to do? *(SEBASTIEN goes to ERIKA. The MAITRE D' HOTEL signals the orchestra to play a slow dance, and the three dance together. SEBASTIEN wipes ERIKA'S tears as the MAITRE D' HOTEL empties the glasses with great dignity)*

SCENE SIX

A rehearsal at the Peppermill. A musical overture. We see HITLER in prison. Clowning.

OTTO: Visit for you, Sir. Mr. Fritz Thyssen, cannon manufacturer. *(He puts on a mask and comes forward.)*

THYSSEN *(OTTO)*: Have you heard the election results of May the 4th, 1924? No? Why not? It's the 5th today, isn't it? The communists held four seats. They now hold sixty-two. What do you make of that? Do you know on what kind of a scrap heap I'll find myself if you don't stem this Bolshevik tide? And you haven't helped with your despicable failure. When I think of Mussolini...The march on Rome. Now there's a man. You should be ashamed of yourself. God knows there are enough officers in the German army willing to lend a hand. In fact, I'm waiting for...

AN ACTOR: The Head of Staff of what's left of the German army, Sir. *(Clowning entrance of FONNESIQUE.)*

FONNESIQUE: *(lost in thought)* Buggered. They buggered us. It's the Jews.

THYSSEN: My dear Fonnesique, allow me to introduce one of your most fervent admirers.

FONNESIQUE: Sissies. Poor Germany. Nothing but sissies. The real Germans are dispersed over the face of the earth.

THYSSEN: Quite. My young friend here shares your feelings, and...

FONNESIQUE: Austria. Full of Germans, Austria. We'll annex Austria.

THYSSEN: That's exactly what my young friend was saying. Would you -

FONNESIQUE: Poland. Crammed with Germans. We'll annex Poland.

THYSSEN: Precisely, but before you -

FONNESIQUE: Lorraine, Alsace, Czechoslovakia, all Germans there. Switzerland, Belgium, Spain, the Canary Islands. Nothing but Germans. We'll annex.

THYSSEN: If we could just look at the election results -

FONNESIQUE: And Panama. What about Panama? A million oppressed Germans in Panama. We'll annex Panama.

THYSSEN: *(shouting)* The Bolsheviks! What are you going to do about the Bolsheviks?

FONNESIQUE: There are Germans in the U.S.S.R. We'll annex the U.S.S.R.

THYSSEN: Save yourself the trip. There are Bolsheviks right here in Germany.

FONNESIQUE: Jews. Hang them.

THYSSEN: Assuredly. I have here in my office a young man -

FONNESIQUE: All women are whores.

THYSSEN: I understand your legitimate grievances, my dear Fonnesique, but to come back to the Bolsheviks -

FONNESIQUE: What's the name of that general who executed ten thousand soldiers for insubordination?

THYSSEN: Petain. Philippe Petain.

FONNESIQUE: We'll annex Philippe. It's the communists who stabbed the German army in the back. I have that from the socialists themselves.

THYSSEN: My young friend and I hate the communists above all.

FONNESIQUE: Long live Bismarck. Long live Frederick the Great. Long live the 15th Century. Long live the Stone Age. The Republic's a dung heap. What?

THYSSEN: Personally, Frederick the Great leaves me cold. I don't want to find myself sweeping the floor of my own factory for ten rubles a month, that's all. Now listen to me, my dear Fonnesique, what you need are the mercenary and paramilitary organisations of Mr. Hitler. Right?

FONNESIQUE: Wrong!

THYSSEN: Listen, Kurt, I've got him well in hand. As soon as he's finished with the Bolsheviks, we'll ditch him. Right?

FONNESIQUE: Right! They can have the sleeping bags.

THYSSEN: *(to HITLER)* That's a deal. You've already got the sleeping bags. We'll talk about the big money when you get out of this place. Heil Hitler. Guard! Hurry. Out of here, we're getting...

(They bang on the door. The guard (ALEX) comes to open it. But he hesitates, pushes the two men back, and closes the door.)

OTTO: What are you doing?

ALEX: I'm not letting them out.

OTTO: But -

ALEX: I think we need to present a positive figure.

MYRIAM: Have I heard this? It's two o'clock in the morning and he wants to start discussing the role of the positive figure. Now is that wise? Is that wise?

OTTO: All right. You don't let them come out. Go on. Improvise. Let's go back.

176

FONNESIQUE/THYSSEN: Air. Of air in need ve are. Or suffocate ve will. *(ALEX pulls the bolts across the door.)*

ALEX: *(striding to the front)* And that, Comrades, is the end. You know who's in there: the capitalists. Down with the bourgeoisie. Down with international capitalism. So, Comrades, come rally and the last fight let us face. Long live the Revolution. Greetings to the Soviet Union. There. The message is clear, optimistic, positive.

MAGNUS: Yes, but if you show the positive figure of the guard you also have to show the negative figures of the bosses. They'll kick you in the behind and say, "Open that door immediately or we'll put a bullet through your brains." *(This he demonstrates.)* And frankly, when I see an actor who claims to be politicised shout and salute the Soviet Union with his eyes closed, I say that isn't an actor, that's a vulgar propagandist. A brainwasher.

ALEX: I am a communist worker.

MAGNUS: That doesn't have to be synonymous with brainwasher.

ALEX: I am a communist worker and I am aware of the fact that the person addressing me is nothing more than a bourgeois social democrat. And I'm tired of all his clowning. We're not creating revolutionary theatre here, we're simply imitating the same old forms of bourgeois entertainment.

MYRIAM: What's he saying? What's he saying now? Enlighten me, my son. Tell me just what it is I have to do to be allowed entry into the heaven of revolutionary theatre. What? What?

ALEX: Why can't we have a theatre that's as concise as our pamphlets? In any case, Hitler's now in prison. The Germans aren't the same people as the Italians. The German working class is much too politicised for fascism to be a serious threat in Germany. The real danger we face and have always faced is the continual betrayal of the social-democrats. We mustn't forget it was Noske who ordered his friends to be shot, not Hitler. The domination of the bourgeoisie is always the domination of the bourgeoisie, whether you call it fascism or social-democracy.

MYRIAM: *(to OTTO)* How long are you going to put up with this?

OTTO: I don't know. I'm confused. I'm tired. If fascism isn't a serious threat, then we should forget about Hitler and do something else. Anyway, I'll show you the backdrop.

(ALEX lowers the drop. It's been wrecked. There's an inscription:
"JEWS, COMMUNISTS, SOCIAL-DEMOCRATS...BE PATIENT...WE'LL GET ALL OF YOU." *Blackout.)*

(A few hours later, still at the Peppermill. OTTO and THERESA are finishing the repairs.)

THERESA: That's it. Now they can start again.

OTTO: And we'll repair it again.

THERESA: Until they take to their axes and hack the words on our faces. I'm frightened. If only you knew how frightened I am. I don't understand. I'm the only one who seems to feel so frightened. I feel sick with fear.

OTTO: Come and work with us, Theresa. Fear is best cured by the struggle.

THERESA: And so on and so forth. I don't like you when you talk like a pamphlet. I'll come when Höfgen comes.

OTTO: Höfgen is here. He may not be rehearsing at the moment, but he's still with us. He's a true socialist, Theresa, you're unfair.

THERESA: That's because I want to go to bed with him. I'm going. Are you coming? You're not? Why? Are you waiting for someone? Who? I'm so nosy. Come on, Theresa, come along. It's time to go home.

(She goes out. OTTO turns off the lights. CAROLA comes on.)

CAROLA: Otto?

OTTO: Is that you, my lovely star?

CAROLA: Yes. It's me. Otto. I have very bad news. I feel so sad for you, Otto.

OTTO: What is it?

CAROLA: Lenin is dead. *(Silence. OTTO repeats like a child.)*

OTTO: Dear God, please make it not be true! Please make it not have happened. It mustn't...not now...later...please make it not now, dear God please, not now. What's to become of us?

SCENE SEVEN

*The veranda of **THOMAS BRÜCKNER'S** house. It's a warm September evening. Some are reading, others day-dreaming.*

NICOLETTA is playing a game of patience. The atmosphere is
pleasant and gentle. SEBASTIEN sings, accompanied on the piano
by his father.

THOMAS: Ah. You sing Schübert so well, my boy, and I play so
badly. Whenever I hear those *lieder* I'm reminded of that sentence of
Dostoyevsky's: "The world will be saved by beauty." Is that from *'The*
Brothers Karamazov' or *'The House of the Dead'*? What do you think,
Theo? You must remember.
SARDER: No.
ERIKA: *(curled up in a chair)* It's from *'The Possessed'*.
(SEBASTIEN is taking photographs. EMELYNE, the servant,
follows him, holding an inspection lamp.)
SEBASTIEN: No it isn't. It's from *'Crime and Punishment'*.
ERIKA: Not at all. It's in *'Anna Karenina'*.
THOMAS: Well, wherever it's from, it's a very great thought.
HENDRIK: *(to ERIKA)* Dostoyevsky didn't write *'Anna Karenina'*.
ERIKA: Really? Are you sure?
NICOLETTA: Sebastien, come and take a picture of Erika and me
together.
THOMAS: *(to HENDRIK)* Come and sit next to me for a
photograph, Hendrik. You come, too, Erika. Are you still working on
your poems and songs? I hope so. Ah, my little girl, my little girl with
her thin little legs always covered in scratches. She looked like a boy
with her cropped hair and she used to come to me at night and say:
"Father, father, you who are a great magician you must tell that animal
on my dresser to go away and not to frighten Sebastien." Ah, little
traitor, you've found yourself another magician now and I shall have to
disappear in a puff of smoke. And he's put on such an elegant suit, too.
So, my dear son-in-law...
HENDRIK: *(embarrassed)* Sir..It's strange having a piano on the
verandah.
THOMAS: Yes, that piano gives us a lot of trouble; it's very
demanding. When we cook pancakes or fritters we have to bring it
with us into the kitchen. I have to go away tomorrow...It's such a
shame. We were just getting to know each other.
SEBASTIEN: You're going tomorrow? Why?
THOMAS: They're having a festival in Goethe's honour in Frankfurt.

179

I must go and honour Goethe. It's exceedingly tedious, but what can I do? And I have a strange conviction I'll miss my train.

ERIKA: Ah, yes. By the way. Where is the train time-table? Ha ha ha. There's trouble brewing. I can feel it. (*She goes out.*)

HENDRIK: *(to NICOLETTA)* I'm bored.

NICOLETTA: We're carnivores in a house of herbivores. It's not that easy for the wolf to sleep with the lamb. Theo, take a picture of the two of us.

SARDER: I can never make those machines work.

ERIKA: *(coming back)* Where, but where is the time-table?

SEBASTIEN: Where it always is, on top of the magazines in the lav.

ERIKA: No, damn, it isn't. I've just been there and the time-table is not there anymore. No-one ever puts it back in its place. Theo, what have you done with the time-table?

THEO: *(irritated)* The last time I saw it, it was in the lav. I haven't touched it.

(EMELYNE comes in and serves raspberries, with the help of the chauffeur, LUDWIG.)

THOMAS: The very last raspberries of the season. Smell them, it's the scent of passing time. Emelyne, my dear, have you come to a decision yet? Are you going to marry Ludwig or will you let him stew in his misery?

EMELYNE: I'll let him stew a little and when he's really desperate, I'll give in and marry him.

THOMAS: That's very wise of you, Emelyne, very wise. Ludwig, you're a good-looking lad, but you're not worthy of her, do you understand?

LUDWIG: Yes, Sir. I'm not worthy of her.

ERIKA: Emelyne, my darling Emelyne, will you come to my new house with me? Father, please give me Emelyne; I couldn't think of a better wedding present.

THOMAS: Emelyne, are you willing to leave me and go with Erika to her new home?

EMELYNE: Yes, if I can go with Ludwig.

THOMAS: You've broken my heart, Emelyne...but there we are. *(to SEBASTIEN)* And you, my boy, tell me where have you been? Where are you going? What are your plans?

SEBASTIEN: I've been nowhere, I m going nowhere and I have no

180

plans. Raise your head, father, or you'll have a shadow across your face.

ERIKA: He's lying, Father. He's written two plays and we acted them in Hamburg and Munich.

THOMAS: I didn't know. Yes, the world can be full of malignant stupidity. One gets used to it.

SEBASTIEN: You and I have the honour of featuring in a "Simplicissimus" cartoon.

THOMAS: Ouch.

SEBASTIEN: I actually find it quite amusing. I'm standing behind your chair, leaning a little over you, just like this, and I'm saying, "I am told, Father, that the son of genius cannot be a genius himself. Therefore you are no genius."

THOMAS: Sebastien, my accomplished colleague, I am a most promising father, I have total faith. Theo, why are you sulking over there? I find you exceedingly tedious this evening and so does your charming wife.

SARDER: I'm not sulking.

THOMAS: Go and amuse him, Sebastien.

SEBASTIEN: I can't, I make him angry. I'm against an amnesty for the Nazis; he's for it. We get nowhere.

SARDER: All I said was that if the youth of Germany wants this amnesty, we must be understanding.

THOMAS: We musn't be understanding about everything. We mustn't be complacent.

SARDER: I understand today's youth and its disgust with our continual politicking. I've put my faith in our country's youth.

SEBASTIEN: But...

THOMAS: The young don't always point to the future.

SARDER: The young are becoming radical, at last.

SEBASTIEN: You used to be in love with the sabre; now you're content with the truncheon.

SARDER: I m content with a little psychology.

SEBASTIEN: Yes, you can justify anything with a little psychology, including the use of the truncheon. Hitler is about to be given an amnesty. In less than nine months, he'll get out of prison and reorganise the Nazi party. And that's all going to happen because people like you are quaking before a couple of youth organisations.

181

And what really kills me is that I'm talking to you about my own generation.

SARDER: But-

THOMAS: That's enough, Sarder, you're being exceedingly tedious. Do you know I have to cut down our lane of elm trees?

ERIKA: The elm trees! Why?

THOMAS: It's a disease. And there's no cure for it. All the elms of Germany will die soon and after that, those of the whole world. Do you know that in 1983,'4, or '5, there won't be a single elm left in the world? *(Silence.)*

ERIKA: *(acting)* Mama asks you not to cut down the trees until she's left.

SEBASTIEN: Friends, my dear friends, now that I'm about to leave this house forever, I can't remain quiet, I can't refrain from expressing my deepest feelings....

ERIKA: Theo, do Trofimov.

SARDER: Humanity is marching towards the supreme truth, towards the greatest happiness, and I'm at the forefront.

SEBASTIEN: There isn't much time left. We must go. Who's smelling of herring here?

ERIKA: Goodbye, dear house, dear ancestor. Winter will pass, spring will come and you'll no longer be here. They'll have pulled you down.

HENDRIK: *(to ERIKA)* Do you know the whole of *'The Cherry Orchard'* by heart?

ERIKA: I've known it since I was ten.

HENDRIK: You, too, Sebastien?

SEBASTIEN: We used to say all of Act Four on summer evenings with Nicoletta. Erika and I always ended up in tears.

ERIKA: Just one more little moment. I'm going to sit down. I feel as if I've never seen these walls before, this ceiling. And now my eyes feast on them and I feel such tender affection. When we're gone, there won't be a soul left here.

SEBASTIEN: My friends, let's get into the carriages. The train will be in soon.

NICOLETTA: Goodbye, house. Goodbye, old life.

SARDER: Greetings to the new life.

ERIKA: They go. Liouba and Gaiev are left alone and throw themselves into each other's arms. They cry silently, trying desperately

182

not to be overheard.

SEBASTIEN: My sister, my sister....

ERIKA: My orchard, my dear, my beautiful, my treasured orchard. My happiness,...goodbye.

NICOLETTA: Mama!

ERIKA: We're coming.

SEBASTIEN: They go. There is a sound of footsteps and Freers, the old servant, appears through the door on the right. He's ill.

THOMAS: It's all locked. They've gone...they forgot me. It doesn't matter...I'll rest here. Life's already over and it's as if I never lived. I'll lie down. There's no strength left in you, you useless old lump, none at all. In the distance, a sound is heard, as if coming from the sky, the sound of a chord snapping slowly and sadly dying away. Then nothing is heard but the dull thud of the axe against the trees far away in the orchard.

INTERVAL

SECOND PROLOGUE

THE ACTOR: *(to the audience)* 1925, 1926, 1927, 1928 1929. The years went by and they paid too little attention to those years. Even the depression of 1929 and its brutal repercussions could be explained away as part of the natural upheavals of modern society. And upheavals, they said to themselves, were self-contained. They didn't necessarily provoke other upheavals. And indeed, 1929 didn't provoke anything new, because everything was already there, lying in wait. And then, at last, the rats came out of their hiding and they saw that they were many. And in September, that warm September of 1930, they were forced to open their eyes and count the numbers. A pale Germany, a red Germany, a dark Germany had given birth to a putrid carcass, and even their delicate nostrils had to breathe in the stench.

SCENE EIGHT

HENDRIK and ERIKA'S home. Breakfast. HENDRIK has just finished reading a letter and puts it down on the table

HENDRIK: They want to see me in Berlin. Several theatres are making me very...interesting offers. Even Reinhardt wants to meet me. You're not interested, are you? You're not even interested in what I'm going to say to them.

ERIKA: Are you going to accept?

HENDRIK: Of course not. I'll turn them all down. Because I've given my word.

ERIKA: When do we get the results?

HENDRIK: *(distracted)* What results?

ERIKA: Hendrik. The elections!

HENDRIK: Otto's waiting for them at the printers. I'll have them before they've even reached the news-stands. *(Pause.)* I'm stuck here, tied down by my word of honour. Mind you, there isn't really anything to keep me in Hamburg after *'Faust'*. I haven't committed myself to anything for next year. What? - The Peppermill. What did you say? What?

ERIKA: I didn't say anything.

HENDRIK: I have to turn my thoughts to the Peppermill.

ERIKA: You might do a little more than turn your thoughts to it.

HENDRIK: Would you mind explaining to me precisely what you meant by that remark?

ERIKA: Nothing. You know, as far as I'm concerned, world revolution-

HENDRIK: Darling, when I need advice on revolutionary tactics, I'll go to someone who knows something about it.

ERIKA: Otto's so fond of you, he melts my heart.

HENDRIK: You don't understand a thing, do you? Otto's a Comrade. We are part of the same struggle, we share the same ideology. Feelings don't come into it. It doesn't make any difference whether he's fond of me or not. *(HENDRIK is having difficulties with his egg.)*

ERIKA: You should try it my way. Break the egg into a glass, add a lot of pepper, a pinch of salt, sauce piquante and a drop of lemon.

HENDRIK: Would you do me an enormous favour, my darling, and try not to make fun of me every time I behave differently from your venerable Papa? In the Brückner household eggs are eaten in crystal goblets with a clove from Zanzibar and sprinkled with Siamese pepper. In my house, we ate them with salt. Please forgive me for displaying such appalling lack of originality. You see, I'm only a simple human being.

184

ERIKA: I have some letters to type. Give me your letter; I'll answer it for you. *(She takes the letter from the table, but HENDRIK snatches it away.)*

HENDRIK: Leave it. It's not that urgent. I can dictate an answer tomorrow. We have more important things to worry about today.

(At this moment, EMELYNE brings in OTTO and THERESA.)

ERIKA: Sebastien! Hurry up! Otto's here.

(SEBASTIEN comes in, wearing his bathrobe. OTTO has all the newspapers and the table is cleared for them. He sits. MAGNUS and MYRIAM come in.)

OTTO: *(reads)* "Total number of registered voters: 43,000,000. Total votes cast: 39,260,000. Or 82 percent."

MAGNUS: That's the best turn-out since the first elections of 1915.

OTTO: *(reads)* "Social Democrats: 143 seats. 24 percent of the vote."

MAGNUS: We've lost ten seats and more than 5 percent of the vote.

OTTO: *(reads)* "Communists: 77 seats. 14 percent of the vote."

MAGNUS: They had 54 seats and 10 percent of the vote. They must be pleased.

OTTO: *(reads)* "National Socialist Party: 107 seats. 6,407,000 votes. It becomes Germany's second-largest party." *(Softly.)* They too must be pleased. *(Silence. They freeze. LUDWIG comes in and joins EMELYNE.)*

MYRIAM: *(coming to herself, to MAGNUS)* So what's happened to the walking encyclopaedia? Come on, numbers! Numbers! How many seats did they have, how many are they taking, how many of them go to bed before midnight? What are you waiting for?

MAGNUS: They had twelve seats. 810,000 votes.

OTTO: *(reads)* "German National Party: 41 seats. Probable coalition of Nazis and Nationalists: 148 seats."

SEBASTIEN/ERIKA: It's not possible, it's just not possible.

THERESA: It's like trying to run in a bad dream.

SEBASTIEN: *(reads from a paper)* "6,400,000 men and women of voting age have added their voice to the dullest, most empty and vulgar charlatanism imaginable."

THERESA: *(reads from another paper)* "The Fifth Reichstag of the German Republic is the most despicable parliament this country has ever elected. Let us hope its existence will be brief."

OTTO: *(from another paper)* "3,336,000 unemployed as of last week.

185

Ten million Germans are currently affected by unemployment. Those who remained silent about those figures yesterday have no right to make an outcry today."

MAGNUS: *(opening the last paper)* "The Red Flag, official organ of the Communist Party: September 16th, 1930. The final victory of communism has been confirmed by the present socialist defeat. The social-democrats will never recover from the blow they received on September 14th. Not only did they lose 600,000 votes, they also had to forgo their majority in Berlin. Of even greater significance are the clear indications that the Communist Party is at last making inroads into the working class, which was once totally dominated by the socialist camp." They really do seem pleased. *(to OTTO)* Well, Comrade, are you pleased?

HENDRIK: I don't understand. I don't understand any of it. Could you please explain to me, Comrade Otto, where is the victory of your party? Because I'm desperate, you see, I'm desperate.

THERESA: So what? We're not interested in your despair, Hendrik. Leave him alone.

SCENE NINE

The Hamburg Theatre. THERESA, MYRIAM, MAGNUS, ERIKA, HENDRIK, OTTO, MRS. EFEU. The whole company are there for the rehearsal of 'Faust'. HENDRIK plays Mephisto; OTTO, Faust.

MEPHISTOPHELES: Good friend,
You view things as they're generally viewed,
We must do better, 'ere the joys of life
Escape us.
So up!
Quit thought, and out into the world with me!
I tell thee, sooth, a carle who speculates
Is like a beast upon a barren heath
Led in a circle by an evil sprite,
While beautiful green pastures lie all around.
FAUST: And how do we begin?
MEPHISTOPHELES: We just go out.
Why, what a place of martyrdom is this?

186

Is this to be call'd life - to bore to death
The youngsters and thyself? Leave that, I say,
To neighbour Paunch! Why should'st thou vex thyself
With threshing straw? The best that thou can'st know,
Thou dar'st not tell the lads. Even now I hear
One o' them in the passage.
FAUST: I cannot possibly see him now.
MEPHISTOPHELES: Poor boy! He has
Waited long while, and should not go away
Uncomforted. Give me thy cap and gown!
The mask will suit me excellently.
Now leave me to my wit! I only want
A quarter of an hour; meanwhile thyself
Prepare for a fine journey!
(MEPHISTOPHELES in Faust's long gown)
Reason and Knowledge do thou only scorn,
The very highest strength of human kind,
Do but allow thyself to be confirm'd
In blinding magic by the Prince of lies,
Then shall I have thee unconditionally.
Him hath Fate gifted with a spirit which
Spurning all bounds, forever forward hastes,
One whose o'er-rash impetuous impulses
Overleap all the pleasures of the earth.
Him will I trail thro' the wild ways of life,
Thro' weary ways of Inutility,
Sprawl shall he, be benumbed, cleave to the dust.
And for his insatiety shall float
Viands and drinks before his greedy lips,
Refreshment shall he supplicate in vain,
And even tho' he had not to the Fiend
Render'd himself up, still he must be lost!
(MIKLAS, who is playing the student, comes on, carrying his script.)
STUDENT: I am but just arrived here, and I'm come-
HENDRIK: Aren't you off the book yet?
(MIKLAS gives his script to MRS. EFEU.)
STUDENT: I am but just arrived here, and I'm come
Full of devotion-

HENDRIK: Stand in for me, Otto, will you? Now let's try to lift this scene from the quagmire of boredom we fall into every time we do it. And whatever happens, let's not blame Goethe. For once, it isn't the writer's fault.

MIKLAS: I am but just arrived here, and I'm come
Full of devotion to address and make
Acquaintance with a man whom all do name
With reverence.

MEPHISTOPHELES: Your courtesy delights me
You see a man like many more. Have you / applied elsewhere?

MIKLAS: I beg you will receive me!
I come with all good disposition,
Moderate means, and innocent young blood;

HENDRIK: Start again.

MIKLAS: From the top?

HENDRIK: From the top. Why? Already tired? Stop there. Go back one step; take a half step to your right. That's where you stand. Now start. *(MIKLAS goes off and comes on again.)*

MIKLAS: I am but just arrived here-

HENDRIK: I thought I showed you where to stand. That's your place. There.

MIKLAS: I am but just arrived here, and I'm come
Full of devotion to address and make
Acquaintance-

HENDRIK: Again.

MIKLAS: I am but just arrived here-

HENDRIK: Again.

MIKLAS: I am but just-

HENDRIK: That's awful. Again. *(MIKLAS remains silent.)*
I thought I told you to start again.

MIKLAS Tell me at least what I'm doing wrong, Mr Höfgen.

HENDRIK: Wrong? What are you doing right? Start again.

MIKLAS: I'm waiting for your instructions, Mr. Höfgen. You're the director. It's your job to help me.

HENDRIK I'm trying, Miklas, I'm trying. It's very difficult.
(MIKLAS goes off and comes on again. He's about to open his mouth.)

HENDRIK: Where do you stand? *(MIKLAS corrects his place.)*

MIKLAS: I am but arrived here-

HENDRIK: That's not what Goethe has written.

MRS. EFEU: *(prompting)* I am but just arrived-

HENDRIK: Who asked you to prompt? Miklas, we're all waiting for you. *(ERIKA leaves. MIKLAS tries.)*

MRS. EFEU: I am but just arrived-

HENDRIK: I thought I told you not to prompt. You're not running the theatre yet, Mrs. Efeu, whatever you may think. It's not because you've managed to get a few more votes for your cretinous party of beef-wits that you can start ruling the country, my poor woman.

MIKLAS: May I ask what party you mean, Mr. Höfgen? Is it the National Socialist party?

HENDRIK: He's awake!

MIKLAS: I am a member of the National Socialist party, Mr. Höfgen. The National Socialist party is the party of the working class and I will not allow it to be criticised. No one in this Jew-infested theatre has a right to speak against the Party. I will not tolerate it.

HENDRIK: You won't tolerate it? Well, you can thank me for not having to tolerate anything anymore in this Jew-infested theatre. Magnus, I formally request that the Nazi Hans Miklas be excluded from this company.

MRS. EFEU: No! You can't do that!

HENDRIK: We've heard rather enough from you, Mrs. Efeu.

MRS. EFEU: Half the theatres in the country are closed. If you throw him out, he'll have nowhere left but the doss-house.

HENDRIK: What have you decided, Mr. Gottchalk?

MAGNUS: *(after a silence)* I don't like the idea of throwing him out to join the three million unemployed. I won't ask him back next season, that's all.

MRS. EFEU: Can't you see how sick he is?

HENDRIK: Sick? Sick? The whole of Germany will be sick if we don't do something about it soon. *(to MAGNUS)* You're the perfect illustration of social-democratic cowardice in the face of the Nazi threat. When are we going to show those thugs they can't get away with it? When are we going to show them they have to stop somewhere? When? Gottchalk, make up your mind.

OTTO: Magnus has already given you his answer, Hendrik. Given the present political situation I really think we should avoid turning Hans

189

Miklas into a martyr. He's nothing more than a little creep who'll wake up one day crying and screaming that everyone's tricked him.

MIKLAS: Stalin's a murderer.

(*HENDRIK spits in MIKLAS' face. MIKLAS goes for him. The others try to separate them. OTTO intervenes and ends up fighting with MIKLAS.*)

MRS. EFEU: Leave the poor boy alone, leave him alone. He's sick. You're all so sure you're right, but you're blind, all of you, you're blind.

HENDRIK It's simple: He goes. Or I go. Choose, Magnus.

MAGNUS: Don't be stupid. Miklas is going. *(to MRS. EFEU)* And so are you, Mrs. Efeu, if I hear one more word from you.

SCENE TEN

The Railway Bridge. It's night. OTTO, HENDRIK, THERESA.

THERESA: What about Magnus?

HENDRIK: I adore Magnus, Theresa. I admire Magnus. Magnus has taught me everything I know; well - almost everything. I love Magnus. But I feel he's beginning to get on. And our political views are so different. And he's seen better days. And - I need to feel free. What a night! Look at the stars. *(A train goes by.)* The train to Berlin. Will I ever be on that train? Oh God, when will I take the train to Berlin? Hendrik Höfgen: The great leading actor - of Hamburg. What a joke! And it's the same for you, Otto. Even the Peppermill would be more effective in Berlin; they're ready for that kind of work there. Listen, Otto, I have an idea: I'll go up to Berlin, and when I've made a name for myself I'll bring you all there and we'll start another Peppermill. Well? What do you think?

THERESA: Magnus has already announced the next season and we're all in it.

HENDRIK: Which is more important? The Hamburg Theatre season or the Struggle? In any case, the rest of you will stay on. It'll take me some time to get everything ready. I'll have to find the right café or restaurant for the Peppermill. Make some money...films....you can make films in Berlin. Otto, Otto, I know it's a cruel decision to make. If only you knew how painful it was for me to make it. But it's time to break off and we must break off. And since we have to go to Berlin, let

190

us go to Berlin.

(As the train goes by, HENDRIK embraces OTTO and THERESA and leaves. The train moves away. THERESA looks carefully at OTTO'S face. He turns his head away. He's in tears.)

THERESA: "God knows we needn't blush at our tears, they are like rain on the dry dust of our hearts." I like Dickens. Time for you to go home, Comrade, and get a good night's sleep.

(OTTO goes. ERIKA comes on.)

THERESA: *(coldly)* I suppose you re looking for your husband.

ERIKA: I've just met him.

THERESA: And you aren't already on your way to Berlin?

ERIKA: I'm looking for Otto. Theresa von Herzfeld, let me ask you something: I do a little writing: songs, pamphlets, short scenes. Is there any way I could make myself useful at the Peppermill?

(The two women embrace.)

SCENE ELEVEN

A rehearsal at the Peppermill. CAROLA, SEBASTIEN, NICOLETTA, MAGNUS, OTTO.

OTTO: *(singing)*

> I'm the prince of lies
> in the country of lies
> I make the trees bloom blue
> and the sky rain green.
> My lies are fantastic
> my lies buzz like flies
> in the hot air.
> It's already November
> and summer is here
> the trees are in flower
> the violets bright yellow
> and at the front
> no-one will be wounded
> no-one, no-one
> ha ha ha ha.

191

(Refrain)
Lies, lies, lies
lying's so good
lying's so fair
makes you lucky
makes you healthy
makes you rich
makes you famous
and then it's easy
because at the front
no-one will be wounded
no-one, no-one
ha ha ha ha.
(Refrain)
What I want
I lie for
and the world
applauds
because after all
I'm the prince of lies
in the country of lies
lies are soft
lies are delicate
lies make you quiet
rock you to sleep
make you dreamy
make you still
as death

Wake up quickly and throw the truth at the vile mask of lies. Only truth can triumph over adversity. *(The deafening ring of a telephone.*
***MRS. GRUNTBOUM (ERIKA** as a clown), the landlady, enters with a newspaper under her arm, the* 'Volkischer Beobachler'.*)*
MRS. GRUNTBOUM *(ERIKA)*: Coming. Coming. Never a moment's peace around here. I can't even go to the neighbourhood rallies anymore. Look at this bunch of shifty-eyed sheep, look at these vegetarian vegetables. What a country! What are you doing here, anyway? Why aren't you at your neighbourhood rally? Well? Why? Why? You get a free lecture, you learn something there, grass-brains.

It's going to change, that's what they said. About time, too. Quick turn of the screw. That's what they said. About time they took things in hand, that's what I say. *(She reads her paper.)* You don't mind if I read, do you? Aah. Look at that. Isn't that nice. Yes. Oh, and what about this now? I didn't know that. Did you? You didn't, did you? Do you know what's wrong with this country? No? Can you guess? Come on, guess. No? Well, my little darlings, it's those telephones. You didn't know that, did you? I didn't either. I knew absolutely nothing about it when I came here, but now I know, I'm sure, I'm smothered in sureness, it's written right here: The telephone is at the root of all our problems. That's right. Well, actually, I had my suspicions the first time I saw one, didn't you? It's obvious. And when I think that some people still don't know that all our troubles have their root in the telephone, that we're poisoned from the root up by the telephone, that the telephone has been poisoning our roots for millions and millions of years...Oh, really? That's a long time, isn't it - millions of years? But it's written here and yet, it's true, it's absolutely true. Is there anyone here with a telephone? Raise your hand if you're harbouring a telephone and come and see me in my office later. I'll take down your names. I'm in charge of taking down names now. It's like that with them; one day you're a nobody and next day you're in charge of names, you're petrified with importance. *(The telephone rings.)* Listen to that. Just listen to that. It has the gall to call me right here in my cosy polished sweet little German home. No manners. Disgusting. Just rings when it wants without so much as a by-your-leave. And me, with Germany's fate here on top of my two shoulders, I'm expected to get up and answer it. And mark my word, it's going to ring until dawn, with its filthy foreign habits, polluting my pure little home; listen to it, damned cosmopolitan race of dangerous insinuators trying to wriggle itself into a proper German home. *(Pause.)* That was well put. And they're all over Germany now, breeding like rabbits, taking over our nice clean pure little country; foreign trash. I hate them. Anyone here have any objections to hate? No? Good. *(The ringing stops.)* See? That shut it up. A little authority and it stops. I always knew telephones were cowards. Not like us. *(It rings.)* What! *(She shouts. Silence.)* See? I don't even have to say anything. One look and it stops. *(She reads.)* Oh, really? Yes...mmm...Oh? Extermination? Isn't that going a little far? No, no. They're right.

Absolutely right. *(She reads.)* Think what will happen to us if we don't stop them now. Yes. *(The phone rings.)* I'm collapsing with fear. No. Steady. Steady. Bang, bang, bang. *(It rings again.)* Boom. *(Silence.)* Got it. *(She reads.)* Yes, yes. What are we coming to? Well, it's a good thing to be well-informed. And you out there, you mutton-heads, drugged up to your earlobes, you'd better read this and find out what kind of danger you're in. Well. What are you waiting for? What? What? *(MISS LINNAMUCK, the cleaning lady, comes in.)*

LINNAMUCK *(MYRIAM)*: Dear, dear, dear, what's happening here? I've never heard such screaming and shouting! But you're alone, Mrs. Gruntboum, what's happening?

GRUNTBOUM: It's because it's true. It's all true, absolutely true. Linnamuck, you're a woman swimming with intelligence, you're sinuously subtle, sensationally sensible, sensually senile. In a word, you're a pure German, your ancestors were pure German from the beginning of time, your descendants will be German 'till the end of time. From one pure German to another, answer me this: Do you have a telephone?

LINNAMUCK: Well, no, you see, I've been thinking of getting one, but -

GRUNTBOUM: Ah Linnamuck, you poor starry-eyed little ewelet, ah, you narrow-minded dumb blonde, repeat after me: "The telephone is a fiend."

LINNAMUCK: "The telephone is a fiend."

GRUNTBOUM: "The telephone is a fiend."

LINNAMUCK: "The telephone is a fiend." Is that so, Mrs. Gruntboum?

GRUNTBOUM: Yes. It's written here. Just go and look at its mug if you don't believe me.

LINNAMUCK: You know, I think you're right. The other day the telephone rang me to tell me my cousin had broken his foot. It gave me ever such a fright.

GRUNTBOUM: I told you it had a fiendish tongue.

LINNAMUCK: But do you still believe in fiends, Mrs. Gruntboum? You're so educated, so advanced, so modernised.

GRUNTBOUM: I believe in the fiends of progress, Linnamuck, I believe in the fiends of liberalism, the fiends of civilisation, of intelligence. Look at us. We're simple ordinary everyday women.

194

We're not related by blood, by friendship, we're not even related by neighbourhood, but now we're united. Now we've got hate. Hate. We hate the telephone. Why? Because we know the telephones are ruining this country.

LINNAMUCK: You're such a good speaker, Mrs. Gruntboum, and now that I look at the telephone, I can see it's dirty, it's disgusting, it's smelly...I'm going to throw it straight out of the window.

GRUNTBOUM: Wait. Our time has not yet come.

LINNAMUCK: As typical representative symbolic ordinary middle-of-the-road in-no-way-outstanding city dwellers, we proclaim the telephone a national threat.

GRUNTBOUM: What do we know about the telephone?

LINNAMUCK: That it's shit.

GRUNTBOUM: What do we say about the telephone?

LINNAMUCK: That it's shit.

GRUNTBOUM: The telephone is-

LINNAMUCK: Shit. *(Increasing energy. THERESA, playing the Baroness, comes in.)*

BARONESS *(THERESA)*: Heaven above, what is going on, Mrs. Gruntboum? Is this an election?

GRUNTBOUM: Forgive us, your ladyship, but everyone's so excited these days and I myself have become a little nervous.

BARONESS: I too am feeling a surge of excitement, Gruntboum.

GRUNTBOUM: Your worshipful Baroness, in the name of all the honest people of our nation, in the name of the masses that stand behind me, in the name of your respectworthy name, I beg you to lead the way and get rid of your telephone.

BARONESS: *(troubled)* There's something bewitching in your words, Mrs. Gruntboum; they're so exotic, quixotic, idiotic, erotic. Yes, yes, I will get rid of my telephone.

OTTO: Blackout! *(The working lights go back on.)* Let's see what the censor finds to complain about in what you've written there, Erika.

CAROLA: My dear, why worry about the censor? No one pays attention to the censor anymore. We're no longer in 1931, unfortunately for us. The S.A. will be in the audience tonight, as they were the other night, but this time they'll smash your heads in, that's all. They've even started to come to the theatres where I play my innocuous

195

Shakespeares. It seems I'm a stinking Jew.

ERIKA: And I'm a flat-footed hyena.

CAROLA: I'm the propagator of syphilitic culture.

THERESA: My ugliness would put off the most determined rapist.

ERIKA: Cosmopolitan hermaphrodite.

NICOLETTA: *(to ERIKA)* Witless dyke.

CAROLA: Diarrhoeic ape.

MYRIAM: Turkish-bath spittoon. *(Pause.)* Yes. It's written in the *'Popular Observer'*: Myriam Horowitz is small, fat, ugly and displays as much humour as one might find in a Turkish-bath spittoon.

(They burst out laughing, nervously. THEOPHILE SARDER comes on. He is shaking. ALEX follows him in.)

SARDER: Woe to us all! I bring you tidings of woe. Let us sit upon the ground and weep. The light of reason is being extinguished. Dark clouds are gathering over our beautiful country. This morning, the grand master of Hell, Adolf Hitler, was named Chancellor of the Republic. The Nazis are in power. God has turned his face away from our nation and soon torrents of tears and blood will cascade through our streets.

OTTO: *(to ALEX)* What now? A general strike?

ALEX: The Red Flag is calling for a general strike but with 7 million unemployed, it's pointless.

OTTO: What are our instructions?

ALEX: To remain calm. *(He reads:)* "The workers must avoid any action which would give the new government grounds for taking measures against the Communist Party. The party must remain unharmed until the next general election, when it is sure to triumph once and for all over the Social-Democrats." And the usual analysis from Moscow: "Nazism is the last phase of a moribund capitalism and will sooner or later cause its final downfall."

MAGNUS: And the Social-Democrats?

ALEX: They're against a general strike. They want to wait for the next elections.

SEBASTIEN: The unions?

ALEX: The confederation of unions refuses to interfere. Management is still management. *(Silence.)*

SEBASTIEN: What day is it today?

MYRIAM: Monday, January the 30th, 1933. The horoscope says

Pisces will receive money from unexpected quarters but must go easy on the drink. I'm a Pisces. *(Silence. OTTO suddenly throws up.)*

SCENE TWELVE

Still at the Peppermill. SARDER, NICOLETTA, SEBASTIEN, ERIKA, CAROLA, OTTO, ALEX, and THERESA are there. The telephone is ringing, but no-one can be bothered to answer it.

OTTO: Carola, you can't afford to lose a minute. You have to go. You have to go today, do you understand? Not tomorrow. Today.
CAROLA: Yes, Otto. I know. I'll leave...tonight.
SARDER: Can you tell me what our generation was able to offer the young? We're the ones who taught them to despise intelligence. We thought we could make a clearing in the human spirit. But we wrecked it with the carelessness of bad woodsmen, who instead of thinning a forest only succeed in decimating it.
NICOLETTA: You're going, too, Theo. You like the South of France. Go and take a little trip to the South of France.
SARDER: Alone? Are you telling me to go alone? Aren't you coming with me?
(ALEX goes to answer the telephone, and the ringing stops.)
NICOLETTA: I'll come and visit you, Theo, but what is there for me to do in the South of France? You're a writer, I'm not. I don't know. We've been sitting here for hours asking ourselves what we can do to change the course of events, but there is nothing anyone can do, absolutely nothing. We will have to come to terms with that. As for me, I'm only an actress.
ERIKA: What does it mean to be "only an actress"?
NICOLETTA: It means I'm not a rich little princess. The earth is turning the wrong way around all of a sudden, but what can we do about it? *(ALEX comes back and speaks to SEBASTIEN.)*
SEBASTIEN: Erika, we have to go home. It's our father. Some students at the University wrecked his study. They beat him. He's back home now. They burnt his manuscript. He was crying on the telephone.
SARDER: Yes. It will all happen very quickly now. Erika, my little one, we're coming with you.

197

ALEX: I'm coming, too.

SARDER: Yes. It will all happen very quickly now. Until this moment, I was able to say to myself, this is the twilight, yes, but we can still hope, we can still think, that it's a twilight which presages the dawn. It is a morning twilight. Today, we must resign ourselves to the truth. It was a twilight that presaged the evening that was coming and soon it will be night.

(Blackout.   CAROLA and OTTO)

OTTO: Where will you go, Carola?

CAROLA: To America, I suppose. They've been begging for me to come. I'll make films. My English is good.

OTTO: Carola?

CAROLA: Yes....yes, Otto?

OTTO: Carola. Go to Moscow. Go somewhere where this is a new dawn. Join those who have made it happen. You can work there, they have wonderful directors in Moscow: Eisenstein, Donskoi, Poudovkine Meyerhold. They need people like you there.

CAROLA: Yes, but I'm afraid to go there, I'm afraid. They say things haven't been going well for the last seven years. Apparently, they're throwing artists in prison.

OTTO: It's only propaganda to try and discredit our cause. And even if it were true, all the more reason to go and fight against any betrayal of the revolution. Carola, go to Moscow.

CAROLA: I'm afraid. But yes, my love; yes, I'll go to Moscow.

SCENE THIRTEEN

The Berlin Opera. Chandeliers dripping with light. Rehearsal of Verdi's 'The Force of Destiny'. HENDRIK appears.

HENDRIK: *(to the wings)* The mirror! The mirror isn't straight. The audience must see itself the moment the curtain goes up. It must recognise itself. It's the audience that is acting in this opera. During the whole performance, the audience remains face to face with itself. *(He sings; he strides.)* La la la la la la la la la la la la la la. Are you ready? Now. Careful. AND - houselights down. Footlights up. Yes, that's right. And now, the curtain. Slowly. More slowly. I said slowly. Now. A spot on the mirror, dim at first, then bright, brighter, burning. Take it up another ten points. Good. And now the character comes on. Excellent. Tomorrow we'll put it all together with the orchestra. And if they play a different tempo from the one on the recording, I'll go and hang myself. Thank you. I'll see you all here tomorrow morning.

(The lights go off, leaving only the work lights. There's a sound in the wings.)

Who's there? I can't see anything. Answer me. Who is it?

(It's JULIETTE, with a suitcase.)

HENDRIK: *(terrified)* What are you doing in Berlin? You must be mad! And in this theatre, too. The way things are now. No, no. Keep out of the light. Someone could see you. What do you want?

JULIETTE: When you left Hamburg, you said you'd bring me to Berlin.

HENDRIK: That was two years ago! Anyway, I wrote to you. I told you to be patient. It was too soon.

JULIETTE: And now?

HENDRIK: It's too late. You'll have to go.

JULIETTE: "Go". Go where, Hendrik?

HENDRIK: Try to understand, Juliette. I love you, you know that. But you could get me into a lot of trouble here. You must try to understand my position. If anybody ever found out that you...that I...that you and I...that I had relations with a non-Aryan, they would -

JULIETTE: Who's "they"? The people you work for?

HENDRIK The people I *have* to work with, Juliette. I have no choice. Please try to understand, Juliette. You don't want to harm me, do you? You don't want to get me into trouble? Serious trouble? And all because of you? You don't want that, do you, Juliette? Then you must leave. Listen to me: Go to Paris. Think of it. A dancer like you in Paris, you'll be the toast of the town in no time. Look at what happened to Josephine Baker. I'll tell you what: I'll even pay for your trip.

JULIETTE: So you're dropping me.

HENDRIK: I'm not dropping you. I'm looking after your safety. I'm sending you to Paris!

JULIETTE: I don't give a pig's ear for Paris. I don't speak a fucking word of fucking French. My father was German. I feel German.

(HENDRIK bursts out laughing.) That makes you laugh, does it?

You think it's funny. You don't give a shit about me, do you; you don't give a shit about anything except your shitty career. You never cared about me. You never cared about your friends. You never even cared about communism. If you had, you wouldn't be working here today with the people who are killing the communists. Go out into the streets, Hendrik; get out of your precious little theatre and have a look. They're killing your friends in the streets, Hendrik. They put their corpses in sacks, sew them up and throw them in the river.

HENDRIK: That's enough now.

JULIETTE: "That's enough now"! For years, let me tell you, I had to play at being your savage. You never even asked me if I wanted to, did you? But now Hendrik Höfgen is big and tough. You don't need me to slap you around anymore, do you; there's enough of that going on in the country for your cravings. Are you happy now, Hendrik; are you getting your satisfaction?

HENDRIK: If you don't leave, Juliette, I'll have you thrown out.

JULIETTE: *(screaming)* Just you try, Superman.

HENDRIK: *(whispering)* Shht. Don't shout. Please. Let's calm down, shall we? I'll write you a cheque. Here. You can take a sleeper. *(He writes a cheque and gives it to JULIETTE.)*

JULIETTE: Seems Paris is really cheap these days.

HENDRIK: I promise I'll send you more. But you must go. Promise me you'll go.

JULIETTE: I don't have any cash. I need cash.

(HENDRIK empties out his pockets and gives her what he has. JULIETTE is about to go.) By the way, I almost forgot. I saw your friends in Hamburg. Your wife, too. She was much too good for you, your wife, wasn't she? I told her I was coming to see you. I asked her if she wanted me to give you a message, from her or from your friends.

HENDRIK: *(moved)* Well?

JULIETTE: There's no message. *(She goes out.)*

SCENE FOURTEEN

The Hamburg Theatre. JOSTHINKEL, the new theatre manager, is there. So are MR. KNURR, MRS. EFEU, OTTO, MAGNUS, THERESA, and LORENZ.

JOSTHINKEL: Knurr: Stage doorman. How long have you held this position?

KNURR: Oh, since the war, Mr. Josthinkel, Sir.

JOSTHINKEL: Have you ever been a member of the Communist Party?

KNURR: No, certainly not, Mr. Josthinkel, Sir. I've been a paid-up member of the National Socialist Party since 1925.

MRS. EFEU: That's right, Mr. Josthinkel, Sir. I can bear witness to that, Mr. Josthinkel, Sir.

JOSTHINKEL: Would you both stop calling me Mr. Josthinkel Sir? I am the new superintendent of the Hamburg Theatre and you are to call me by my exact title. Call me Superintendent.

KNURR: Certainly Mr. Superintendent, Sir.

JOSTHINKEL: Mr. Knurr. It has been brought to my attention that you are fond of a joke.

KNURR: Oh yes, I like telling a good joke, Mr. Superintendent, Sir.

JOSTHINKEL: Tell me the one about the Englishman.

KNURR: The one about the Englishman. Well - the one about the Englishman,...no, I can't remember any jokes about Englishmen, no...

JOSTHINKEL: Lorenz, you told me -

LORENZ: Yes, Mr. Knurr. The one about the Englishman who goes back home and says what he thinks of the Germans.

KNURR: Oh, that one. Oh yes. It's not a very good joke, Mr. Superintendent, Sir. It really isn't.

JOSTHINKEL: Tell it anyway.

KNURR: Well. There's this Englishman who comes back from a visit to Germany. He meets his friend on the street. "Well", says the friend, "what did you make of the Germans? " "Oh," he says, "the Germans. They're wonderful people, charming, and they have three great virtues. First of all, they're national socialist. Secondly, they're honest. And thirdly, they're intelligent..." *(KNURR sniggers nervously.)*

JOSTHINKEL: Go on.

KNURR: It really isn't a very good joke.

JOSTHINKEL: Go on.

KNURR: "The trouble is," says the Englishman, "they never have these three virtues at the same time. If they're honest and national socialist, then they're not intelligent. If they're intelligent and national socialist, then they're not honest, and if they're honest and intelligent, then they're not national socialist." *(Pause.)*

JOSTHINKEL: Were you aware, Mr. Knurr, when you told this joke, that you were spreading filthy propaganda invented by the Jews and the Bolsheviks?

KNURR: Oh no, Mr. Superintendent, Sir, I wasn't aware of that.

MRS. EFEU: He wasn't aware of that at all, Mr. Superintendent, Sir, not at all.

OTTO: Since when are jokes forbidden in Germany, Superintendent? Surely the freedom to express -

JOSTHINKEL: *(interrupting)* Since yesterday, Mr. Ulrich. *(He reads:)* "In order to protect the people and the state against communist acts of violence we decree the suspension of articles 114, 115, 117, 118, 123, 124 and 153 of the constitution. We authorise restrictions on personal liberty, on the right to free expression of opinion and on the freedom of the press. We also authorise, beyond the legal limits prescribed in the constitution, violation of the privacy of postal, telegraphic and telephonic communications." *(He folds the decree carefully.)* Presumably you are aware of the events that led to the signing of this decree.

OTTO: The burning of the Reichstag, I suppose.

JOSTHINKEL: That is correct. The burning of the Reichstag by your communist friends, Mr. Ulrich.

OTTO: Unfortunately, the communists didn't burn anything.

JOSTHINKEL: Withdraw the word "unfortunately" forthwith or I shall report you as an accomplice in the burning of the Reichstag, Mr. Ulrich.

OTTO: I withdraw the word "unfortunately."

JOSTHINKEL: To draw this meeting to a close, let me remind you once again that henceforth your repertory must consist solely of the great German classic or contemporary German plays whose national and political integrity cannot be questioned.

OTTO: Like your own plays, Mr. Superintendent.

JOSTHINKEL: Possibly...The concept of art for art's sake is a perverse invention of decadent bourgeois democracies. Art is valid only insofar as it serves the revolution and its people.

OTTO: *(to THERESA and MAGNUS)* Have you noticed that there are some statements which act like the belladonna plant? Meant to be a cure, in the hands of murderers, they become poison.

JOSTHINKEL: The new management of the Hamburg Theatre also notes with concern that it does not presently include among the members of its company a young leading actress of pure Germanic type. Nor indeed does it have an actor capable of playing the heroic roles of the classic German repertoire. The management considers this situation intolerable, Mr. Gottchalk.

MAGNUS: Could you explain to me what you mean by a young leading actress of pure Germanic type?

JOSTHINKEL: You cannot be unaware that your wife, to take but one example, is not a young leading actress of pure Germanic type.

MAGNUS: My wife is not a young leading actress, Superintendent, of pure Germanic type or any other type. My wife is forty years old. One is no longer a young leading actress at the age of forty. What's all this about?

JOSTHINKEL: The management wishes to inform you, Mr. Gottchalk, that you would be allowed back as artistic director of this theatre were life's vicissitudes to separate you from your present wife.

THERESA: In a word, Magnus, divorce your wife and marry a young leading actress of pure Germanic type. It's very simple. Don't make such a song and dance about it.

JOSTHINKEL: I have not yet made a final decision regarding your contract, Miss von Herzfeld, as my inquiries are not yet complete, but I am obliged to point out that your irony will not help your case.

THERESA: If there was only my irony wrong with me. When you find the name of my grandmother, Superintendent, you'll be most upset. And since I can't divorce my own grandmother, I prefer to give in my notice now, while I can still afford that little luxury.

JOSTHINKEL: That has saved us both valuable time.

MAGNUS: Laws! Where are the laws forbidding a man to be artistic director of a theatre because he's married to a Jew! Where are the laws forbidding Theresa von Herzfeld to appear on the stage because her grandmother was a Jew? Where are they?

JOSTHINKEL: You want laws, Mr. Gottchalk, don't worry, they won't be long in coming. In the meantime the management finds itself unable to renew your contracts. Ladies and Gentlemen, you're free. Heil Hitler. Lorenz, return the contracts. *(LORENZ hands out the papers.)* Where will you go, Mr. Ulrich? To Moscow?

OTTO: Moscow? Why Moscow? I am German. And these will be

203

interesting times, even for an unemployed German like myself. No, Mr. Josthinkel, I have no more intention of leaving Germany than you do.

SCENE FIFTEEN
The Railway Bridge. ALEX, OTTO, THERESA.

THERESA: "Theresa," I said to myself, "you never know. There's no dictatorship without an underground, there's no underground without pamphlets, there are no pamphlets without a duplicator."' The duplicator is the backbone of the underground. So I decided to steal the theatre's duplicator. And you, Otto, what have you decided?

OTTO: I don't know yet. I have to find a way to earn a living, like the rest of you. I've been offered a Shakespeare in Vienna, two months' work. But I'm afraid they won't let me back in if I leave Germany. I'm sure there'll be some kind of resistance organised soon, but at the moment all of my friends seem to be in prison. I don't know where to start, I don't know who to contact, I don't know what to do. Any idea what to write in your pamphlets, Theresa?

THERESA: Listen. It's the train to Berlin.

OTTO: *(imitating HENDRIK)* Ah, Berlin. Will I ever be on the train to Berlin, Theresa?

(They smile as the train goes by.)

ALEX: So many things have happened in the last few months, at least you can't complain of boredom. Last night, I went home on foot. It was a warm evening, like this one, so I said to myself: "Don't take the tram, Alex; walk, it's cheaper." I turn down Ferdinandstrasse, to the Blue Café. I open the door. Place is packed with S.A. men. I close the door. I walk. I keep walking. I get to this bridge and stop a moment. I hear a train start up. I look at the time: fourteen minutes past midnight. There aren't any trains that leave Hamburg at fourteen minutes past midnight. It's a cargo train. It goes by...I didn't understand. I stood here, on this bridge. The train gained speed. And then I did understand. There were screams coming from the cattle trucks. Screams of rage, of pain, of indignation. I stood here. Frozen. "If they're screaming,"' I said to myself, "it's because they want to be heard. So Alex, Alex, stay here and listen." One carriage after another. Some were shouting their names and addresses. "Alex, Alex, carve

204

those names into your brain." I close my eyes. Out of dozens and
dozens I managed to remember four names: Holtz Karl, Stresemann
Strasse. Fritz Gigah, Chemitzstrasse. Johan Kralik, Katherinen
Strasse. Hans Gusti, I didn't get his address, but I'll find it. Then the
noise died down. There was only the night left and the fog beginning to
thicken. I stayed here, listening, until the only sound I could hear was
the blood drumming in my ears. I stayed here. No-one else about.
Just me. Alone.

OTTO: A minute ago we couldn't think what to do, but now we know.
We have to let everyone know what you've just described, Alex. We
have to say to the Germans: listen. Listen to the trains moving across
your country every night. Those trains are loaded with men and
women. Today it's the communists and socialists. Tomorrow it'll be
the Jews and then it'll be you. Block the tracks, Comrades, and refuse
to drive the trains. Refuse to mine the coal that fuels the trains. Refuse
to lay down the tracks that carry the trains. Refuse to serve, friends,
refuse to cooperate. Theresa, my friend, what else is there for us to do
but follow you to your house?

(He takes the duplicator on his shoulders.)

SCENE SIXTEEN

*The dressing-room of the Berlin Theatre. **HENDRIK** and
NICOLETTA are at their make-up tables.*

NICOLETTA: I couldn't bear it anymore...I simply couldn't bear it.
He would sit all day long on the terrace, staring out at the cypresses
and moan. He moaned every hour of the day, day in, day out.
"Nicoletta...Nicoletta...stay with me, stay close, it's so awful. I hear
the men and women being tortured in Germany. The wind carries their
screams to my ears. The executioners play gramophone records in the
torture chambers, but I can still hear the screams of pain." And a lot
more nonsense of that kind, a lot of sentimental raving. Theo is a
wonderful man; he is a genius. I know that and I love him. But he is
also outside of his time, he lives outside of reality, and that's something
I cannot bear.

HENDRIK: Yes, I know. All those emigrés playing at being martyrs on the beaches of the South of France. Listen to me, Nicoletta, they're deserters, nothing more, nothing less than deserters. What can they possibly do from over there?

NICOLETTA: I couldn't bear it anymore...I simply couldn't bear it. I kept saying to myself, "Nicoletta, my darling, you're dying in this place. Soon, you'll be dried up. You're an actress, my girl; go home and act." Mind you, it's a good thing you were here.

HENDRIK: Did I tell you they've suggested me for...

NICOLETTA: For what?

HENDRIK: It's a very important position. I don't know...Should I, shouldn't I?...It's so difficult....

NICOLETTA: Of course you should. If you don't someone else will. And so....

HENDRIK: It might as well be me.

NICOLETTA: Quite. And once you're in power, you can be...you can...help...people....

HENDRIK: I'll be able to stop some of the....

NICOLETTA: Exactly!

HENDRIK: You see, we are the ones at the front. If you want to change things, it's better to be here, on the inside, not in Sanary or Cassis. Are you ready? It's our turn. *(He gets up.)*

NICOLETTA: You never told me in whose honour we're doing this gala.

HENDRIK: I don't really know but all the greatest German celebrities have agreed to take part and they were so keen to have me, I couldn't turn them down. *(He comes close to her.)* Kiss me...my beauty, my torment...

SCENE SEVENTEEN

The Hamburg Theatre.

JOSTHINKEL: *(to LORENZ)* Bring in Hans Miklas. *(LORENZ is about to go.)* Lorenz, let me see your plaything again. It fascinates me.

(LORENZ shows him a weapon consisting of a metal base to which are attached steel balls.)

JOSTHINKEL: And what do you call this?

LORENZ: Steelworks.

JOSTHINKEL: Steelworks. How simple. How poetic. Ah. The masses make us drool with admiration when it comes to violence. Lend me your toy, will you, Lorenz? *(LORENZ salutes and goes out. JOSTHINKEL tries to master the weapon. MIKLAS comes in.)*

JOSTHINKEL: *(reads from a file)* Hans Miklas. Born November the 9th, 1903, in Thalburg. Son of Joseph Miklas, accountant, and Hildegarde Breker. Your father was killed in 1916, as was your older brother. One of your sisters is married to Joseph Strepper, butcher in the suburbs of Hamburg. It is this same Joseph Strepper who sponsors you when you join the party in 1923. You are unmarried. You have never been abroad. And since your arrival in Hamburg you've resided at the same boarding-house, the Rosa-Monica. You've often helped your neighbourhood detachment of S.A. with propaganda spectacles and with the distribution of food to the unemployed. However, you have never actually joined the S.A. Is there anything else you know about yourself which might be of interest to the superintendant of the theatre before whom you now stand?

MIKLAS: Yes.

JOSTHINKEL: What? We've left something out? What could that possibly be?

MIKLAS: I'm an actor. You've left that out.

JOSTHINKEL: So we have. So we have. It's not written anywhere in this file. Hans Miklas: national socialist actor. *(He writes this down.)* You've put yourself up for the part of the student in the Hamburg Theatre's next production of *"Faust."* You will play the student. And I am now in the fortunate position of being able to tell you that we will be honoured with a special guest appearance by Hendrik Höfgen, whose extraordinary interpretation of Mephisto has earned him such renown. You will have the privilege of playing opposite our greatest national-socialist actor. Heil Hitler. *(MIKLAS begins to leave. JOSTHINKEL calls him back.)* But I see you've already worked here and were dismissed at Mr. Höfgen's request. Hans Miklas, come back here for a moment. *(Pause.)* You see, it may be that I share your feelings about Mr. Höfgen. I too may have some doubts as to the authenticity of Mr. Höfgen's national-socialism.

MIKLAS: He was a communist. *(JOSTHINKEL writes this down.)*

JOSTHINKEL: A communist...yes, well...it's not because he had a little flirtation with communism...Many nazis, both humble and highly-placed ones, had little flirtations with communism. But it's been said...there was a liaison with a prostitute...a non-white....

MIKLAS: The whole theatre knew about that. *(MIKLAS suddenly realises that JOSTHINKEL is writing down everything he says.)*

JOSTHINKEL: You see, Hans Miklas, if there was someone in this theatre who could watch and warn me of any such...funny business, I would find that most helpful. What do you think?

MIKLAS: I don't know what you mean, Superintendent. Could we please discuss my wages?

JOSTHINKEL: You know, my boy, the sexual submissiveness some of our great German artists are showing before the erotic wiles of Jewish and Black women is giving us serious cause for concern.

MIKLAS: Superintendent, I'd like to discuss my wages.

JOSTHINKEL: That's why I'd like you to be my watchdog, my Moral Minister, as it were. Well? Do we have anything concerning Höfgen and his mistress that might serve to avenge you, my boy? Can we get him with some concrete evidence? I've said a great deal, Hans Miklas; it's your turn now.

MIKLAS: I don't look for my enemies in bed, Superintendent, nor on the lavatory pan.

JOSTHINKEL: What do you mean? I order you to make yourself clear.

MIKLAS: I mean that when I joined the party ten years ago, Superintendent, it wasn't with the ambition of ending up as your spy or your peeping Tom. My ambition was to witness the triumph of the national socialist revolution. I wanted to see the return of Germany's honour and the greatness of the German people re-established. I hated the Jews because I was told: "No more Jews, no more capitalism." But now I notice that a lot of Jews are leaving Germany, but capitalism is still rampant. I notice that there are no longer any Jewish professors at German universities, but there aren't any more boys from the working class than before. I notice that Jewish magistrates have been dismissed, but there's still one law for the rich and one law for the poor. It's still the rich who reap the benefits and the poor who receive the promises. And if that's not capitalism, then I wonder what capitalism is. And I wonder if we started our revolution to make Germany national-socialist or to fill the theatres with informers instead of actors. You've betrayed

us. You've abused our anger. And now you want to dishonour me as well. Wretches that we are, poor, poor wretches. What have we done to deserve the horror of such masters? *(LORENZ comes running on. MIKLAS shoves him aside and runs out like a madman.)*
JOSTHINKEL: *(recovering)* Follow him, Lorenz, and take all the measures necessary to keep him from doing something silly. Bolshevik propaganda has wormed its way into his mind and he's capable of anything. *(as LORENZ is about to go.)* Take this, Lorenz. You may need it. *(LORENZ takes his weapon and goes.)*

SCENE EIGHTEEN

The Hamburg Theatre. MIKLAS is on the stage, playing the violin. MRS. EFEU and KNURR are at their usual places. MRS. EFEU is playing the piano. LORENZ appears. In the wings, there are four shadows.

MIKLAS: *(to LORENZ)* And now I'm even playing music written by the son of a Jew and a Gypsy.
KNURR: *(to MRS. EFEU)* Come...we had better leave.

(MRS. EFEU is dragged off by KNURR. MIKLAS moves towards LORENZ. He is still playing the violin.)

SCENE NINETEEN

The Railway Bridge. MYRIAM and MAGNUS. MAGNUS holds a letter.

MYRIAM: So? This letter?
MAGNUS: Another reply. From the Little Theatre in Dresden: "Honoured to have qualified as a purely German theatre for many years now - therefore impossible to consider your application. Should circumstances free you from the unfortunate attachments which hamper your career, would be pleased to hear from you again," and so on and so forth. Heil Hitler." What do you expect? They're idiots.
MYRIAM: Idiots. Idiot. Talk of the schlemiel calling the schlemazel black. Why can't you divorce me and take me back as your mistress?

209

It'd be like that film that made me cry so much, *'Back Street'*.

MAGNUS: Myriam, we've broken too many dishes discussing that subject. There's no more to be said. But you mustn't worry, my dear, we'll pull through as we've always pulled through, with grace.

MYRIAM: Worried? Who's worried? The baker, maybe he's a little worried. The others won't give us any more credit, so why should they worry? He's a nice man, that baker, or maybe he's Jewish, how do I know? We'll leave him a little note of apology if something happens to us.

MAGNUS: If something happens to us you can't expect us to start worrying about the baker. But why do you want something to happen to us?

MYRIAM: Did I say I wanted something to happen to us? All I said was *if* something happened to us. If they...if we...that's all I said.

MAGNUS: Something could happen to me alone. Or something could happen to you alone. That would be awful.

MYRIAM: Yes, that would be awful. I think it's better if something happened to both of us at once. I understand, Magnus, I understand. But do you understand?

MAGNUS: I understand.

MYRIAM: Do you really understand?

MAGNUS: Do you want me to understand something in particular?

MYRIAM: Do I want him to understand something in particular, he asks. When you say to someone: "do you understand", it's always because you want them to understand something in particular. Otherwise, you wouldn't have to insist so much, would you? I mean, do you understand that I've understood, or don't you?

MAGNUS: I understand, Myriam; don't get irritable.

MYRIAM: Irritable! Who's getting irritable? *(Pause.)* Is your shirt clean?

MAGNUS: Yes.

MYRIAM: And your underpants. What about your underpants? Are they clean?

MAGNUS: Myriam!

MYRIAM: Myriam. Why Myriam? My mother always used to say: "Myriam, my daughter, if you had an accident and your underpants were dirty, think what a disgrace it would be to the family."

MAGNUS: Myriam, I'm as bright as a button.

210

MYRIAM: Good. I feel better now. *(Silence.)* We've had a good life, Magnus.

MAGNUS: Yes, but it was useless. We couldn't stop anything.

MYRIAM: We did what we could, Magnus. Who can say our life was useless? Maybe one day in 20, 30, 50 years, somebody will hear that a German actor by the name of Gottchalk killed himself rather than repudiate his wife the way they asked him to. And they'll say: "There's a man who said no in his own way." And for a minute, they'll think about us. And for that minute, we'll live again.

MAGNUS: Yes. Perhaps.

(They hold hands. They are sitting on the rail. A train whistles in the distance.)

SCENE TWENTY

THOMAS BRÜCKNER's house. The Veranda. SEBASTIEN, ERIKA, LUDWIG, EMELYNE.

SEBASTIEN: You really think we should leave, Ludwig?

LUDWIG: Yes, Mr. Sebastien. You must leave Germany. Both of you. Especially Miss Erika. Because of her Bolshevik cabaret.

SEBASTIEN: And our father?

LUDWIG: Let him stay in Switzerland. He can extend his holiday. Miss Erika, please listen to me when I tell you to go as quickly as you can. If they catch up with you...

SEBASTIEN: It's all right, Ludwig, we're going. Stop worrying. Go and prepare my things. *(LUDWIG is going out.)*

ERIKA: Ludwig? Who told you it was a Bolshevik cabaret?

(LUDWIG stops, looks at her, doesn't answer, and goes. EMELYNE stays.)

ERIKA: Emelyne?

EMELYNE: Yes, Erika?

ERIKA: What are you thinking?

EMELYNE: Ludwig's been working for them for several years. He used to tell them everything that went on in this house. But he's fond of you, so now he's telling you what is being planned there. What'll happen to me? I'm his wife. They'll turn him into a mad dog. He's

211

already like that sometimes. They'll make monsters out of all of us.

ERIKA: Come with us, Emelyne. We'll take you to America.

EMELYNE: No, Miss Erika, you can't take all of Germany into exile. You'll have to leave me here. I'll pack your case.

ERIKA: I'll take one small bag.

SEBASTIEN: This nightmare can't last.

EMELYNE: Yes, Sir. It will last. *(The telephone rings.)*

ERIKA: Hello? Father! Sebastien, it's the magician. *(EMELYNE indicates the telephone might be bugged and they must be careful.)*.Yes, yes, Father. No, no, rest there for a few more days. In fact, we were thinking of coming to see you for a little while. Tomorrow? No, absolutely not. The house is in a frightful mess. It is, Father....Father...

SEBASTIEN *(takes the telephone)* Hello, Father? It's raining, too. We're having a dreadful March. It's snowing, actually. *(to ERIKA)* He says the weather's bad in Switzerland. Listen to me, Father, listen, there are storms on the way. No, they're not spring storms. *(to ERIKA)* He says he doesn't care, he wants to come back.

ERIKA: Hello, Father? Listen to me. Don't come back. You're no longer safe in Germany. We're not either. Is that clear? We're leaving. There. Understood? We'll be with you day after tomorrow. Lots of love.

(She hangs up and goes, followed by EMELYNE. LUDWIG comes on with a suitcase. SEBASTIEN takes two glasses of cognac. He serves LUDWIG and himself.)

SEBASTIEN: It's the first time we drink together, isn't it, Ludwig?

LUDWIG: Yes, it's the first time.

SEBASTIEN: But it doesn't matter anymore, does it?

LUDWIG: No, it doesn't matter anymore.

SEBASTIEN: We didn't drink to anything. But what is there to drink to? *(ERIKA comes in with EMELYNE.)*

SEBASTIEN: It's time for us to go.

(He shakes LUDWIG'S hand and kisses EMELYNE.)

LUDWIG: Have a good trip, Mr. Sebastien. And I wish you a bright future abroad, Miss Erika.

ERIKA: Have a bright future in Germany, Ludwig.

(LUDWIG takes the suitcases out, followed by EMELYNE.)

SEBASTIEN: It's time to go.

ERIKA: Just one more little moment. I feel as if I'd never seen this room before. When we're gone there won't be a living soul left here.

SEBASTIEN: My sister, my sister.

ERIKA: My orchard, my dear, my beautiful, my treasured orchard. My happiness, goodbye. *(THERESA comes in, carrying a suitcase.)*

ERIKA: Theresa! We're leaving.

THERESA: So am I. The Gestapo came and arrested Otto yesterday. Alex, too. I'm all that's left of the Peppermill.

ERIKA: And me. We'll take it with us, Theresa, we'll take it everywhere we go.

SEBASTIEN: And every word we write, every truth we utter, will do them harm, a little harm.

SCENE TWENTY-ONE

The Hamburg Theatre. HENDRIK, playing Mephisto, takes a solo bow to tumultuous applause. JOSTHINKEL brings a microphone onto the stage. He's in full evening dress and holds a telegram in his hand.

JOSTHINKEL: *(to the audience)* Minister, General, ladies and gentlemen, it gives me the greatest pleasure this evening to commit an indiscretion. This telegram was not addressed to me. But a quasi-diabolic intuition allowed me to guess its contents and authorised me to open it. This telegram is addressed to our great national-socialist actor, Hendrik Höfgen. I will, however, read it to you all forthwith. *(Applause.)* "Fully aware of the services rendered by the actor Hendrik Höfgen and knowing how much the prestige of the theatre of our Third Reich will be enhanced by his future successes, I have decided to name Hendrik Höfgen Administrator of all the theatres of Prussia." And it is signed...it is signed: "Adolf Hitler. Our Führer." *(Applause. Bows. JOSTHINKEL brings NICOLETTA from the wings and she stands beside her husband.)*

JOSTHINKEL: *(reciting)* "Open the ball, divine couple, pair beloved of the gods, sovereign royalties of the nether regions, bewitching angels. Lead us to the depths of the earth, to the primeval caves oozing with blood, where the warriors make love and the lovers make war, and where the beauty of death entwines with the beauty of love in a sublime

213

and unique feast."

(Applause. More bows. Suddenly, the theatre is empty.
NICOLETTA and HENDRIK remain alone. They're silent, frozen.)
NICOLETTA: Aren't you getting changed, Hendrik? They're waiting for us at the Grand Hotel.
HENDRIK: I don't want to go.
NICOLETTA: You have to go, Hendrik. The reception is in your honour. Don't forget Goering himself has come to Hamburg to embrace his dear Mephisto and drive him back all the sooner to Berlin. It's too late, Hendrik, you have to go. I'll wait for you in the foyer.
(She goes out. A figure appears on the gangway.)
HENDRIK: Who's that? Otto? Otto! My brother, my friend, you *are* here. They told me- *(He runs towards OTTO.)* You've come at last. I'm saved! *(But he stops in front of a man who's staring at him in silence.)* Who are you? I've never seen you here before. Everyone's left the theatre, you shouldn't be here. You have no right-
(The man comes forward, slowly. HENDRIK tries to close the curtains but the man leaps onto the stage and reaches him in a few steps.)
HENDRIK: Don't touch me! Help! Knurr!
ALEX: No need to shout, Administrator, I've come to bring you Otto's greetings.
HENDRIK: I don't know who you're talking about.
ALEX: You don't remember Otto? Your friend, your brother, Otto. Otto is dead and sends you his greetings.
HENDRIK: Listen, my friend, I'm not afraid of you, but I should tell you that you're not safe here-
ALEX: Otto was beaten for nine days. In the end, he had no face left. His body was a mass of bleeding sores, broken bones, and all I could recognise of him were his eyes. But when they took him away for his last interrogation, Otto managed to say - it was difficult to understand him, his mouth was full of blood - he managed to say: "When you've reached this stage, you no longer make mistakes. I know now that we'll win. I'm sure of it in a way I never was before. We'll have to fight for a long time, but in the end, we'll win."
HENDRIK: Why are you telling me this?
ALEX: So that your friends in the government will learn about it. So that the scum you keep company with, those men who stink of urine,

214

will hear of it from your own mouth. Otto died without revealing a single name. They threw his body from a third-floor window. I am now going to name the murderers so that they will be damned for the centuries to come: They were the S.A. Witske, the S.A. Kubik, the S.A. Moder. Listen carefully, Administrator: Witske, Kubik, Moder.

HENDRIK: How do you know all this?

ALEX: I shared Otto's cell. They transferred me after his death and I jumped from the lorry.

HENDRIK: Well, you didn't die, did you? You got yourself out of it, you let Otto down.

ALEX: I'm still alive, yes, unfortunately for you, Administrator. Unfortunately for all of you. But no, I'll never let Otto down. They wouldn't allow anyone at Otto's funeral, so do you know where his memorial service took place? In Dachau. They heard of his death through one of the prisoners' wives. And one night, a man started to sing. Then another joined him. And another. Six thousand prisoners sang for Otto and there was nothing anyone could do to stop it. No-one will ever sing like that for you, Administrator.

HENDRIK: Don't come near me. I'll give you some money.

(NICOLETTA comes on. HENDRIK grabs her purse.) Give me some money, quickly. This man's threatening me. He wants money.

NICOLETTA: No, Hendrik. He doesn't want your money. Good evening, Alex. You've come too late. There is nothing you can do for us anymore. I think you had better leave as soon as you can. The rot has set in and we are beginning to stink. Go. Go quickly.

HENDRIK: Get out or I'll call the police. Go to Hell!

(ALEX goes. HENDRIK nestles against NICOLETTA and begins to cry.)

HENDRIK: What do they all want from me? Help me. Protect me.

NICOLETTA: Be quiet, Hendrik. We mustn't say anything. There is nothing left for us to do now but to go in mourning for ourselves. Get dressed. They're waiting for us.

HENDRIK: Why are they tormenting me? I haven't done anything. What can I do? I'm only an ordinary actor.

(The lights fade.)

END

THIS PLAY IS DEDICATED TO:

HANS OTTO
actor, communist
tortured and assassinated by the
Gestapo in Berlin
November 24, 1933

ERICH MÜHSAM
anarchist poet
tortured and hanged at the
Oranienburg concentration camp
July 10, 1934

MADAME MÜHSAM
disappeared in the Soviet Union,
most probably during Stalin's
purges

CAROLA NEHER
actress
emigrated to the Soviet Union
deported by Stalin
disappeared in 1936

KURT TUCHOLSKY
pacifist writer and satirist
committed suicide in Sweden
December 21, 1935

ERNST LUDWIG KIRCHNER
painter
committed suicide in Switzerland
June 15, 1938

CARL VON OSSIETZKY
journalist, pacifist writer
died of starvation after three years
of imprisonment
May 4, 1938

WALTER HASENCLEVER
playwright
interned at a camp at Milles,
France
committed suicide
June 21, 1939

EGON FRIEDDELL
historian
committed suicide in Vienna
1938

ERNST TOLLER
poet
committed suicide in New York
May 22, 1939

CARL EINSTEIN
poet
interned at a camp at Gurs, France
committed suicide
July 3, 1940

WALTER BENJAMIN
writer, essayist
committed suicide in France at the
Spanish border
September 26, 1940

RICHARD OEHRING
poet
committed suicide in Holland
1940

WILLI MÜNZENBERG
writer, editor, communist
excommunicated from the party
found dead in Grenoble
1940

HERWARTH WALDEN
writer, theoretician
disappeared in the Soviet Union
1941

JOACHIM GOTTCHALK
actor
committed suicide with his wife
and son
November 1941

JAKOB VAN HODDIS
poet
interned near Koblenz,
assassinated in a gas chamber
April 30, 1942

STEFAN ZWEIG
writer, pacifist
committed suicide in Rio de
Janeiro
February 22, 1942

SHIMON DUBNOV
historian
assassinated in a Soviet
concentration camp
1942

PAUL KORNFELD
playwright
assassinated in a concentration
camp
1942

ERNST OTTWALT
communist writer
assassinated in a Soviet
concentration camp
1943

ALFRED WOLFENSTEIN
poet, critic
committed suicide in Paris
January 22, 1945

ERIKA MANN
actress, pamphleteer
1905-1969

KLAUS MANN
writer
committed suicide in Cannes
May 21, 1949

HARSH ANGEL

by Maria Avraamidou
Translated by Rhea Frangofinou

The play was first produced in 1986 by the Cyprus Theatrical Organisation. Directed by Phaedros Stasinos with Lenia Sorokou and Jemy Gaitanopoulou as Antigone and Ismene.

CHARACTERS:

ANTIGONE, 45 years
ISMENE, 43 years, sister of Antigone
FATHER, 75 years
MOTHER, 68 years
ALEXANDER, their son, brother to Antigone and Ismene - 47 years
ELLI, Alexander's wife - 40 years
MRS. MARIA, a neighbour - 55 years
PARIS, a young student, writer and neighbour.

ACT ONE, SCENE ONE

The hall of a refugee house. We see at first glance that the inhabitants have books - everywhere - on a makeshift bookcase, on shelves, on chairs. To the right, French windows open onto a small yard dominated by a pear tree in blossom. To the left, a staircase. In front, another door leads to the kitchen. In the centre is a table with a bowl of fruit, two armchairs and a low table near the entrance. The furniture generally is old-fashioned and displays a discreet, perhaps fallen gentility. On the walls are some traditional tapestries with embroidered mottoes such as: "This too will pass", "God is our hope". In a prominent position is a framed religious poem: "Where there is faith there is blessing, where there is peace there is hope; where there is hope is God; where there is God, there is no need". Under the stairs there is a clock with a pendulum on a carved base.

As the curtain rises, ANTIGONE is typing slowly and steadily on an old typewriter. She stops and reads what she has written.

ANTIGONE: "Oh, how distant it all is, so long forgotten. It seems the stars, the sun and the moon are dead. Dead. All that I loved - places, people, my friends, one after the other bade me farewell and were lost at the turning of the road. And yet on some nights, my senses long for your voice, your face, your lips..." *(She sighs, rises and goes to open the French windows. With a sudden movement, she draws the curtains, closes the door, returns to the table and nervously resumes her typing.)* "Oh such nights I wander through the streets looking for you, to crush you with my love." *(She stops typing.)* Imagine! "To crush you with my love..."

(Suddenly, from upstairs, we hear a song on a record. It is Brahms's "Lullaby". The record is very scratched. ANTIGONE stops at the foot of the stairs. Calmly.) Mother, how many times have I told you to throw away that record. Why don't you tell him a story?

MOTHER'S VOICE: I can't Antigone. I don't feel well tonight. Come and say something to him.

ANTIGONE: *(controlling her nerves)* I can't. I've told you, I've started a new job. Leave him alone, he'll go to sleep.

(She moves towards the typewriter. She starts to type. The door opens and ISMENE enters. She is dressed like a much younger woman - a red jacket and beige full skirt. She is holding a book. It is the latest poetry anthology by the poet Montis. She thinks aloud as she reads.)

ISMENE: Oh, no, I don't agree, Montis.

ANTIGONE: Have you finished work? Isn't it a bit early?

ISMENE: It was the boss's daughter's birthday. He let us off early.

ANTIGONE: And you rushed straight to the bookshop?

ISMENE: *(annoyed)* If we give up books what will we have left? Listen to what Montis says here: "To life...If you see us again, let us know." Do you hear? He believes it all ends here.

ANTIGONE: *(with contempt)* And where do you think it all ends? In Paradise? *(She resumes typing.)* I've never had any hopes for this or for any other life. *(She reads aloud.)* "And on such a night I will make you the heroine of my most tragic tale..."

ISMENE: What are you typing?

219

ANTIGONE: It's a novel by the confectioner's son. He heard that I take in typing and he brought me his novel. He wants to take it with him to Athens to find a publisher for it.

ISMENE: It sounds quite good.

ANTIGONE: I wouldn't know. I just copy.

ISMENE: How much will you charge him?

ANTIGONE: *(annoyed but trying not to show it)* I don't know. What I always charge. I haven't discussed it.

ISMENE: *(surprised)* You haven't discussed it? What if he cheats you like the building contractor who hasn't paid you for three months?

ANTIGONE: He won't. When you meet him you'll see.

ISMENE: Oh...

(She opens the curtains to the French window and looks out.)

ANTIGONE: For heaven's sake, close the curtains.

ISMENE: It's still light out... *(Pause. Almost to herself.)* And my pear tree doesn't like to be alone outside.

ANTIGONE: Stop this nonsense. Draw the curtains.

ISMENE: *(approaches ANTIGONE. Softly.)* You're in one of your moods again. What's wrong?

ANTIGONE: Nothing's wrong.

ISMENE: It's spring outside.

ANTIGONE: I don't care.

ISMENE: Everywhere is so unbearably...beautiful.

ANTIGONE: *(harshly)* To me everything is so unbearably indifferent.

ISMENE: *(with a nervous laugh)* Even indifference is a luxury for us. *(She touches ANTIGONE'S shoulder. The latter is uncomfortable, and ISMENE lowers her hand. She goes to look out again.)* Let's walk in the yard.

(ANTIGONE stubbornly remains seated and turns to her work, and ISMENE lifts the curtain, looks out. She sighs.)

ISMENE: Daises have grown even in mother's vegetable patch. Yellow daises, white ones, and the lime tree and the lemon tree are covered in blossom. But my pear tree is something else. It's...an offering. *(Sighs. Moves to ANTIGONE.)* Last night I dreamt about it. Can you believe it?

ANTIGONE: Well, if you've got nothing better to dream about ?

ISMENE: I dreamt we were in our village in Bellapaix, on the balcony. Everything was blurred, as if wrapped in gauze, but underneath the balcony, in our orchard, was my pear tree...
I don't know why, but I'm sure it was the same one. In the middle of the clouds I could see it clearly - upright, almost austere. And all round everything was quiet. And suddenly, opposite me, our old Granny appeared. You know, Theodora, standing watching me. "Granny, where have you been all this time?" "I was over there, my dear." "Do you remember when you used to comb my hair and tell me I was the star of the East?" "I remember, my dear." "But now, Granny, I've changed, I'm tired." "I was the beginning, my dear, but you are the tree...and you've no other choice..." What do you think she was trying to tell me? "You have no other choice..." I heard it clearly.

ANTIGONE: *(suddenly angry)* I know very well what our grandmother wanted to tell you. But what good is it? Can it bring back Bellapaix, our balcony, our youth?

(From upstairs an undefined noise is heard - something like a laugh, then an elderly voice sings a lullaby out of tune.)

ANTIGONE: *(more softly)* Listen to that. Can you stand it? *(Goes near the stairs.)* Mother, I've told you a thousand times to close your bedroom door. Do you want the whole neighbourhood to hear us?

ISMENE: Don't shout at her.

ANTIGONE: How many times have I got to tell her to shut that door.

ISMENE: She's an old woman. She forgets.

ANTIGONE: I don't care.

ISMENE: She's our mother.

ANTIGONE: Did she think of us? Then?

ISMENE: Don't start all that again.

ANTIGONE: Didn't I tell her? Mother, it's dangerous at your age. But would she listen? *(Mimics her mother's voice.)* I'm not God, my dear, I don't decide. *(Scornfully.)* You know, if he hadn't been born, I'd be married now, with children. Perhaps even grandchildren...

ISMENE: *(almost to herself)* I'd be married too...

ANTIGONE: Sophocles and I were about to get engaged. But then his mother persuaded him...to leave me...

ISMENE: *(to comfort her)* You're better off without him.

ANTIGONE: *(almost to herself)* I've never loved anyone else.

ISMENE: I loved Sotiris too...

ANTIGONE: *(angry with herself)* What are we doing, sitting around thinking of old stories?

ISMENE: You're at home too much, your nerves are in a state. You should try to get a job. If you like, I'll talk to my boss.

ANTIGONE: *(rises angry)* I'm fine where I am. And if I got a bit of money from you occasionally I'd manage the house perfectly but you spend it all.

ISMENE: It's my money.

ANTIGONE: You know our parent's pension isn't enough.

ISMENE: *(slightly annoyed)* Alright, alright. As soon as I get paid, I'll give you some money.

ANTIGONE: *(more softly)* I've been hearing that for months now. *(Pause.)* It's six o'clock and father's not home yet.

ISMENE: You know him. He'll have wandered off somewhere. *(Door bell rings.)* Speak of the devil. *(Goes to the door.)* He's forgotten his key again.

VOICE OF PARIS: Hello. I wanted Miss Antigone...

ISMENE: *(a little surprised)* Antigone? My sister? Come in. *(PARIS enters, young, presentable, wearing jeans and a tight white T-shirt.)*

ANTIGONE: *(rises to meet him)* Come in Mr. Paris, have you come to see how I'm getting on?

PARIS: *(awkwardly)* Mrs. Antigone...Miss I mean, if it's not too much trouble... I've brought some poems. I read that the Labour Bank is holding a competition. Nothing much of course, but it doesn't hurt to try my luck, does it?

ANTIGONE: Of course, of course. Do you want them typed before your novel? How many copies did you want?

PARIS: Four, if you can. Better leave the novel for the moment.

ISMENE: So you write poetry too? Do you like it?

PARIS: *(modestly)* Very much.

ISMENE: Have you seen Monti's latest collection?

PARIS: No Mrs...

ISMENE: Miss, Miss Ismene, or just Ismene.

PARIS: Antigone, Ismene...

ISMENE: *(laughing)* Our father had a passion for the ancient Greeks.

PARIS: *(suddenly interested)* Really? I wish everyone had the same passion. Our language wouldn't have deteriorated so much. As soon as I came into this house I realized that it's not...an ordinary house.
ISMENE: What do you mean, not an ordinary house?
PARIS: I mean, all the books, and the garden with the pear tree.
(ISMENE and ANTIGONE exchange relieved looks. ANTIGONE exits upstairs.)
ISMENE: The books cost a thousand sacrifices. As for my pear tree, it's my pride and joy.
PARIS: So, Mrs...Miss I mean...
ISMENE: Call me Ismene since we're neighbours. I'll call you Paris.
PARIS: Alright, Ismene, so you like the Cypriot poets? Well, we do have some good ones, but not like the Greeks. Which of our poets can compare with Elytis, or Seferis?
ISMENE: You're wrong. Wait a minute while I find a collection by Pantelis Mechanicos. His complete works were published recently.
(She goes and returns with a book.) Here you are. You don't appreciate the Cypriots! Here, read this.
PARIS: *(reads)*

> The bird is silent now
> The tree bears no fruit
> The seed gives no miracle.

ISMENE: *(recites softly)*

> Harsh angel
> Bleed
> Bleed my insides
> And lead,
> Lead me again
> On the hard road of suffering
> To the miracle,
> Else my soul dies
> My soul does not laugh.

PARIS: You know it by heart. You're right, it's wonderful.
ISMENE: "Else my soul dies, my soul does not laugh." Sometimes, sometimes I think those verses were written for me.
PARIS: Why?
ISMENE: I don't know. They suit me.
PARIS: *(smiling)* Mourning becomes Ismene?

223

ISMENE: I think so.

PARIS: Think of something else, something beautiful. Your pear tree for instance. So sure of itself, determined to blossom every spring.

ISMENE: You seem sure of yourself too.

PARIS: Well...I know what I'm doing as I've no other choice. Do you understand?

ISMENE: *(sighing)* I understand.

ANTIGONE: *(coming downstairs)* Still here, Mr. Paris? Don't worry, I'll finish your typing as quickly as I can.

PARIS: *(moving to the exit)* Thank you. As regards the fee...I don't know. Whatever you say...

(The door bell rings. ANTIGONE goes to answer it.)

ANTIGONE: We'll discuss it another time. *(ANTIGONE opens the door and FATHER enters. Severely.)* Father, have you forgotten your key again?

FATHER: I left it in my coat .

ANTIGONE: You haven't got a coat.

FATHER: If I haven't got a coat, where would I have put the key?

ANTIGONE: Stop being clever and go up and help mother.

FATHER: I can't, I've got a lot of work to do...

ANTIGONE: *(goes upstairs)* A lot of work. I see... *(Sighs.)*

FATHER: *(quietly, to ISMENE)* Have you got ten shillings? I would venture to say that...

ISMENE: I gave you money last night.

FATHER: My dear, I beg you, ten shillings, or even one pound. At the post office they told me I should send my letter to Queen Victoria registered to make sure she gets it.

ISMENE: Elizabeth. The Queen's called Elizabeth. I've told you a hundred times. Paris, let me introduce my father - a retired schoolteacher. Mr. Paris is a neighbour - he's a student of literature.

FATHER: Oh, how do you do? Paris, eh... Paris Alexander, the son of Priam...and you're studying literature too. But you know, times were hard then...yes, yes...where was I? I would venture to say...*(To ISMENE.)* When my cheque comes I'll... Please Ismene...

ISMENE: *(quietly)* It's the end of the month. *(Loudly.)* My father knows all of the Odyssey and the Iliad by heart, in ancient Greek.

PARIS: Really? I've been studying for years and I can't remember three lines, except for - "Tell me, Muse, of the man of many devices..."

FATHER: When we were children we used to really learn things *(Recites from Odyssey.)* "The day will come when Priam and his people will vanish..." What do you think sir, has the last judgment arrived? I don't lose hope though, and I venture to say...struggle, I struggle...If I had ten shillings, I'd serve a sacred cause - I'd send a registered letter to Queen Victoria.

ISMENE: Elizabeth.

FATHER: I'd plead with her to intervene to put a stop to all wars. You see what's going on in the Lebanon, in Iraq? And as a guarantor power to Cyprus, she should carry out her responsibilities...and make the Turks go away.

PARIS: If only it were that simple, sir.

FATHER: But that's our mistake. Taking things as being too difficult whereas, I venture to say, at bottom they are simple. Justice is simple, the world is simple - who said that?

PARIS: Seferis.

FATHER: Seferis. A great poet. *(Quietly.)* Have you got ten shillings on you, my boy? I venture to say...when my cheque comes...*(Loudly.)* If only the politicians would let me. I would solve the Cyprus problem. *(To ISMENE.)* I'm going to send a copy of my letter to the committee of the Nobel Prize. You never know, my dear girl, your father might become a Nobel Prize winner. Can you imagine that? You'd be proud of me. You and Antigone, and Alexander and... *(Pause.)* Ismene, now that I remember, your brother phoned me at the coffee shop, he's coming to lunch on Sunday.

ISMENE: Alexander's coming on Sunday? Alone?

FATHER: With...his wife...but...

ISMENE: Ah. *(Pause.)* Did he mention the children?

FATHER: *(pause)* I think...not.

ISMENE: Ah. *(Pause.)* Antigone!...Antigone!

ANTIGONE: *(from upstairs)* Don't shout. What's got into you?

ISMENE: Alexander 's coming to lunch on Sunday with his darling wife.

ANTIGONE: *(indifferent)* Really? How did that happen?
(Comes downstairs. The clock strikes.)
I thought you'd gone, Mr. Paris.

PARIS: I'm sorry, I came for five minutes and I'm still here. *(To ISMENE.)* I've probably bored you...

225

ISMENE: It's been ages, years, since I've met someone like... I mean, I'm very pleased to have met you, Paris.

PARIS: You're very...you're all wonderful people, all of you. I'm honoured to have such neighbours. *(Secretly tries to give FATHER a pound as he shakes hands with him.)*

FATHER: I'd venture to say...

(Looks at his hands, puzzled. The pound falls to the floor.)

ANTIGONE: *(severely)* Father, you should be ashamed...from strangers. Come upstairs and help mother please.

FATHER: I'm sorry Mr. Paris.

PARIS: It was only a pound. I dropped it.

FATHER: Yes, yes only a pound. And I must...I must post the letters.

ISMENE: *(sighs)* Problems, problems...

PARIS: We all have them. The thing is not to let them ruin our lives.

ISMENE: I try. I do try, but inside me...something always seems to be weeping, as if something's broken down, for ever.

PARIS: I feel you're all very sad here. If there's something I can do...

ISMENE: No, no thank you. I wish you all the best. Just come here whenever you like. We'll talk - and I'm sure your novel will be marvellous and your poems delicate, and sensitive, and beautiful like you. Forgive me, I don't know what I'm saying. Anyway, I'm going to help Antigone with the typing. We'll finish it quickly, and don't worry about the money.

PARIS: No, no. I'll pay the full fee. All the best to you too. *(Exits.)*

ISMENE: *(going towards the verandah)* What was my grandmother trying to tell me? I'm the beginning, but you are the tree...the tree?

SCENE TWO

ISMENE is tidying the room. She is dressed and made up. ANTIGONE comes downstairs.

ANTIGONE: I can't understand why Alexander has suddenly remembered us.

ISMENE: Have you left him alone?

ANTIGONE: He's asleep.

ISMENE: Asleep? At this time?

ANTIGONE: Well, yes, I gave him a bit too much of his medicine. Did you want your sister-in-law to come here and get upset? You know how she is.

ISMENE: I know, I know.

ANTIGONE: And why shouldn't we sit down to a meal like human beings? Not with the fear...We're entitled to that, aren't we?

ISMENE: I don't know... I suppose so.

ANTIGONE: That dress is new. Where did you get it from?

ISMENE: Another interrogation? I stole it.

ANTIGONE: You think it suits you? All covered with flowers. And it's too thin for this time of year.

ISMENE: It's Easter next week. *(Chants.)* "Easter, Holy Easter"... summer will be here soon. The meadow beneath our balcony will turn yellow. The walnuts will ripen at Episcopi, and the Turkish helpers will come up from Kazafani towards our house. The reeds down by the river will dry and when the wind blows they 'll touch each other...so gently, so gently...chick, chick. How I loved to hear them, especially at night. And in the shadows the foxes will move silently and the hares and the bats...

ANTIGONE: Oh, Ismene...

ISMENE: Towards noon Sotiris and Anna and Eleni will come, and we'll go for a bathe at Pachyammos. How wonderful the water is there, green and blue and always so tranquil, as if it sleeps in the arms of the sand.

ANTIGONE: Forget it all.

ISMENE: I can't.

ANTIGONE: It's gone. We've lost it.

ISMENE: Look at my trees. They're in blossom. Come and smell. When they grow, the verandah will look like a balcony... If I plant all round...

ANTIGONE: Where is our balcony? Our orchards, our gardens? Our life, our youth, our people...where are they?

ISMENE: We'll find new ones.

ANTIGONE: Find new ones! Are you forgetting you're forty-three years old? You think because you spend your money at the hairdressers and on clothes, you're still a girl? You think anyone will ever turn and look at you...or me?

ISMENE: But...when will we live?

ANTIGONE: Accept it, say - we were never born, that all this - the war, our misery, is just a bad dream. Some day, if you've no hope, no hope at all, you can rest.

ISMENE: I don't want to hear this.

ANTIGONE: Come on. Let's set the table. The old people will be back from church soon. Is the roast done?

ISMENE: I've had it in the oven since eight.

ANTIGONE: I wonder why Alexander's coming?

ISMENE: Maybe he's missed his parents.

ANTIGONE: *(ironically)* Oh, yes, he's missed his parents. When mother was ill he didn't visit her once, and suddenly he remembers her now. No, no, something's going on. I'm convinced of it.

(The clock strikes .)

ISMENE: Whatever it is we'll soon know. *(Pause.)* Do you think they'll bring the children?

ANTIGONE: Madame wouldn't let them see... *(Indicates upstairs.)* and get them upset. As if he were a monster. *(Door bell rings.)*

ANTIGONE: Your father's forgotten his key again.

FATHER: I forgot my glasses and couldn't see to put the key in the door.

MOTHER: *(anxiously)* Aren't they here yet?

ANTIGONE: It's only 10.30...

MOTHER: *(looking upstairs)* Have you left him alone?

ANTIGONE: *(slightly guiltily)* He's sleeping.

MOTHER: *(as she goes upstairs)* That's odd. Could he be ill?

FATHER: *(sniffing the roast)* The fatted calf for the Prodigal Son, and tomorrow we fast...

ANTIGONE: It's just as well. We might manage to pay what we owe the grocer.

FATHER: *(reading the newspaper)* The Holy week hymns move me... I venture to say they move me greatly...

ISMENE: Me too father. We mustn't miss any of the services this year.

ANTIGONE: *(as she lays the table)* I must finish the typing. We need the money.

ISMENE: Give me the manuscripts if you like - I'll finish them at the office. My boss is away in England...and my typewriter's better.

ANTIGONE: *(suspiciously)* Why?

228

FATHER: It would be wonderful if he brought the children...

ISMENE: To help you.

ANTIGONE: Or take the money for yourself!

FATHER: Anthony must be - how old? He must be a teenager now...

ISMENE: He's doing his national service, he's almost nineteen. Anita's sixteen and Robert was ten the other day. *(To ANTIGONE.)* Is it absolutely necessary to take money from him?

ANTIGONE: *(controlling her anger)* I've been waiting for that money to try and make ends meet, and here you are telling me not to take it! The old people's cheque just disappears at the beginning of the month. And we owe money to the grocer, the chemist...Your brother's medicine is finished. Who would dare to ask the chemist for more?

ISMENE: Alright, I only mentioned it.

ANTIGONE: And why shouldn't we take money from Paris? Is he a relation, or a friend? We didn't even know him two days ago.

FATHER: I've always disagreed with the names... Anita...Robert...They're not even Greek.

MOTHER: *(coming downstairs)* It's very strange, he's asleep. Do you think he could be ill?

ANTIGONE: *(harshly)* No mother, he's not ill. If you really want to know, I gave him a slight overdose so that he'll sleep and give us a bit of peace.

MOTHER: *(calmly)* You shouldn't have. What harm has he done you?

ISMENE: It's only a tranquilliser, it won't hurt .The doctor said so.

ANTIGONE: You know what harm he's done me.

FATHER: *(to ANTIGONE)* I venture to say...if you played some music for him...he likes music.

ANTIGONE: He likes music! Children's rhymes! I can't bear to listen. You stay at home for an entire day and see if you can bear it.

MOTHER: I can bear it.

ANTIGONE: You have to. You don't have any choice, do you?

MOTHER: What do you know?

ISMENE: Come outside.You'd think a white cloud has descended on our garden. Smell the blossom. I think this year there'll be enough for flower water.

MOTHER: I don't really feel like it, dear. I've such a pain in my side. It's so bad at times... Let's set the table.

229

ISMENE: No, you sit down.

MOTHER: Do you think they'll bring the children? At least the little one, Robert.

ANTIGONE: You know very well they won't.

FATHER: I don't agree with the names. With so many Greek names...

MOTHER: I haven't seen him for three years. Who does he look like now?

ANTIGONE: He must want something.

MOTHER: He wants to see us. I've been ill. We are his parents...and old. If only he'd bring the children...

ANTIGONE: He's lucky - he's got away.

(Enter ALEXANDER and ELLI. She is gaudily dressed, covered in jewellery. He is in a dark suit.)

ALEXANDER: *(to ANTIGONE)* Hello. Hello. How are you all?

ELLI: Hello Antigone. You look well, you've put on weight, suits you.

ANTIGONE: I've put on weight?

MOTHER: You haven't brought the children. At least Robert...

ELLI: You know how children are nowadays. He wanted to go to some friends. They're all going to the match this afternoon. And Anita was up late at a party so we let her sleep in.

ALEXANDER: You know how young people are these days.

FATHER: Yes, yes, I venture to say that today's youth is different. In my days I recall...I recall that...

ELLI: *(to ISMENE)* That's a nice dress. And your hair looks lovely. Only, you should start putting some colour in it.

ISMENE: I dyed it yesterday.

MOTHER: I was really hoping you'd bring...

ELLI: But the roots are all grey. Oh how lovely and roomy it is in here! Have you bought new curtains?

ISMENE: No. We just washed them. It's Easter you know.

MOTHER: I've missed you, my son.

ALEXANDER: I know, but you can't imagine how busy I've been.

ELLI: *(outside)* You've a whole orchard out here. Just look - she's planted apricot trees and lemon trees, and how the pear tree's grown. Alec, come and look at the garden.

FATHER: Ismene takes care of it all, bless her. When we were in Bellapaix we had a very large garden...but I venture to say...

ELLI: Where do you find the time?

ISMENE: They don't need much care. A little watering and pruning from time to time.

MOTHER: I was ill - you didn't come and see me.

ALEXANDER: *(tenderly)* I couldn't...I couldn't... *(Pause.)*

MOTHER: I'm not completely well yet. I get such pains - here in my side.

ALEXANDER: Well you are getting older you know. You mustn't forget that.

MOTHER: You should have brought the little one. I've missed him.

ALEXANDER: He's missed you too, but you know what women are...

MOTHER: I don't know anything any more.

ANTIGONE: Well brother, why did you remember us?

ALEXANDER: That's not fair, I always remember you.

ANTIGONE: Once every two years.

ELLI: *(enters)* This house stands out from all the others in the settlement. It's, how shall I say, more aristocratic. It has character. *(To her husband.)* What happens once every two years, darling?

ALEXANDER: Antigone's been complaining we haven't been for two years.

ELLI: We didn't just come to see you, Antigone - we've come on business.

ANTIGONE: Oh! You've come on business.

ALEXANDER: The roast will get cold. Did you light the oven in the yard, or did you cook it in the store?

ISMENE: Now that the trees are in bloom we don't light the oven. I'm afraid it might harm them. *(Puts flowers in a vase.)* I don't like cutting my flowers, but for you, dear brother...

ANTIGONE: You said there was something you wanted, Elli?

ALEXANDER: About the pain you get, mother. I'll come one afternoon and take you to a friend of mine, a doctor.

MOTHER: I don't want to put you to any trouble, dear.

ANTIGONE: *(to ALEXANDER)* What did you want to talk about?

ALEXANDER: Nothing, that is...*(He looks at his wife.)*

ANTIGONE: Elli, what did you want to talk about?

ELLI: Darling, we agreed that you would speak.

ALEXANDER: I didn't agree to anything. You're the one who arranged it all.

ELLI: You've always been spineless.

FATHER: Now what was I saying? Oh yes, yes...it always escapes me...but I venture to say, I'm very pleased...that...

ANTIGONE: Well, since we've nothing more to say, let's eat. I'll just go and bring down our brother.

ISMENE: Antigone!

ELLI: Bring him down? But how will you do that? What an idea!

ANTIGONE: Alexander will help me. He's his brother too.

ALEXANDER: Alright, but-

ISMENE: Calm down. It's just one of your sister's tasteless jokes. He's asleep.

ANTIGONE: Why shouldn't we wake him? He's a member of the family.

FATHER: *(timidly, to ANTIGONE)* My child, sometimes...I don't recognise you.

ELLI: *(relieved)* It's true, you do overdo it sometimes. Why wake him if he's asleep? *(To ALEXANDER.)* If you won't speak, then I shall.

ALEXANDER: At least wait till after lunch.

ELLI: Before, after, what difference does it make?

ALEXANDER: Do as you like.

ELLI: You remember mother, when you first came from the enclave at Bellapaix, the first house they gave you at Strovolos. It was very far from Ismene's work, and a little small, and it wasn't convenient for...

MOTHER: Yes, I remember.

ELLI: And then my mother suggested that you exchange with her, because she felt sorry for you.

ANTIGONE: She didn't feel sorry for us. She simply preferred Strovolos. She'd be closer to her friends.

ELLI: Well anyway, now my mother's changed her mind.

ISMENE: Changed her mind?

ALEXANDER: You could have let them eat first.

ELLI: You know, now that my sister's widowed, she lives with my mother, and the house just isn't big enough. You do understand, mother? She's in a difficult situation.

MOTHER: Yes my dear.

ANTIGONE: And what is this to do with us?

ELLI: My mother wants her house back.

MOTHER: Her house?

FATHER: Which house? The fact escapes me...which house...I can't...which house?

ISMENE: What do you mean?

ELLI: Well, this one of course - my mother's old house. *(Pause.)* The house in Strovolos isn't bad you know. It's nice and full of light. You'll have good neighbours. They'll help with anything you might need and it'll be better for... *(Indicates above.)* No stairs - easier to move him around.

ISMENE: *(to ALEXANDER)* What's she saying, are they going to take our house away?

ELLI: No, you're simply going to move back to your own house. The one they gave you - that's in your name.

MOTHER: But my home is in Bellapaix. Near the castle. It was my dowry from my father.

ANTIGONE: I won't move a step from this house. Not one step.

ELLI: This house is in my parents' name. They can throw you out whenever they choose.

ANTIGONE: Then let them throw us out.

ELLI: They won't throw you out. They'll get the police to do it.

ISMENE: Alexander?...

ALEXANDER: That's how things are - just as she says. They can evict you at any time. I asked a lawyer.

ELLI: Why do you say we're going to evict them? It's just that the silent agreement made to exchange houses has ceased to exist. Each family must go to its own home. So you spoke to a lawyer, did you?

MOTHER: My home is in Bellapaix. Next to the Castle. Sometimes I get such pain. Such pain...

(Exits slowly, followed by FATHER.)

FATHER: Which house?

ALEXANDER: There's nothing I can do, do you understand?

MOTHER: As I get older, I understand nothing, nothing.

FATHER: The words...escape me...I can't comprehend...which house?

ALEXANDER: Stay and eat at least.

MOTHER: I don't want anything.

ELLI: Why are you making such a drama of it? You're simply going from one house to another. The only difficulty is that it's a little far from Ismene's work. But there are buses all day. And I haven't told you the most important part. They're building an old people's home nearby. I've asked, and they told me they'd take him. He sits on a chair all day - he wouldn't be any trouble. The director said they 'd take him. Of course there'd be a fee. Not too much though, and there's the old people's pension. For the present we can't help. Anthony's going to University this year. We need three thousand a year for his fees and quite a bit for Anita. You know how expensive the English school is. Anyway, I've discussed it with Alec and we thought it was a good idea to-

ALEXANDER: God damn you, shut up!

ELLI: Alec...

ANTIGONE: *(to her brother)* So you want to take our house, do you? Do you want to keep on punishing us for existing? You'll never be rid of us. Never! We're in your blood. We are your blood. My poor brother, you don't even have the guts to tell that bitch to be quiet.

ELLI: Don't you dare! I came all the way here so that you wouldn't find out from strangers.

ANTIGONE: Nobody's more of a stranger than you and him.

ISMENE: *(to ANTIGONE)* Don't go too far.

ANTIGONE: I haven't even begun. Haven't you understood what's going on here? Word got around that you've created the most beautiful garden in the settlement - Madame's mother saw it and suddenly remembered that her house is too small and she wants to come here. No. Let the police come here. I won't budge.

ELLI: Let's go. Your sisters are just as stubborn as you. *(He does not move.)* Are you coming or am I going to leave alone? *(To the sisters.)* And as for your moronic brother - you can send him to the asylum. You'll be joining him there soon. As if I'd ever bring my babies to this madhouse. And thank you for lunch. *(She exits)*

ALEXANDER: Don't be angry with her, please. She didn't mean it.

ANTIGONE: She may be right, who knows?

ALEXANDER: Is there anything I can do? *(Car horn is heard.)*

ANTIGONE: Go to your wife. Everything will take its course.

ALEXANDER: Do you think...there's a curse on us?

ANTIGONE: Perhaps...perhaps...who knows?

ACT TWO, SCENE ONE

One month later on the verandah

FATHER: Yes, yes...I'm very pleased my boy.

PARIS: Did you send the letter you were telling me about? If you'd like some money?...

FATHER: As soon as I receive my cheque. But, my boy, I venture to ask, do you think it's all in vain?

PARIS: What?

FATHER: All my efforts, the letters to those in power...Words, so many words. Appeals...what else can I do? I'm old...old. *(Pause.)* And I wish to return to my village, my home.

PARIS: I do too, sir.

FATHER: Yes, yes...but I venture to ask, does it hurt?

PARIS: Does what hurt, sir?

FATHER: When you think of your village, the house where you were born and grew up, does it hurt? How can I say? The words escape me... desperately... irrevocably, as I suffer? Often my boy - forgive me, I talk too much, everyone tells me so. Antigone says I talk nonsense, but I forgive her. She's felt pain too...yes...Where was I?

PARIS: You were speaking of your house.

FATHER: Yes, yes...Do you know what hour I loved best? Twilight. When I sat on the balcony and listened to the sounds of evening, the villagers returning from the fields, saying "Good evening", the dogs barking. Down on the Kyrenia plain the lights would come on, one by one, and everything was imbued with the scent of the meadows. Then my boy, it seemed...

PARIS: It seemed...

FATHER: It seemed the night was a tender and beloved woman who took you in her arms and promised...promised...everlasting bliss. Don't you find sir, that Cyprus, its beauty I mean, has been unfair to us?

PARIS: Unfair?

FATHER: Yes, yes, unfair. In my village everything was so beautiful. Full of promise, which gave one the idea of eternal happiness. And I, my child, was carried away by this.

PARIS: In what way?

FATHER: I thought it was my duty to be happy, carefree, but deep inside me there was a great sadness.

PARIS: You have two wonderful daughters. You know that Miss Antigone has typed my manuscripts without a single mistake. Without one spelling mistake. And how beautiful they've made your home, this garden. It's like being in the country.

FATHER: Yes, yes my boy, but in a few days we must...but it is of no matter. What grieves me is my wife. I feel great sorrow for her. But please say nothing, nothing... *(Enter ISMENE.)*

ISMENE: Father, stop bothering people.

PARIS: No, not at all. We were talking about many interesting things.

ISMENE: Still, you'd better go upstairs. Mother might need something.

FATHER: Correct, correct...but Ismene...

ISMENE: Yes father?..

FATHER: We should call a doctor. I have some money.

ISMENE: You took her to hospital this morning, and they told you there was nothing wrong with her. Where did you get the money?

PARIS: *(clumsily)* I've brought the money for Miss Antigone. Ask her how much I owe her, and give her my congratulations. She didn't make a single spelling mistake. Not one.

ISMENE: Antigone, a spelling mistake! She was the first in her class. She took all the prizes.

PARIS: Shall I call her and pay her?

ISMENE: She told me she doesn't want any money. Take it as a token of our friendship, she said.

PARIS: No, no. I know you need the money. I have money. My father's bakery does good business. *(Enter ANTIGONE.)* Miss Antigone...

ANTIGONE: Yes, Mr. Paris.

PARIS: About the money I owe you. Ismene said...

ANTIGONE: Oh Mr. Paris, have you come to pay me? You've been sent by God. I was thinking that we might need a doctor tonight for my mother, and you know that home visits are at least ten pounds. I'm only charging you the same as everyone else. Five shillings a page and three for the poems. How many pages were there?

(ANTIGONE exits with FATHER..)

236

ISMENE: Else my soul will die, my soul will not laugh.

PARIS: Don't be upset.

ISMENE: I'm ashamed. Once she was so proud, so beautiful. The most beautiful girl in Bellapaix. You don't believe it, do you? Everyone at the high school was in love with her. Even the teachers. Do you believe in fate?

PARIS: I haven't thought about it.

ISMENE: What do you know of tragedy? How well I remember that school fete, the end of the year. The graduates were to present *"Antigone"*. When our Antigone stood before Creon and said: "For me no marriage songs were heard, no bridal wreaths on my head", I felt something strange... that there was nothing more to say.

PARIS: Ismene, there's something I wanted to tell you. I don't know if this is the right time. I've never met anyone, I mean a woman like you. I've lots of friends, but there's no-one I can talk to as deeply as I can to you. I often long to talk to my friends about beautiful verse, about a good book - they listen for a while, and then they get bored. Imagine! I haven't told a soul that I've written a novel, and poems. They don't understand me so they label me strange...peculiar. I've decided to leave Cyprus, although I love it. I can't breath. I'll go and live in Athens. I've found work there.

ISMENE: Don't you have a girlfriend?

PARIS: I've tried but...

ISMENE: But?

PARIS: I couldn't stand them - none is...

ISMENE: Worthy of you.

PARIS: No, no none is...like you.

ISMENE: Me?

PARIS: You, the things you say are full of...full of tenderness. Ever since I met you...

ISMENE: Years ago there was enough tenderness in me to warm the whole world, but now...

PARIS: Now?

ISMENE: I have nothing.

PARIS: I have something.

ISMENE: What?

PARIS: My friendship.

ISMENE: Ah, your friendship?

PARIS: Yes.

ISMENE: A wonderful thing, friendship, without it, life would be a nightmare - Who said that? *(Laughs hysterically.)*

PARIS: If I've made you happy...

ISMENE: If happiness is like despair, then you could say I'm happy.

PARIS: I don't understand.

(FATHER enters.)

FATHER: I'm pleased, you're so cheerful Ismene. Tonight my heart 's so heavy, but say nothing, nothing.

ISMENE: Father, Mr. Paris has offered me his friendship...

FATHER: What? Oh yes. A tried and trusted friendship is a precious thing. *(Wanders off again.)*

ISMENE: The sun's set. Look. The sky's red. It's not cold anymore. The days will get longer, warmer...and terribly beautiful.

PARIS: I like to hear you talk.

ISMENE: Kiss me.

PARIS: Ismene.

ISMENE: Kiss me, on the lips.

PARIS: But...I...

ISMENE: No-one has ever kissed me. A man, I mean, on the lips...*(An awkward silence.)* I disgust you.

PARIS: No, no, you don't understand.

ISMENE: I'm old.

PARIS: No, no. I can't. Do you see? I can't...

ISMENE: Ah, you can't. How quickly time passes. Or perhaps the clock's not working properly. Perhaps. It's so old. Father says it's over a hundred. Imagine, counting the hours continuously for a hundred years. One after the next. Always the same dull, boring hours.

PARIS: Forgive me, forgive me...

ISMENE: Have you ever read Montis? I told you to read Cypriot poetry. We have such good poets. How does that verse go? "If it weren't for that small thing - our self deception would be smaller"

FATHER: *(appears, disturbed)* It's very strange...

ISMENE: What ?

FATHER: I believe, or rather I'm certain...

ISMENE: What's wrong?

FATHER: It seems that...your mother...I think that your mother...I'm certain...she's stopped breathing.

ISMENE: What are you saying? *(She exits.)*

FATHER: *(to PARIS)* My wife, sir...it seems...no, it is certain...she is dead...dead, sir.

SCENE TWO

Preparations for moving. Boxes and crates everywhere. A neighbour is helping, holding a framed tapestry.

MARIA: I used to have exactly the same picture.

ANTIGONE: Wrap everything well, Ismene. We don't want any of the plates to break. You can't get this quality any more.

ISMENE: *(to MRS. MARIA)* If you like it, you can have it.

ANTIGONE: But it's one of mother's...

ISMENE: Why this sudden love for mother?

(FATHER comes down.)

ANTIGONE: Don't come down yet, father. We're still packing. The newspaper has come. Take it up with you and read for a while.

FATHER: He's quiet.

ANTIGONE: Yes?

FATHER: I believe...I'm certain...

ANTIGONE: What is it?

FATHER: It has wounded him. I'm certain that...I venture to say that he is deeply grieved.

ANTIGONE: If you can't go up, go out to the verandah with the paper. We must finish packing.

FATHER: I saw him. He was weeping, tears were flowing down his cheeks.

ANTIGONE: Weeping? *(Goes upstairs with FATHER..)*

MARIA: At least your poor mother is spared the sight of you being thrown out of your home.

ISMENE: *(to MARIA)* We're so obliged to you - you've stood by us so much. I wanted to ask you another favour. Could you come here from time to time to water my garden, and do a little weeding?

MARIA: With pleasure. But how? I can't come into a strange house.

ANTIGONE: *(entering)* He's asleep. Father was right, he seems to miss mother. But what can we do?

MARIA: Now that you mention it, yesterday when you were at the cemetery, the baker's son came here. What's his name?...Paris. He said to call him if you wanted any help.

ANTIGONE: Thank you, but it won't be necessary.

MARIA: He seems a nice boy, kind,but you know what they're saying.

ISMENE: What are they saying?

MARIA: Of course I don't believe such things...

ISMENE: What are they saying?

MARIA: That he's one of them. Of course I don't...

ISMENE: One of whom?

ANTIGONE: Whatever someone is - is his own business.

MARIA: That's right. But it's a pity if it's true - such a good-looking boy...

ISMENE: One of whom?

ANTIGONE: Help me with this Mrs. Maria.

(Enter FATHER.)

FATHER: I must write a letter at once. Queen Victoria hasn't replied, but I'll persevere. Perhaps King Constantine...

ANTIGONE: Write it later. We must finish before dark.

FATHER: I will appeal to all those in power. I must not forget the Nobel Prize committee, the Queen of Sweden, Norway, Denmark... However, Ismene if you could spare ten shillings...for the good of Cyprus. As soon as my cheque comes...

ANTIGONE: If it's money you want, forget it. Who'll pay Kostas for the move?

FATHER: When my cheque comes...

ANTIGONE: Then we'll pay the grocer. You don't want us to leave debts behind us, do you? Mother wouldn't have wanted that either.

FATHER: No, no...but I venture to say, just ten shillings...

ANTIGONE: *(ALEXANDER enters)* What wind brought you here?

ALEXANDER: I thought you might need some help.

ANTIGONE: We're almost finished.

ALEXANDER: *(to FATHER)* Since I was a boy I always remember you bent over a table, writing, and Ismene with a book in her hand - or with a spade in the garden.

ISMENE: We were young then.

ANTIGONE: Mrs. Maria's helped us. Without her I don't know what we'd have done.

MARIA: I'm only sorry we're going to lose such good neighbours.

ANTIGONE: Let me introduce you. My brother Alexander, Mrs. Maria.

MARIA: Ah, your brother. Pleased to meet you Mr. Alexander, you should have moved heaven and earth to prevent this injustice. Having to move house after all that's happened. *(An awkward silence)* Well, if you don't need me, I'll be going. All the best - and I'll keep an eye on the garden, whenever I get the chance. *(MRS MARIA exits)*

ALEXANDER: What are you writing? You seem so involved.

FATHER: "Dear sirs, my country Cyprus is suffering"...

ALEXANDER: What are you trying to say?

FATHER: "Strongly from...the Turkish...Turkish"...

ALEXANDER: Invasion - is that the word you're looking for?

FATHER: Troops...the words occasionally escape me..

ALEXANDER: You're doing fine.

FATHER: Yes, yes only...You didn't bring the children to the funeral. Her soul will find no rest.

ANTIGONE: Father...

ISMENE: She was their grandmother, after all.

ALEXANDER: I wanted to, God knows I did.

ISMENE: She was your mother. Your mother.

ALEXANDER: I can't eat, or sleep.

ANTIGONE: Why? Why?

ALEXANDER: I keep thinking of you all. And I have such dreams. Last night I dreamt we were all together in our garden, at Bellapaix - and we felt such joy, such joy. Even...our brother was there...and he was well, handsome even. Mother was dressed in white. Her hair was loose and she was laughing... laughing. I cut a white rose and pinned it on her hair. Then she took my hand and said: "Alexander, do you love me?" "Of course I love you. I love you very much". "Well, if you love me, look after my white roses", she said, and she vanished - like a shadow.

ANTIGONE: Let the shadows be. Come into the kitchen. There must be some coffee and a pan somewhere. Come and rest awhile.

ALEXANDER: I don't want anything. Antigone, I know it. Her soul won't rest while she feels she's left him behind her.

ISMENE: What can we do? Kill him?

FATHER: *(to ISMENE)* How you express yourself at times.

241

ANTIGONE: What can we do? It's our duty.

ALEXANDER: I was thinking...

ANTIGONE: If it's anything to do with an institution, forget it.

ALEXANDER: But why? He wouldn't be the first or the last. And the others there - haven't they got feelings too?

ANTIGONE: Yes, but they might not have relatives. There are the two of us, thank God, and father. For the present there are enough of us - and later, we'll see.

ALEXANDER: A friend of mine, a doctor told me of a new place for cases like this. Only it costs a lot. I thought of getting a second job, in the afternoons. I could help out. I'll give private lessons. You know how much money there is in that. And I don't have to say anything to Elli. Think about it.

ANTIGONE: Our brother will stay with us. For as long as I live, at least. Don't worry, we'll manage. Word has got around that I type without mistakes, and I know good Greek and English. I have trouble fitting in all the work they bring me.

ISMENE: Why don't we think about it? It's a new institution after all. It may be very good, who knows?...It may do him good.

ANTIGONE: I know these places. I've been to see them. They're like morgues. While I live our brother will share our home. And if you don't want to help, I'll manage on my own.

ALEXANDER: Why won't you think it over?

ANTIGONE: Nothing can change. You know very well the decision isn't mine.

ALEXANDER: I'd better be going.

ISMENE: Yes, go. And if you know what's good for you, you'll forget about us.

ALEXANDER: What do you think I've been trying to do all these years? To get away so I could breathe again. But it only takes one little thing - a word, a gesture, a stranger's voice - and you all come into my life again. Eating into my soul like worms in wood. I'm tired of fighting.

ANTIGONE: Let's look at Ismene's garden for the last time. See how her pear tree's blossomed. And the smell of jasmine! Isn't it strange? I've lived in this house so many years, and I've only just begun to come out into the garden. I used to watch Ismene raking and watering. "What's the use of it all?" I'd say. It just takes a little care, a little

242

watering and pruning - and there Ismene's trees stand before us - giving so much. Life is sacred, in all its forms. Mother knew that.

ALEXANDER: You used to be hard - a rebel.

ANTIGONE: But don't you see? This is my last stand. At last I'm happy.

ALEXANDER: Happy?

ANTIGONE: Happy.

ALEXANDER: With all this. Losing your house? Happy?

ANTIGONE: Happy. *(ALEXANDER kisses her hand.)* Kiss me properly. We haven't kissed each other since we were children. *(They embrace.)*

ALEXANDER: As soon as you've settled down in the new house, I'll bring the children over.

ANTIGONE: Yes, yes.

ALEXANDER: The little one keeps asking about his grandmother. What is death, he asks over and over again. One of these days I'll take him to see her grave.

ANTIGONE: Her soul will be glad. She was so sad towards the end. Let's go in. I must collect some things from upstairs. *(They enter.)*

ALEXANDER: I must be going too. I'll come and see you tomorrow. With the children.

ISMENE: I told you - for your own good, forget us for ever.

ALEXANDER: For my own good, I'll never forget you. Never again. Goodbye, little sister.

ANTIGONE: I'm going to finish upstairs. Father, go and find Kostas at the coffee shop and tell him that we're almost ready. Ask him how much he wants. Don't forget.

(ISMENE is left alone.)

ISMENE: Else my soul will die...*(Door bell rings.)* I'll get it.

(Enter PARIS.) Hello. We're in such a mess.

PARIS: I came to see if you need any help. I only heard the other day that you were moving. Why didn't you tell me?

ISMENE: Why burden others?

PARIS: I'm your friend.

ISMENE: I don't know who my friends are, or my relations. I know nothing anymore.

PARIS: I've brought some work for Antigone. A friend of mine wants his thesis typed. He's in no hurry. When she's settled in the new house.

ISMENE: I'll call her.

PARIS: Wait...-

ISMENE: Yes?

PARIS: About the other day...I wanted to say, I'm not leaving.

ISMENE: Why?

PARIS: Cyprus is where I belong.

ISMENE: It's made us so bitter.

PARIS: But when there are people like you, we'll find a way to bring back the dream...Poetry...joy...life. I need you. I'll make you the heroine of my most tragic tale.

ISMENE: You're too late.

PARIS: I could love you so much.

(FATHER enters.)

FATHER: It's almost time. Mr. Kostas...

PARIS: Sir, if you need any help. I was just saying to Ismene-

FATHER: You're very kind, but what could we need...now?

PARIS: Anything you do need...I'll bring work for Miss Antigone...Sir, I'd like to say again that I consider it a great honour to have met you. A great honour.

FATHER: I too...venture to say...

PARIS: Everything will be alright. *(Exits)*

FATHER If I were a poet...but the words...

ISMENE: You're talking to yourself.

(Enter ANTIGONE.)

ANTIGONE: Did you tell Mr. Kostas that we're waiting for him?

FATHER: He's coming.

ANTIGONE: How much does he want? Did you ask him?

FATHER: He said he doesn't want any money.

ANTIGONE: To move a whole house?

FATHER: He said he'd rather lose his right arm than take money from good people.

ANTIGONE: What did you say?

FATHER: That he would rather lose his arm than take money from good people and the neighbours are all sorry that we're leaving.

ANTIGONE: Did he really say that? Did you hear that, Ismene? The neighbours are sorry that we are leaving.

ISMENE: I heard. It's almost evening. There's a chill in the air.

ANTIGONE: Shall I bring your cardigan?

ISMENE: No.

ANTIGONE: At the new house...

ISMENE: Yes?

ANTIGONE: I thought we could plant some jasmine in the front, on a trellis so that it can climb high, like our jasmine on the balcony at Bellapaix. Remember?

ISMENE: I remember.

ANTIGONE: And a pear tree too, and some limes. I love lime blossom.

ISMENE: So do I. *(A car is heard.)*. It's time.

ANTIGONE: Yes, it's time.

FATHER: Mr. Kostas is here...my paper...my letters..."Dear Sirs, my country Cyprus...is suffering..." Oh the words...the words escape me.

END

VERONICA FRANCO
COURTESAN AND POET

by Dacia Maraini
Translated by Siân Williams and Marion Baraitser

The play was first performed in the Roman amphitheatre at the Festival of Taormina in Sicily in August 1991.

DIRECTOR: Gino Zampieri
DESIGNER: Enrico Luzzi
MUSIC: Giacomo Zumpano
CAST: Alvise Battain, Isa Gallinelli,
Andrea Tidona, Marco Balbi,
Antonio Mercone, Clara Colosimo,
Renata Zamengo.

CHARACTERS:

VERONICA FRANCO, courtesan and poet, about 33 years old.
ANZOLA, a young nun
DOMENICO VENIER, an elderly senator
PAOLO FRANCO, Veronica's husband
GASPARA GREGHETTA, a servant, in her 50s
MARCO VENIER, a poet, Veronica's age
KING HENRI III OF FRANCE
RIDOLFO VANNITELLI, a young tutor
MAFFIO VENIER, a young poet and eventual Bishop
MONSIGNORE, a member of the Tribunal of the Inquisition

Set in sixteenth century Venice, during a time of plague.

ACT ONE
Plague hospital. Bodies are strewn on the floor. There are large windows through which a gentle light streams, illuminating a scene of squalor and neglect.

VERONICA: Dying people all around, for god's sake, dying people all around...What in god's name am I doing here? *(She looks around. She bends over one of the shrouded shapes. She uncovers just its head.)* And this one? A young man. What long eyelashes! He seems to be sleeping...What are these two black marks on his temples? *(She stretches out a hand to his mouth.)* He isn't breathing...he's dead! Sister! There's a dead man here and no-one's taking him away! Two black marks, two fingermarks...as if the plague had squeezed him tight by the temples...like a midwife does when she brings a child into the world. He's been dragged over there into the world of ...delight. A meadow of sweet, sweet, green, fig trees, a clear river and the rustling wind...But why, to go to such a beautiful place, must they drag you along by the temples, making your breath stink in your throat? *(Walking back and forth.)* "Your glands are swollen signora, you have two lumps here which say quite plainly: you're ill". "Me, ill? You're raving Signor Doctor!" "Ah no, my dear, you really are ill" "I'm not ill, you brazenhead." "If you continue to talk like a whore I'll pack you off to the dying" "But I am a whore you filthy beast." "If you are, you don't seem like one." "Thank you, I've spent my whole life learning the art!" "The art, ha, ha.." "Yes, go on laugh, Signor Know-all, what do you know about art? You are an artist perhaps? No, well be quiet then." And he, brurubum, threw me in here amongst the dying...Heavenly Father help me! You who know about wounds, pains...But what would you know about a harlot who's eaten her heart out! What would you know about her!...Where's the mirror sister? Where's the mirror? I must have a look at myself in the mirror sister, I must have a look at myself in the mirror...Where's that bitch of a mirror, where is it? These damned people have taken everything from me...I had a mirror in my pocket...I had money...Where have they hidden them? I must have a look at my face...I must...If I lose my face sister, I lose everything: house, clothes, food...everything depends on this female face...Mother of God where have they put my mirror? What can I do with a face that's swollen, bruised, sick? *(Touching herself.)* I can feel that it's swollen, I feel it...I'm ugly...what shall I do? Stupid beastly little plague! You're taking someone who needs her body like a baker needs flour...What the hell do you want with me -what do you want? Don't you see that I don't want you, I don't want you!

247

(She falls to the floor. Gets up. Falls down again.) These pigs - not even a bed, I'm dying on a stone floor...Sister!
(Falls down again, appears to be dead Enter a nun, ANZOLA, carrying a candle and humming to herself. She uncovers the dying. Closes the curtains.)
ANZOLA: *(singing)*

> They were made for me a pair of shoes -
> Made, yes - but paid for no.
> And they call out when they see me go -
> "Pretty little blonde, are you paying, yes or no?"
> Thursday night, Friday night, Saturday no -
> And they call out when they see me go:
> "Pretty little blonde, are you paying, yes or no?"

(She continues to sing.) This one's dead. *(She makes the sign of the cross.)* Requiem eterna dona eis domine, requiescat in pace, amen. This one's gone, Requiescat. This one's dead too...Requiescat - Oh no, she's breathing...she's still alive. Do you want some water, signora? Signora, can you hear me? She isn't black at the temples...And what beautiful shoes! Signora! What beautiful shoes! Exactly like Saint Barbara's...*(Humming to herself.)* "Beautiful little blonde, are you paying yes or no? Do you want some water? No? If you don't want any, I'll drink some - I'm thirsty.*(Drinks.)* Am I falling ill too? If it's time I'll go. *(Beginning to sing again.)*

> I had a pair of shoes made for me,
> Made for, yes, paid for no..."

VERONICA: Give me the water, whore!
ANZOLA: So you're all right then!
VERONICA: The water!
ANZOLA: I'm sorry, I drank it...I thought you were dead.
VERONICA: Not on your life!
ANZOLA: *(laughing)* But you're very well! You look like a goose that's just come out of the water.
VERONICA: *(looking at her)* You'll catch it too!
ANZOLA: If I get sick, I get sick. If I don't get sick, I don't get sick. As Saint Barbara wills it.
VERONICA: Does Saint Barbara cure the plague?
ANZOLA: No, she's my saint. I talk to her at night. And she nods.
VERONICA: Go and get me some water, sister, I'm dying of thirst.

ANZOLA: I'm going. As long as when I get back I won't find you dead.

VERONICA: But what do you mean, dead? I'm very much alive.
(As she says this she falls to the ground as if dead.)

ANZOLA: She's gone. Poor lady. Didn't even have time to drink a drop of water. May God bless her! Amen.

(ANZOLA goes off singing. Lights fade on VERONICA. In the centre of the stage is a picture which is illuminated. DOMENICO VENIER enters, limping.)

DOMENICO: Veronica, my angel...I don't know if you've ever reflected on old age. It suddenly sneaks into your bones, twists and deforms you without your knowing. The heart is emptied, it takes on the colour of deserts, of dull burnt honey. Rain is not enough to wet it -it would want an ocean of sweet water - and all you see are the pathetic traces of a few black drops piercing its surface like so many holes made by termites...Veronica, my angel, where have you hidden yourself? Since I saw you the other day in the street with your stomach swollen and protruding, I don't know why, you've heated my blood...Could I be the father of this creature, tell me? Do you hear me? But you act as if you know nothing. Yet I know I could be the father. I confess I wouldn't be displeased to have made you pregnant. Certainly the child would get beauty and grace and intelligence from you. But from me I would like it to get only a certain clear and cavilling intellect, a certain fertile indolence of the mind - the only thing that functions in my body...

(Enter PAOLO, VERONICA'S husband.)

PAOLO: And if it were my son?

DOMENICO: Ah, it's you Paolo.

PAOLO: If it were mine?

DOMENICO: It would have two long ears, like a rabbit's.

PAOLO: Don't worry yourself Signor Domenico Venier, the child's not mine - but it's not yours either.

DOMENICO: How can you be sure of that?

PAOLO: The father's a wealthy and generous gentleman who, you see, has made me a present. This gold locket encircled with rubies. Do you like it?

DOMENICO: Did he make you a present of it, or Signora Veronica?

PAOLO: What difference does it make seeing we're married?

DOMENICO: I'm sure he gave it only to her.

PAOLO: Husband and wife - a single unit.

DOMENICO: Yes, a single bandit! I'm only joking.

PAOLO: Do you object to the welcome we always give you Signor Domenico?

DOMENICO: What are you talking about? Excellent suppers, excellent wine...

PAOLO: Despite your deformities, the fact that you limp, have arms like chicken's necks, your everlasting headaches, your nerves which sometimes make you fling your arms about like a windmill - despite this you've always been given a king's welcome, admit it. And I believe Veronica's affection has never been lacking.

DOMENICO: Satisfy my curiosity: Why did you marry her?

PAOLO: Oh, why does one marry? For love?

DOMENICO: It amazes me that you're not a whit jealous.

PAOLO: If you marry a woman like Veronica you have to give up any vain ambition of owning her. The punishment is appearing ridiculous.

DOMENICO: Such wisdom, Signor Paolo, but to be frank, I think Signora Veronica doesn't need you.

PAOLO: So you say.

DOMENICO: Yes, that's what I think.

PAOLO: And who would my wife need?

DOMENICO: Someone erudite, someone very assured, someone with a great deal of patience, and someone with a great deal of money.

PAOLO: Someone like yourself in fact. But you are good for a lover. For a husband, she wanted a young man who was rather well-padded and rather handsome.

DOMENICO: Have you looked in the mirror?

PAOLO: Shall I pour you a drink while we're waiting?

DOMENICO: Like her mother, always late.

PAOLO: Did you know the beautiful Paula?

DOMENICO: At old Tron's house. He kept a lavish table. You could eat there at all hours. There were always three or four courtesans who livened up supper - lutes, singing, rhymes...Then everyone would end up in bed...*(Tired of waiting.)* Hah...tell her I'll come back tomorrow.

PAOLO: One moment...excuse me...if you'd like to settle a little bill meanwhile. *(PAOLO gives DOMENICO a sheet of paper.)*

DOMENICO: So this is what you call a little bill!

PAOLO: Settle it another time, whenever you want.

DOMENICO: I'll pay it when Signora Veronica asks me to, slave.
(Exit DOMENICO followed by PAOLO. Darkness.)
(Lights up. Enter VERONICA, nine months pregnant followed by GASPARA.)

VERONICA: Give me paper and pen Gaspara, I must make a will.

GASPARA: Again? But this is really and truly a mania of yours.

VERONICA: And what if I die in labour?

GASPARA: You had Achillino without even noticing. I know very well this one will be fine too.

VERONICA: Didn't my cousin die after labour even when her child had been born? And didn't my mother die after having her thirteenth? I've inherited her profession, so I could inherit her death too.
(GASPARA goes to get pen and paper.)

GASPARA: Here you are.

VERONICA: *(writing)* "In the event of my death during labour I leave this house and all the furniture in it, my jewels, my clothes and one hundred ducats which are hidden - put your fingers in your ears Gaspara -

GASPARA: Under the last brick at the bottom of the wall in the kitchen.

VERONICA: How do you know?

GASPARA: In the event of your death, your son should know where his inheritance is.

VERONICA: What a stupid fool! *(Starting to write again.)* "One hundred ducats which are hidden under the last brick at the bottom of the wall in the kitchen." I would like it to be a girl...I'd leave her some clients...a profession all set-up.

GASPARA: And what if she wanted to be a nun?

VERONICA: Nuns are all mad, because of praying, fasting, obeying and keeping silent. Instead of brains, they have chicken pap - and they don't even lay eggs.

GASPARA: Is the will finished?

VERONICA: No wait...I've forgotten the two silver plates, the pearl necklace -

GASPARA: And the gold scissors.

251

VERONICA: Of course, the gold scissors with the silver case.

GASPARA: A beautiful antique.

VERONICA: The ruby ring, a present from Senator Domenico Venier.

GASPARA: But we sold that - in a lean moment.

VERONICA: That's true...well, no ruby...And the garnets?

GASPARA: Those went as well. To pay your husband's debts.

VERONICA: It doesn't matter why. They've gone.

GASPARA: Are you sure that the little bag with the ducats is still in its place in the kitchen?

VERONICA: I don't remember Gaspara.

GASPARA: Did you ever mention it to your husband Signor Paolo?

VERONICA: Why is it important? If I die I won't have to think about it and if I live I shall earn some more.

GASPARA: You're too careless about money. You'll find yourself an old woman without a penny.

VERONICA: Domenico Venier thinks this child is his. If I were to tell him it was, he would stuff me with gold.

GASPARA: And why didn't you tell him that?

VERONICA: The truth, Gaspara. The truth lasts longer than gold.

GASPARA: A courtesan who tells the truth exists neither on earth nor in heaven.

VERONICA: It amuses me to tell the truth. Have you seen the faces they make? They believe it the most subtle and acute lie ever invented. And instead, it's only the truth.

GASPARA: Signor Aretino, God rest his soul, said that a courtesan's wisdom lay in her telling such lies that they'd confuse those around her. That way she'd become more beautiful and desirable.

VERONICA: My memory's too short to rattle off untruths - I'd get mixed-up and that would be it. I'm not the whore I should be.

GASPARA: Whore, whore - don't put yourself down. A courtesan is not a whore.

VERONICA: Subtleties, Gaspara. My mother said it too. "We are whores, my daughter and there's nothing wrong with that. They need us to keep the others at home."

GASPARA: Your mother was very intelligent. You're not quite up to her ,but you're more successful, while you've learned to write poetry, something Signora Paula disdained, grande-dame that she was.

VERONICA: To write poetry, to sing, to play. Who taught me if it wasn't her - Signora Paula Franco, Venetian courtesan - at ten scudi an hour. Do you remember the price list?

GASPARA: That's wicked! They put you down at two scudi. And now you're the most respected courtesan in Venice.

VERONICA: Years ago, when I began, I used to charge two scudi, just so.

(VERONICA'S house. PAOLO is alone on one side.)

PAOLO: In my day, says granddad, debts were twenty scudi at most, but now my grandson squanders two hundred scudi at a time - and he'll grow up to produce another big spender.

(VERONICA is writing on her bed. PAOLO slides down next to her.)

PAOLO: He's healthy, he's beautiful, we've named the boy after him. Now we should proceed to the attack.

VERONICA: We're not at war, Paolo.

PAOLO: We should give that arse-hole a good grilling.

VERONICA: I don't like to hear you talk like that about my clients.

PAOLO: That's what I think about him.

VERONICA: I like him, he's nice.

PAOLO: Leave it to me.

VERONICA: No, Paolo, you're too brutal.

PAOLO: And you're too sentimental. This is a business, not a salon.

VERONICA: They come here to talk, drink, play cards. It's not a quick sale on the street.

PAOLO: This is business Veronica, business!

VERONICA: I write poetry, Paolo. I play. I like to flirt. If it's business, I'm bored.

PAOLO: You sell and they buy.

VERONICA: I sell, yes. I sell courtesy, pleasant evenings, music and tenderness.

PAOLO: Balls!

VERONICA: You're so pure , you only love money. I only love money for what it gives me, that's the difference.

PAOLO: You've got too many butterflies in your head, Veronica. Trust me.

(The hospital. VERONICA is lying on one side. ANZOLA enters.)

ANZOLA: *(singing)*
           The women from Gaeta were weaving silk,
           They wove it with thread for a son born dead...
(Counts the dying.) This one is dead. This one's gone...Saint Barbara, how close it is. Have you seen what Venice is reduced to? Heat, a rotten smell. It seems as if the water in the canals is sick too. If you hold some in your hand it makes you hot, as if the water here were fever-ridden...And the boats full of the sick keep on coming. There's no more room, Saint Barbara - we have to throw them on the ground, like animals...The child too is dead.
VERONICA: Sister!
ANZOLA: And that one? That one's still alive - Sacred Madonna. Water - I promised her water...How are you? Can you hear me? How do you feel? Are you still thirsty?
VERONICA: You drank it all, damn you!
ANZOLA: I'll go and get it now.
VERONICA: Damn you!
(ANZOLA goes out. VERONICA alone.)
What horrible dreams! Is it true that when you see your past flash before your eyes you're about to die? Paolo, Paolo...Trust - he used to say. What a disaster! I was put out on the street because of the debts...If he hadn't had those soft lips...
(ANZOLA comes back with the water.)
ANZOLA: Here's the water. Shall I help you to drink?
VERONICA: *(drinks)* Is it possible to get pleasure in kissing a man whom you don't respect and who doesn't respect you? Someone who is inside you, should you hold him tight, you think to yourself: "But who is this man? I don't know him, I don't like how he thinks, how he feels, how he acts. Who is he?"
ANZOLA: The body of Jesus Christ is perfectly cold, and if you were to kiss that - certain ideas wouldn't enter your head. I'm going to get a crucifix for you.
VERONICA: No. Give me a little water.

254

*(Lights down. Lights up on **PAOLO** alone, packing.)*

PAOLO: Never marry a courtesan, you get your fingers burnt, poor idiot! Never marry a courtesan, you'll find yourself arse-over-tip and goodnight! I gave all of myself to her - youth, health, elegance. Service, inside and out the house. Consolation, company, I gave it all and what did she give me? Nothing...yes, a few dishes of pheasant, some honey puddings, some clothes, a jerkin edged with gold, some suede shoes, a ring. What were those compared to the life of freedom I sacrificed for her? And the women I didn't have while I stayed with her to look after other men's children? If I lined them up, they'd make a queue as long as my arm. The truth is, I'm fed up. It's not she who's tired, it's me, Paolo Panizza, who's saying - enough! Goodbye! I'm not staying...she hasn't even given me a son, blasted woman! And I'm going to take the silver plates and the jewels and the brocade clothes and the gilded wood frames .You'll never see them again my dear Veronica!

*(**PAOLO** leaves. Darkness. Lights up on the hospital.)*

VERONICA: He's taken everything, everything, Paolo! What a swine!
ANZOLA: Don't get upset signora...there's no Paolo here...Here's some water.
*(**VERONICA** takes the jug and drinks greedily. **MARCO VENIER** has meanwhile appeared on the stage. Enter **GASPARA**.)*

MARCO: Would you like to tell your mistress I'm here?
GASPARA: I'm going. *(She continues to cook.)*
MARCO: What's she doing. Sleeping?
GASPARA: She's not sleeping. She's thinking.
MARCO: Is she thinking about me?
GASPARA: I don't think so.
MARCO: Call her please.
GASPARA: I'm going.
MARCO: You say I'm going, but you always stay here.
GASPARA: She's changing.

MARCO: So tell her I'm here then. That way she'll hurry up.

GASPARA: I don't think she'll hurry up.

MARCO: Why not?

GASPARA: Because, as far as one can judge...

MARCO: Do you remember who I am?

GASPARA: Marco Venier - the beautiful. You are a Venier, like Domenico. But you're handsome while the senator is ugly.

MARCO: What nonsense you're talking...If you don't go and call Veronica, I'll go.

GASPARA: *(exiting)* I'm going, I'm going.

VERONICA: *(reciting)*
>Joined to your side so sweetly
>Love's delight I'll make you taste -
>When your left flank is well-schooled,
>I want to pleasure you so deeply,
>That you could call yourself content -
>And even more in love.
>So sweet and pleasing I become
>When I find myself in bed with someone
>Who makes me feel loved and cherished
>*That* pleasure conquers every delight.

MARCO: With every child you have you become more beautiful...

VERONICA: What joy to see you...why didn't you come earlier?

MARCO: I've waited downstairs so many times...

VERONICA: And you didn't come up?

MARCO: You always had so many people.

VERONICA: I'm alone now, as you can see. Will you stay to supper with me?

MARCO: Thank you. I've already eaten.

VERONICA: Stay though.

MARCO: I haven't come for myself this time.

VERONICA: For whom?

MARCO: For someone you value very highly.

VERONICA: Since when have you been playing ambassador?

MARCO: Do you know the great Henri the third of Valois?

VERONICA: How would I know him - haven't even seen his portrait!

MARCO: I think you've heard of him.

VERONICA: Ah yes, as everyone has. What has he done?

MARCO: He's decided -

VERONICA: To wage war on Venice?

MARCO: He's decided to call on you Veronica Franco, the wisest, most elegant, most extraordinary courtesan in Venice, and to spend the night with you, talking, listening to you sing, write poetry and, who knows, perhaps even kissing your foot.

VERONICA: And who suggested he call on me? You, I suppose. Didn't you say that you'd studied with him at Tubinga? And maybe, between one drink and another, you talked about me and aroused his curiosity.

MARCO: It's true, I did talk to him about you...Do you realise what great honour this visit gives you? You should start to get the house ready immediately. It should shine like a palace.

VERONICA: And you enjoy all of this! Not jealous?

MARCO: If I were jealous of you Veronica, I'd throw myself in the sea with a stone round my neck.

VERONICA: You say you love me?

MARCO: In fact, I do.

VERONICA: And you joyfully hand me over into someone else's arms?

MARCO: Someone else? He's the King of France!

VERONICA: Not the tiniest bit of emotion?

MARCO: I have no respect for jealousy, it's stupid.

VERONICA: It's a sign of love.

MARCO: The less one loves, the more jealous one is. Devotion, detachment and desire for the other's happiness - that's true love.

VERONICA: What wisdom! Where did you get these theories from?

MARCO: Watching my father become jealous of my mother - the day that he stopped loving her...And my brother was never as jealous as when he was in love with a courtesan whom he desired but did not love. I love you as I love Venice - I want others to enjoy her too.

VERONICA: That's a pity. I actually love you as a person, not as a city.

MARCO: You can't be jealous of me because I'm all yours and you're the only one I think about.

VERONICA: Well, when is this king coming?

MARCO: On this occasion, I want you to be extremely beautiful.

257

VERONICA: My hair's a mess.

MARCO: I'll send you the best hairdresser in Venice.

VERONICA: And what should I do to please the king?

MARCO: Be yourself, with your fears, your truths, your rhymes, your songs -

VERONICA: Should I wear jewels?

MARCO: No, no jewels. He sees so many of them at court. One single strand of pearls at your neck which you should leave bare, like your arms...and a touch of perfume, that cornflower which suits you so well.

VERONICA: You seem exactly like a mother getting her daughter ready for her first night of love.

MARCO: Perhaps there is something maternal about me. Venice is like a daughter to me and I want her to be splendid in her youth.

VERONICA: What song shall I sing?

MARCO: Ours...Veronica please, be marvellous.I want Enrico to remember his meeting with you his whole life.

VERONICA: Are you giving me in exchange? In exchange for... what?

MARCO: I need nothing from him. I only wish that the most beautiful courtesan in Venice and the greatest king in the world meet for one night.

VERONICA: Aren't you afraid that I might fall in love with him?

MARCO: It would be silly to fall in love with a king who's leaving the next day for France - you'll never see him again in your life.

VERONICA: In short, you think of everything.

MARCO: You'll see how highly people will think of you in the city. Goodbye Veronica, and good luck!

VERONICA: You didn't even live off my money Marco...

(MARCO runs off.)

VERONICA: And if I were to be jealous? Here I am. I get dressed, I get undressed, I look out of the window, I sleep. I eat...and you come, leave, go, travel. Your freedom makes me curious. Torments me. *(GASPARA enters)*

VERONICA: Gaspara, Gaspara, we must polish the whole house, wash these old cushions, beat the carpets, change the bed linen, get out the silver dishes, buy new crystal glasses-

GASPARA: You'd think the king of France was coming!

VERONICA: Exactly, Gaspara, exactly.

GASPARA: A visit to a whore - the king of France?

VERONICA: A courtesan is one thing, a whore another, didn't you say?

GASPARA: You said so.

VERONICA: I can say it, you can't.

GASPARA: He comes, goes to bed with you and then goes. What do you call that? I hope that he pays well, at least.

VERONICA: He's paying nothing. It's an honour, don't you understand? He's not coming to make love to me. If he wanted that he could find a hundred younger and more beautiful than I. He's coming to taste my spirit...

GASPARA: Spirit? No wine?

VERONICA: He's a king...He needs sighs

GASPARA: Surely something else as well.

VERONICA: Perhaps - but seasoned with sighs. What do you understand? Go into the kitchen and prepare.

GASPARA: Sighs, sighs...

(VERONICA leaves. GASPARA is alone.)

GASPARA: The pharmacist won't give any more credit and the upholsterer has come three times. He sits on the door-step and won't go away. "Would you like a coffee Signor Upholsterer?" "No, I want money." What should I do? He didn't even want the rice pudding with raisins and cinnamon...The house, the house...Achillino needs new sheets, the towels need renewing. And the plates - all the plates have to be bought again. Last week eight of them got broken, and eight the week before. No, it's not that child, Nicodema's fault. She's too little - at seven, she shouldn't be spending the day washing plates - but that wretched mother of hers says that without Nicodema's money they can't manage. Eleven in one room and Nicodema's the only one who works. The father has whooping-cough, the mother has dropsy. The eldest girl will die very soon...There's no doubt the one who handles the plates breaks them, not the one who's using the pen and ink. If there's no money coming in here we'll sink...Poor house...Signor Paolo went off with the silver...As for Vannitelli, he eats,and how he eats! He comes into the kitchen as soon as he gets up ".What's in the saucepan Gasparina?" He takes a piece of bread and digs and digs. When I turn around the sauce's gone...Signor Marco hasn't paid for weeks. Senator Domenico has paid already. Now we have a king coming. And you are so simple and happy that you won't ask a penny of him. I've never known such foolishness, I swear, never.

(KING HENRI enters. Looks around. There's no-one to receive him. He takes his gloves off slyly.)

HENRI: Where is the mistress? A Venetian house of the most Venetian of Venetians. *(He moves to a window and pulls aside the curtain.)* You can see the water...two, three gondolas...in a hurry...Where's the famous geometry of Venice?

(VERONICA enters wearing an enormous red wig and a formal gown. She bows.)

HENRI: Where have you been hiding yourself, signora?

VERONICA: I wanted to observe you unseen. They didn't tell me you were so young and attractive. Good lord - you are a handsome man!

HENRI: I should be the one giving compliments for beauty. You gave me no time.

VERONICA: That I might be attractive was foreseeable. Your beauty has caught me by surprise.

HENRI: Kings are ugly on principle?

VERONICA: You have to admit that the Archduke of Austria and Charles the fifth couldn't exactly be called handsome, not even pleasant. You don't need to be beautiful, that's why its a surprise for me.

HENRI: Marco Venier told me about you. More extraordinary than her beauty is her intelligence, her fascination...I see he was right.

VERONICA: I've had four children and nursed them all...

HENRI: Must one talk to kings about such matters?

VERONICA: Would you like clichés?

HENRI: I like you as you are...offer me something to drink, I'm a little warm.

VERONICA: Some sugar water? Spanish wine? Venetian liqueur of cornflowers? Or some limeblossom tea with honey?

HENRI: You haven't even offered me a seat.

VERONICA: I always imagine kings to be standing, like portraits. However, there's a chair. Do you always need someone to tell you what to do? Just let yourself go and you're on it.

HENRI: You're rather like my Parisian aunt who every time she saw me, told me how ill-mannered I was.

VERONICA: Was she pretty - your aunt?

HENRI: Extremely pretty - two little moustaches which the barber tried to thin out a little every morning. Two hands like sticks - very suitable for slaps. One eye open and the other closed - in sum, your portrait.

VERONICA: *(laughing)* I could be an aunt for you. Did she use a whip or a cane?

HENRI: Would you be very strict?

VERONICA: Extremely strict.

HENRI: Do you think I desire you?

VERONICA: From the way you look at me, yes.

HENRI: I do desire you, in fact. I like your voice, I should begin with that.

VERONICA: And what would you do with my voice?

HENRI: I'd reduce it to silence with a long kiss.

VERONICA: You're not very original. Your desire is too much like all the others.

HENRI: But it is a king's desire.

VERONICA: Once you're naked, and without all these bejewelled, embroidered clothes, how shall I recognise this desire as a regal one?

HENRI: Do you want me to show you?

VERONICA: No, thank you. .If you start acting like any quartermaster, I shall not have the joy of seducing your Majesty...

HENRI: No courtesan would dare to say no to a king. I could have you shut up in prison...

VERONICA: Really? And have my head cut off, I suppose.

HENRI: I will refrain from having you decapitated just as long as you immediately embrace me very passionately.

VERONICA: What a hurry you're in! You're in the house of a famous courtesan. If you're in such a hurry you could go to any whorehouse. There are so many of them in Venice. You could choose a younger, more beautiful girl. You wouldn't be raping anyone.

HENRI: You are insolent - and I shall punish your insolence...But you make me curious Veronica...You make me want to hit you...

VERONICA: If you want to, go ahead, I shall give you a good

beating

HENRI: Insolent and rebellious...may I touch your breast?

VERONICA: My breast is a little painful at the moment. I'd prefer you didn't.

HENRI: You know when I was little, the nursemaid let me taste her milk when it was my brother's turn to feed - when it was my step-brother's too. The nursemaid said "Ouch", but she laughed. May I try your milk Signora Veronica? I will bite your breast a little, only a little, but I swear I won't hurt you in the slightest.

VERONICA: No, Majesty, the milk's for my son.

HENRI: You know I feel I love you madly already. Will you come with me to Paris?

VERONICA: To do what?

HENRI: Oh!.. the king's mistress...wouldn't you like that?

VERONICA: I'd prefer to stay in Venice and be a courtesan - although they've made so many laws against us. When we go out we have to wear a yellow bow on our breast, we have to live in the Rialto district and must not go to church on sundays...But you know, no-one keeps the law. A courtesan in Venice is like a queen.

HENRI: May I kiss the hand of the queen of Venice?

VERONICA: Would you like to kiss a foot? Marco Venier told me that you, as a great king, would kiss my foot as a sign of respect.

HENRI: Why not? I'll kiss your foot as a sign of humility. A king should bow before beauty and female intelligence. *(The King goes to kiss VERONICA'S foot and then attempts to embrace her.)*

VERONICA: What a hurry you're in Majesty. Don't you know the delights of waiting? The evening's hardly begun. First you should listen to me sing and then we'll dance together. And if our bodies purr, like cats, then perhaps...

HENRI: You know the art of living well. I recognise it...I like your game, Madame...I'm young enough not to lose my desire in waiting and I'm old enough not to lose patience while I wait.

VERONICA: Will you recite one of your poems, your Majesty?

HENRI: Who told you I wrote poetry?

VERONICA: All great gentlemen do. I imagine that a king does too. More and better than other people.

HENRI: Now you're flattering. I write rhymes, like everyone, but they're not worth much.

VERONICA: Let me judge.

HENRI: If you want...*(Begins to recite.)*

        I love you as I love my life

        Cruel woman - yet do you take my part

        And ease the torment of love's dart?

VERONICA: But these are my verses.

HENRI: *(laughing)* Do I have a good memory?   *(Reciting.)*

        How is it that within

        The soft, the white, your sweet, fine breast

        Is closed a heart so pitiless?

VERONICA: If you're capable of learning a courtesan's rhymes by heart, you are an extremely shrewd diplomat and a gifted governor...You have conquered me.

HENRI: Sing me your song...be cruel then - Veronica you have immediately understood my tastes...I don't love accommodating hearts, but ones which are severe and obstinate.

(VERONICA takes the mandolin and sings. The King, fascinated, first listens and then approaches her and kisses her ear, then her neck while she continues to sing. Lights fade on HENRI and VERONICA.)

(Lights up on GASPARA. She rocks a baby as she opens the curtains.)

GASPARA: Sleep, sleep little chicken bone...your mama's neck hurts...your mama is the most beautiful...your mama is the plumpest..."Good morning Signora Veronica! Good morning Signor King"..."What a beautiful day" she says. "What a beautiful day!" he, the king replies. And they were here in this house which was cleaned by whom? By Gaspara Greghetta and that's me...And you will say too - "My mama one day welcomed a king, actually, the king of France, Henry the third." And if someone were to ask you, "How? When?" you tell him - "I was in the kitchen with my nanny Gaspara Greghetta when the king went to bed with my mama." It's a great honour my child, a very great honour. If you were a girl, it could happen to you too .But unlike Paula, Signora Veronica here only has boys. First Achillino and then Ulysses and now you Enea..."And not

263

just a king came to my house, but the glorious De Montaigne too, who the whole world honours and who brought my mother an engraved silver plate, not to mention Signor Tintoretto who came to supper every Sunday and painted two of the most beautiful portraits of her"...And it was precisely one of these portraits that your mama, you'll say, wanted to give as a present to the King of France so that he would remember her. How pleased little Henry was with that portrait. How he gazed at it.

(VERONICA sitting in front of her mirror. She's humming as she arranges her hair. VANNITELLI is spying on her from one side. MAFFIO enters and sees him in the mirror.)

VERONICA: Another Venier...How is it, do you pass the word round the family?

MAFFIO: Take care Signora! I am not of the same breed as either Marco or Domenico. I am a solitary Venier. What beautiful hair you have!

VERONICA: Your poetry is ugly and filthy.

MAFFIO: But you do know it...good...I know yours too - it's formal and antiquated.

VERONICA: Did you come to insult me?

MAFFIO: I've come to see you close up. I though you were all false. Like Michelina Brunelleschi.

VERONICA: You visit my house as if it were a fun-fair.

MAFFIO: The elite of Venice bore me - the ladies in lace, the gentlemen in damask, the little dogs, the gondoliers, the servants, the silver plates, the black slaves, the Spanish wine. These are things which deserve to be swept away by a tidal wave. I like them, yes I do - fun-fairs like yours, where you meet everyone, from the Doge to a cultured little priest, from the great Mufti to the Duke of Tuscany, from the court poet to the painter who's the latest fashion. I congratulate you on your success, signora. I couldn't miss out on the fun. They told me that you have a tongue like a knife, and I love everything cutting.

VERONICA: Right now I've lost my dear little gold scissors which I liked so much.

MAFFIO: Are we going to start some needlework now?

VERONICA: And do you know Marco who came here to see me?

MAFFIO: I know him and I don't know him. He's talked to me about you, about this comfortable house, about wines, rhymes...but he doesn't know I decided to come and see you. I didn't even know, until five minutes ago, when I was passing by Santa Maria Formosa and decided to come up.

VERONICA: You did well. A Venier is always gladly welcome.

MAFFIO: Let's be clear. I am not a Venier. I am Maffio. I have nothing in common with the other two.

VERONICA: I understand.

MAFFIO: Domenico has swollen legs, and is dreary and serious. And you see that I, on the contrary, am young, lean, quarrelsome and well-shaped. As for Marco, he's a fop. You only have to know that he's known in society as "a fashionable gentleman" to understand what little significance he has. He's certainly very well-suited to become an ambassador, an advisor, even Doge. But not a poet like me.

VERONICA: So you have introduced yourself. Thank you for sparing me the trouble of investigating.

MAFFIO: Now we've become acquainted I'll go. Instead of flowers I shall send you some rhymes. And remember, before you, you have the greatest Venetian of the century. *(Looking at her intently.)* As a woman you don't seem anything out of the ordinary.

VERONICA: Oh, really!

MAFFIO: I should hear you sing. They say you have a beautiful voice, but now I'm in a hurry. I shall come back.

(VERONICA leaves.)

MAFFIO: *(reciting one of his poems.)*

> In this water of palest crystal
> I see the stones and the shining rubies
> Made from goblets of divers wines
> Which seem to lament my pain.
>
> In these jewels, in these oriental pearls,
> Laugh a thousand little cupids
> Who with the dear childish gestures
> Make carnival for me.
>
> The sight brings this tribute to my heart

Which on feeling unwonted sweetness
Turns my every breath into love.

The one who used me with such pride
Could yet each flavour make me taste
For hers is beauty caring nothing.

(Lights up on GASPARA who is cooking. VANNITELLI enters.)

GASPARA: Shh, be quiet, the baby's asleep.
VANNITELLI: You know that I'm fed up!
GASPARA: I said be quiet.
VANNITELLI: I'm fed up with this house - fed up with Signora Veronica - fed up with Achillino - fed up with being a tutor in the middle of chaos and general indifference.
GASPARA: There you are, I knew it. You've woken him up.
VANNITELLI: Your mistress is in a towering rage because she can't find her gold scissors.
GASPARA: I believe I saw those scissors in your hand just the other day. You were admiring them and even asked how much they were worth.
VANNITELLI: I used them to cut a thread. But then I put them back where they were.
GASPARA: Then they should be there.
VANNITELLI: But they're not.
GASPARA: Go and look for them then.
VANNITELLI: I have looked for them but I don't find them. Perhaps you've seen them.
GASPARA: I've never touched those little scissors. I know how much she likes them.
VANNITELLI: They may have been made of gold, but they were certainly worn out - they weren't even worth ten ducats.
GASPARA: And how do you know?
VANNITELLI: I asked a friend of mine, a goldsmith.
GASPARA: And why did you ask a goldsmith?
VANNITELLI: Just because...out of curiosity.
GASPARA: But with the silver case, they would certainly be worth another three ducats.

266

VANNITELLI: Ah, that had two scratches on one side and-

GASPARA: You asked your friend the goldsmith about that too?

VANNITELLI: Certainly - the scissors go with the case...but both of them together aren't worth much.

GASPARA: You know when you sell something that's not in fashion you get little for it. How much did your friend give you for the scissors and the case?

VANNITELLI: I'm telling you that I've never seen your cursed scissors. I haven't seen them!

(VERONICA enters.)

VERONICA: Ah you're here. Where's Achillino?

VANNITELLI: Your son is a devil. I just don't know what to do with him. Instead of listening to me, he constructs big penises out of paper.

VERONICA: And did you teach him to construct penises out of paper?

VANNITELLI: I did. But for a joke, at carnival time. He does it all year round though.

VERONICA: I pay you thirty ducats a month for you to teach my son how to make paper penises?

VANNITELLI: He's a rascal. He doesn't want to know about Latin and Italian.

VERONICA: What am I paying you to do?

VANNITELLI: If you weren't always in a hurry...if you'd listen to me for a moment...if you'd discuss things with me for a moment, signora.

VERONICA: I'm here. Tell me.

VANNITELLI: Your son is distressed because he's heard it bandied about that his mama's a prostitute...Perhaps he doesn't know what that means but he's understood very well it's an ugly word and implies contempt.

VERONICA: And you, what have you told him?

VANNITELLI: That you are the most beautiful of the beautiful and that...but this is not..Look signora, the real reason that Achillino and I make paper penises is because I can't sleep at night anymore.

VERONICA: I don't understand the connection.

VANNITELLI: I can't sleep at night anymore because if I do sleep, I dream about you naked. And since it's not good to dream about you

267

naked, I prefer not to sleep.

VERONICA: You seem extremely eccentric to me Signor Ridolfo Vannitelli. You should teach my son that I am an honoured courtesan, that my profession is as good as any other, that I have a function in this city along with the doctor, the pharmacist. I treat sicknesses of the feelings and senses. It seems to me that I've demonstrated that I treat them well, courteously and generously. You, on the other hand, what do you do? Make paper penises. I think Signor Vannitelli that I shall have to dismiss you.

VANNITELLI: You have rejected me several times signora. I consider that an insult, not only to me, but my profession. Since you are a prostitute, which you admit, shouldn't you satisfy my desires? Am I not worthy of you? Do you think that I have no intention of paying you?

VERONICA: I don't like you Signor Vannitelli. That's all.

VANNITELLI: Why? You like that half-crippled Domenico Venier and not me?

VERONICA: Senator Domenico Venier is crippled, yes, but he has the most limpid spirit and a mind like a garden in summer. While your spirit, Signor Ridolfo Vannitelli, is crippled and depraved. At least confess that you took my gold scissors with the silver case. I forgive you, but tell me.

VANNITELLI: I didn't take those stupid scissors. I haven't even seen them.

GASPARA: But if you even know how many scratches there are on the case...

VANNITELLI: That was only curiosity. I didn't take your scissors. I wouldn't know what to do with them. I've got enough money to pay you.

VERONICA: Even if you had a thousand ducats I wouldn't have you...And now go away. I shall think later about whether to dismiss you or not.

(Lights up on MONSIGNORE and immediately afterwards on VERONICA.)

MONSIGNORE: Veronica Franco, accused...Are you she?
VERONICA: I am...

268

MONSIGNORE: *(sniffing)* What overpowering perfume!

VERONICA: It's the usual cornflower.

MONSIGNORE: It's good.

VERONICA: I'm consoled by your liking it.

MONSIGNORE: Around here there are always bad smells.

VERONICA: I'll send you a small bottle of it.

MONSIGNORE: Silence! What are you thinking of? Do you think you can corrupt me with a small bottle of perfume? *(Reading.)* "Contra Clara Domina Veronica Francum, annus domini Fifteen hundred and seventy-six." *(Looking at her.)* Do you know that you are charged with serious matters?

VERONICA: Me, Monsignore?

MONSIGNORE: A certain Ridolfo Vannitelli, a tutor, came here. This gentleman works for you?

VERONICA: I don't know about the gentleman, but he does work for me, yes.

MONSIGNORE: *(reading)* "One Veronica Franco, public whore, as she was looking the other day for some of her belongings in her house, made accusation of all those who were in the afore-mentioned house, of having stolen a pair of gold scissors with a silver case, and got angry with the above-mentioned, accusing him of theft"...Is it true?

VERONICA: Very true. He took them.

MONSIGNORE: How do you know?

VERONICA: He told my maidservant Gaspara himself that he had had them valued by a goldsmith friend of his.

MONSIGNORE: That doesn't constitute proof.

VERONICA: I didn't even dismiss him. And he admitted that he and my son Achillino spend their time making paper penises instead of learning Latin.

MONSIGNORE: Paper penises? What for?

VERONICA: Just like that, as a game.

MONSIGNORE: *(beginning to read again)* "In order to find the scissors again, Signora Franco recovered a ring which had been blessed, and an olive twig in addition to a candle which had also been blessed, and some of the purest water taken from the distant church of San Nicola dei Mendicoli, and with a basin full of that water, began to make incantations and invocation to devils so that everyone was scandalised"...Do you realise how serious this is? Reply sincerely,

269

you are before the Tribunal of the Inquisition. Is it true that you denounced this man?

VERONICA: It's true, but it was a game Monsignore.

MONSIGNORE: And what was the result of the blessed water and the candle? Did the guilty person come forth?

VERONICA: Why, do you believe in it too?

MONSIGNORE: Don't talk nonsense. It was in order to understand how events unfolded.

VERONICA: Nothing came forth because we started laughing - so it stopped there.

MONSIGNORE: But your denunciation didn't end. Your tutor asks the Tribunal of the Inquisition to *(reading.)* "punish and have punished the said Veronica Franco and the others who were present in making the said incantations and invocations to demons as the sacred and divine laws command in order that this should be an example to everyone, because in not punishing this witch, public prostitute and cheat, many people would do similar things against the sacred Christian faith"...He accuses you here of dancing, singing, playing cards...Is it true?

VERONICA: Monsignore, you too might have been to a courtesan's house sometimes? What do you do there apart from flirt, listen to music, sing and eat? We play cards. But just like that, as a family does. It's hardly a gambling den.

MONSIGNORE: As you know, Monsignori do not frequent the houses of courtesans.

VERONICA: Yet my house has welcomed several. Would you like me to tell you their names?

MONSIGNORE: No, for heaven's sake...Here you are accused of not ever going to church on Sunday. Is this also true?

VERONICA: But as courtesans we're not allowed to appear in church on Sunday. How could we go to mass?

MONSIGNORE: You have to get up at four and be at mass at five. That isn't prohibited.

VERONICA: Going to bed at two?

MONSIGNORE: You know very well Signora Franco you are accused here of every kind of crime.

VERONICA: What else?

MONSIGNORE: It accuses you of eating meat on Fridays.

270

VERONICA: I must nourish myself Excellency. A courtesan works all day and often all night too and how can it be done? - I can hardly live on boiled fish.

MONSIGNORE: But meat is not allowed on Fridays.

VERONICA: It may have happened once Monsignore. Moreover, at my house on the Friday that Vannitelli is talking about, there were Cardinal Falenghi, Monsignore Guido, Senator Damaso Neva, the Grand Advisor - do you know him?

MONSIGNORE: We shall let it drop.

VERONICA: I'll let it drop too.

MONSIGNORE: It's I who decides.

VERONICA: It's you who decides.

MONSIGNORE: Are you sending me up?

VERONICA: I would never allow myself to.

MONSIGNORE: I could send you to the stake. But I shan't do it.

VERONICA: Wise decision.

MONSIGNORE: I could have you publicly flogged. But since I know that it would be turned into a spectacle for people seeking entertainment, I shan't do it.

VERONICA: Wise decision.

MONSIGNORE: If you continue to make comments, I'll immediately send you to the Piombi prison.

VERONICA: That's not a good idea. Excuse me...I shan't say any more.

MONSIGNORE: But remember - the next time we shall not be lenient. And pay attention because you will be watched! Down on your knees! Go to mass on Sundays even if it does mean you have to get up at four. Don't eat meat on Fridays. And above all, don't spend your time anymore with incantations and devilry.

VERONICA: May I go?

MONSIGNORE: Go.

VERONICA: When you wish, Monsignore, my house is at your disposal. You can spend a pleasant evening, with learned conversation, singing and reading poetry. There will be no lack of delicious food and fine wines.

MONSIGNORE: *(ironically)* I shall ask the Pope if he'd like to come with me. After all it won't be any more scandalous than the king of France.

271

(Lights down on MONSIGNORE.)

(Lights up. VERONICA walks along wearing a black cloak. She's stopped by VANNITELLI.)

VANNITELLI: They didn't lock you up then?

VERONICA: I'm free. So too bad for you.

VANNITELLI: I knew it, pig of a whore, I knew it - how could a poor tutor pit himself against a piece of baggage protected by the most learned fat arses in Venice?

VERONICA: If you know it, why did you do it? You are a disgusting sneak!

VANNITELLI: I knew it, I knew it...Madonna whore!

VERONICA: Watch it Vannitelli, you might run up against the wrath of the Inquisition too if you keep on saying blasphemies. Goodbye, dear tutor - I shan't set eyes on you again.

VANNITELLI: Wait, Veronica..I love you...Wait!

(VERONICA pulls her hood over her head and goes off. Exasperated, VANNITELLI runs after her.)

VANNITELLI: I didn't sell the scissors - I keep them under the pillow to remind me of you. Would you like them back? If you want to have them back you have to look at me at least...Will you look at me signora?

VERONICA: No Signor tutor, you've been just too stupid. Keep the scissors and goodbye.

VANNITELLI: I beg you, I beg you Veronica...

(VERONICA exits.)

VANNITELLI: Damned whore! I hate you! I hate you. You're getting old, you stink of dead cat, your skin's sagging, your eyes are watering, you're ugly, ugly, you make me sick. I hate you! Now I'll go back to that Monsignore and tell him that you've bewitched me with your witchcraft. You've ruined me Veronica... Veronica!

(Black-out on VANNITELLI. Lights up on the hospital.)

VERONICA: I thought I was so splendid, but how petty I was! What pride and arrogance!...I think that the Lord means to punish me.

I talked about love, Anzola, I delighted in the pleasure which I knew how to give...and I wounded our Lord. It was as if I, with my own hands pressed the sponge soaked with vinegar into his wounds...

ANZOLA: Stop tormenting yourself. You're like everyone else, Veronica, neither better nor worse. You didn't press the sponge soaked with vinegar on our Lord's sores. You think you're too important.

VERONICA: And is that the reason He can't make up his mind whether to call me to Him, Anzola? Neither amongst the living nor the dead? Because His eyes glance over my head and rest far away without seeing me?...Is that how it is Anzola?

ANZOLA: That's how it is.

VERONICA: I'm not here as a punishment but from an oversight, from carelessness.

ANZOLA: Just so.

VERONICA: And on the other hand, if He's keeping me in this life for one of his secret purposes which I shall understand later, only later...there is a sweetness hidden in this suspension of judgement, Anzola...Perhaps he's also smelled a light scent of cornflower.

ANZOLA: How you fool yourself! According to you, men are always desiring you. But the Lord, my beloved Lord, does not desire you - just know that. Your cornflower perfume doesn't even touch the laces tied around His ankles. He is perfect and desires only Himself.

VERONICA: It is a sad body that desires only Himself.

ANZOLA: Perfection demands this.

VERONICA: Don't tell me things which could make me swear... Leave me hoping that He wants me.

ANZOLA: A rag like you?

VERONICA: A rag like me...I know He is capable of miracles...Oh God, such pain! *(She collapses. ANZOLA holds her up.)*

ANZOLA: Look, she's going...perhaps the Lord has listened to you...in His infinite goodness...even a whore...an old slipper...Lord what patience you have! There's no limit to Your indulgence. It's too much, I'm telling you honestly - straight from the heart...it's incredible that certain creatures can even seduce Heaven...Go on then, just go right to Him - fortune we know, follows the fortunate...

(Black-out.)

ACT TWO.

The plague hospital.

ANZOLA: Two more steps, over to there.

VERONICA: I can't make it.

ANZOLA: Yes, you can.

VERONICA: I'm falling.

ANZOLA: You're not falling. Let's try...gently, gently, one little step after another...You've seen some people die!

VERONICA: Too many!

ANZOLA: You've got nine lives like a cat.

VERONICA: What do you do with nine lives? One good one is enough for me.

ANZOLA: The grave-digger Raffaele bet three scudi that you'd die by the evening.

VERONICA: What a pig!

ANZOLA: Sister Miranda bet an egg that you'd cheat the angels.

VERONICA: And who ate it?

ANZOLA: She ate it...she...won...And do you know who she bet against?

VERONICA: Who?

ANZOLA: Against me.

VERONICA: You bet that I'd die? - Fine friend!

ANZOLA: You were done for. And then that egg...

VERONICA: Fresh, round, transparent...How long is it since you ate a good hard-boiled egg, sister Anzola?

ANZOLA: Let's see...*(Counts on her fingers.)* Since...one, two, three, seven years. Yes, seven years.

VERONICA: It was better if I died eh? And would you still bet that I'm on my way out?

ANZOLA: To look at you, you seem better...But you never know. The plague is mischievous. It seems to be going away and then, when you've turned the corner, it comes back. It's still possible that I'll taste that egg...

VERONICA: The Lord's given you the mind of a luminary.

ANZOLA:*(annoyed)* No-one's ever called me that before.

274

*(She goes a little way off leaving **VERONICA** alone. **VERONICA** staggers.)*

VERONICA: Wait, please! Don't you see that I can't stand up?

ANZOLA: Die!

VERONICA: Please Anzola. *(She takes three steps towards her.)*

ANZOLA: Without me, you're a lifeless rag. You must obey me absolutely.

VERONICA: *(abject and ironic)* I obey you absolutely.

ANZOLA: Will you do everything that I tell you to?

VERONICA: I will. But don't leave me.

ANZOLA: Well sit down. You're heavy on my shoulder.

VERONICA: No, not on the ground, no. I shan't be able to get up again.

ANZOLA: Stay here for a moment and lean against the wall. I'll go and get you a chair.

VERONICA: No, don't leave me, I'm falling!

ANZOLA: Here, against the door. And I'll tie you with the shawl to this nail.

(ANZOLA does this. VERONICA stays hooked against the wall.)

VERONICA: What a vile end. Veronica, hooked on a nail like a plucked chicken...Sister Anzola, please? Sister Anzola...the whore, I can hear her. She's begun taking bets...Anzola, Anzola!

(ANZOLA comes back with a chair. She unties VERONICA. She helps her to sit.)

ANZOLA: Better like that?

VERONICA: My head's going round.

ANZOLA: Do you want me to tie you to the chair?

VERONICA: No, no, I'll hold on here to the arms.

ANZOLA: Now then...tell me.

VERONICA: What?

ANZOLA: About you. I like your stories so much.

VERONICA: But what?

ANZOLA: You told me about the king...about your husband Paolo... About the other one, what's his name?

VERONICA: Marco?

ANZOLA: Did you love him?

VERONICA: Yes I did. He didn't love me. Or perhaps he did love me - but at a distance. You don't own a courtesan, you share her.

275

They all become friends, allies, accomplices...only real lovers possess
one another...the others share things out, like good comrades...one
likes a breast, another a mouth, a third - the eyes, a fourth - the feet...
ANZOLA: Feet?..Tell me, tell me about feet.
VERONICA: For example Marco - he likes feet very much.

*(Light illuminates the stage. We see MARCO very elegantly
dressed. He comes forward warily.Lights out on VERONICA.)*

MARCO: I beg you, don't be in a hurry...What I love most about love
is precisely that moment of preparation...Let me hear your little shoe
as it falls to the ground, tac...and now the other, tac...You would say
that you were barefoot, yet I hear the light shuffling that your soles
make on the floor...Have you kept your stockings on? I hope not
Veronica, how many times must I tell you that nakedness must be
total - that cotton beneath one's fingers casts me down, it makes me
melancholy...Let me hear the delicate rubbing of feet against the
terrace. I know that you're cold, but then I'll think about how to warm
them up for you...Perhaps you doubt me? My breath? You know that
love has its ass and ox. Take in one's hand a little bare foot, welcome
it between two open palms, like a little new born baby in the arms of
its mother...kiss it, warm it with one's breath until it falls asleep again.
(VERONICA comes in wearing shoes with platform soles.)
VERONICA: Here I am.
MARCO: I was dreaming about you. And you entered my dream
with the delicacy of a mercenary. Why do you wear such shoes? You
know I hate them.
VERONICA: It's the fashion.
MARCO: An obnoxious fashion. Take them off, I beg you.
(VERONICA takes her cloak off. Takes off her shoes.)
VERONICA: It's two weeks since you've been in touch. Where have
you been?
MARCO: I don't know. Perhaps at home sleeping. Perhaps, going
around with friends.
VERONICA: Why are you being mysterious?
MARCO: Are you jealous by any chance?
VERONICA: And if I were?
MARCO: A courtesan should neither provoke jealousy nor feel it.

It's not allowed.

VERONICA: Not allowed by whom?

MARCO: By good sense. By intelligence.

VERONICA: First you seek my love, and then you don't want it. Aren't you a little wanting in logic?

MARCO: In this house, love is an exquisite courtesy, a delicate temerity, a game of chance, an unblemished happiness. Provided that you don't imitate the manners of the people over there.

VERONICA: Which people?

MARCO: The conformists, the "pères de famille", the honest husbands, the faithful lovers, the owners of souls and bodies.

VERONICA: Those people only mimic us.

MARCO: The respectable ladies would like to be courtesans and the courtesans dream of nothing but being respectable ladies.

VERONICA: Perhaps they'd like to be respected as good ladies but have the freedom of courtesans.

MARCO: Life is so boring in this city! Ladies and courtesans - the same broth. However shall a gentleman manage who has a touch of fantasy?

VERONICA: Would you like to have a glass of Spanish wine with me?

MARCO: Don't give me anything to drink. Give me a foot to kiss.

VERONICA: My feet are tired. Those shoes are heavy.

MARCO: Those tubs are real torture for the feet. Feet should be cuddled and caressed, you know. If you treat them badly, they'll have their revenge by giving you corns.

VERONICA: I treat them with sweet almond oil - a drop of Turkish aniseed and they sleep like two babies.

MARCO: I'll be the one to awaken them with a kiss.

VERONICA: Marco, how long have you been coming to see me?

MARCO: I don't know. I don't know how to count.

VERONICA: What if I were to tell you that I'm expecting a baby?

MARCO: Again?

VERONICA: I think so, yes.

MARCO: Do you need money?

VERONICA: Of course I need money.

MARCO: You know that I find new-born babies repulsive. I like children after they begin to read and write. I would like a little girl.

Five years old, called Olympia like my mother, with blonde hair, a fine high forehead. "My most darling papa, can I ask you for fifteen scudi so that I can buy a satin dress with silver bows?" "Dear Olympia, before thinking about dresses with silver bows, I would like you to read this book which your father, with your mother's agreement, wished to dedicate to you."

(Begins to recite a poem. Lights up on GASPARA who is cooking.)

GASPARA: Sleep, sleep little chicken leg, your mama's had her wings clipped... your mama is the most beautiful... and you -and you, are the sweetest little piglet of all my little piglets. Your father Signor Marco doesn't honour you with so much as a glance. He wanted a little girl . How much do you want Gaspara? Thirty scudi? Fifty scudi? But don't annoy me with that little creature - I don't want to see him, he's too ugly. But you and he are as alike as two peas in a pod. He's not in the least like me. He's as ugly as sin. He's little - you'll see as soon as he's grown a bit, how beautiful he'll be! Here you are, I'm giving you another twenty scudi, buy him a new shirt, buy him a little horse, buy him a lute, buy him a rope to hang himself, but don't bring him to me.

VERONICA: *(reads while one foot rocks her new baby's cradle)*
>What I hid in my heart so long
>Challenged my tongue to silence
>Bitter and sweet pains of love
>Awaiting a voice in better times

(she repeats)...bitter and sweet pains of love...pains of love, pains of love...let me feel I'm dying from passion...not to follow him at every hour...*(She counts the syllables)*...not-to-follow-him-at-every-hour-

GASPARA: Do you want the glasses with the gold border or the ones with the lilac line around?

VERONICA: Can't you see I'm busy?

GASPARA: In an hour's time there will be people for supper and here you are still wasting time.

VERONICA: I'm not wasting time. I'm writing verse which I shall recite this evening to my friends.

GASPARA:But you have to get dressed and check the table is properly laid. You have to try the wine and arrange the flowers and

278

light the candles.

VERONICA: You can do all those things very well, Gaspara.

GASPARA: But you've always done them.

VERONICA: This evening I can't. I'm behind with my verses. Do you want me to look bad? Leave me alone, Gaspara, I have to write.

GASPARA: That means the evening will be a real disaster.

VERONICA: All right Gaspara. Just give me five minutes and then I'll come. Now are you happy?

GASPARA: Five minutes, no more.

VERONICA: Five. And take the baby away.

(GASPARA takes the cradle and carries it away.)

VERONICA: Never a moment's peace - never...well. - bitter and sweet pains of love... let me feel that I'm dying of passion... not to follow him at every hour...

(GASPARA re-enters almost immediately.)

GASPARA: Five minutes are up. The pharmacist wants to be paid. Achillino's thrown-up his dinner and now he's crying.

VERONICA: You're always so good at organising everything. Tonight it seems you can't do without me. Why?

GASPARA: When I hear Senator Domenico Venier's stick I get gooseflesh.

VERONICA: Here already!

(DOMENICO VENIER enters.)

DOMENICO: This would be Marco's son?

GASPARA: His name's Enea.

DOMENICO: He could be mine.

GASPARA: Do you like him?

DOMENICO: No, I don't like him.

GASPARA: Not even his father likes him.

DOMENICO: I would have made him better.

GASPARA: He'll be a great man.

(MAFFIO enters. GASPARA exits.)

MAFFIO: Here I am.

DOMENICO: I have been coming here for fifteen years, dear Maffio and I have never seen you here before.

MAFFIO: Since when did you get credit for seniority, as they do in offices of state?

DOMENICO: Oh don't let's squabble. Eh... are you still writing?

279

MAFFIO: You mean you've not read my pamphlet of verse in Venetian dialect?

DOMENICO: I don't read verses in the vernacular.

MAFFIO: That's a mistake.

DOMENICO: Poetry is linguistic sophistication, Maffio. You mix up the everyday with the sublime - you knead, knead - you are a baker, not a poet.

MAFFIO: Always the same incurable formalist, my dear old man. I make words dance, you embalm them.

DOMENICO: You simplify, dear Maffio, you simplify and excite. In poetry, simplification is acquiescence, boredom and banality.

MAFFIO: I talk about creatures of flesh and blood, you talk about ideas. I stand in the street, you in the museums. Where do you think the blood flows?

DOMENICO: I very much hope that it flows around you. I don't like blood, even if it's fake. Your world of flesh and blood is extremely boring and predictable. We are all made of flesh and blood... not to mention tears. That other world interests me, the one made of inventions and eccentricities, of revelations and deliriums. A world in which mountains are made of silk, the sky, paper - the clouds, cotton-wool - the rivers, glass - the lakes, broken mirrors... As for feelings... they are the most refined essence of the most complete absolute artifice.

MAFFIO: You are an old aesthete and your poetry can only be liked by four old fogies tarred with the same brush as you... You can find rhymes on the lips of gondoliers, fruit-sellers, pharmacists, laundry women.. That's the way poetry has to be, popular, otherwise it's a missal only good for the altar.

(VERONICA enters extremely elegantly dressed.)

DOMENICO: At last! How beautiful you are! This boor has done nothing but insult me... and I still don't have a stool.

VERONICA: Gaspara, the cripple's stool.

DOMENICO: You as well Veronica, how coarse!

VERONICA: Excuse me, that's what we call it.

(GASPARA enters with the stool and puts it under the Senator's feet.)

DOMENICO: Look what poetry does, for example - it refines language.

MAFFIO: And cripples the stool... Dear Venier *(Laughs.)* You call the cripples' stool simply a stool and resolve the question. The cripple disappears and the stool is ennobled... Look how you understand how language works then, as a dishonest embellishment of everyday minutiae? The minutiae into which you must plunge your hands, get them dirty, cover them with grease, with sludge. We work with the dregs, without wearing white gloves.

DOMENICO: I'll leave you the dregs. I make you a present of them. I'll keep my white gloves on. Of the two of you, you're the unfair one - mangling Italian to flatter the Venetian public.

VERONICA: Please don't quarrel.

DOMENICO: She knows, she knows the sophistication of rhyme too and uses it.

MAFFIO: Because she too wants to cover up the great landscape of shit which surrounds us.

VERONICA: I don't cover up anything. I speak frankly in my verses and you know it.

MAFFIO: It's true that you always speak the truth - but it's truth all tricked out - artificial and conceited.

VERONICA: Your tongue's got calluses on it from all the insult's you've uttered, Maffio.

DOMENICO: You've swallowed the bait, Veronica. Maffio enjoys it when other people get annoyed... Would you pour me a little wine, Veronica?

VERONICA: Spanish or Cypriot?

DOMENICO: I would prefer the Tuscan one with peach fragrance.

VERONICA: It's not too sweet for you?

DOMENICO: I like the fragrance. It makes me think of when I was twenty and used to go out early and smell the perfume in the garden below the house. There was a twisted little peach tree which bore twisted little peaches but had such a perfume, such a perfume that anyone passing by in the street would stand there transfixed with their nose in the air.

MAFFIO: Trivia!

DOMENICO: *(pretending not to notice)* Veronica, before we sit down at the table, I would like to ask you to read your latest rhymes.

VERONICA: So that Maffio can spit on them? No thanks.

MAFFIO: I swear I'll be good and listen. Everything you do

281

Veronica, excites me... I'm not saying what - it could be something to do with the brain. What do you think? Can a courtesan tickle a man's brain as well as his belly?

DOMENICO: You're insolent, Maffio. I've already realised that you'll ruin this evening.

VERONICA: You recite, Maffio. Something of yours.

DOMENICO: All right then, read - recite so that you'll behave yourself for a bit.

MAFFIO: *(takes a sheet out of his pocket and reads)*

> Franca, by Saint Maffio, believe me
> This is the fourth month I worry
> Should I tarry or advance.
> On the one hand, it's good, I like to see
> You and hear your clever talk.
> On the other, I balk
> To swallow the bitter pill.
> I mean, if a kiss is desired
> Five or six scudi are required
> And if one wants to screw, scarce fifty will do!

DOMENICO: And this is poetry?

MAFFIO: Why, don't you like it?

DOMENICO: No, this is insolence in ballad form. And the ballads are only fit for boatmen to invent.

MAFFIO: In fact, I am a boatman - I carry souls on my boat, here and there on the river... I couldn't carry yours though - It weighs too much. It's not a soul, it's a bag full of holes.

DOMENICO: I'll answer you in rhyme, Maffio. Rhyme for rhyme. You use oars, I use a pen.

VERONICA: Would you like to sit down the table is set.

(GASPARA has brought in a table which is already laid. MAFFIO eats very greedily. VERONICA looks at him ironically.)

VERONICA: I see you're not lacking in appetite.

MAFFIO: *(with his mouth full)* I do have quite an appetite.

DOMENICO: It's obvious.

VERONICA: That you honour my table gives me pleasure. Read us some other rhymes.

MAFFIO: I've got a mouthful of them. *(He laughs at the double entendre.)* I was forgetting the last part of the poem... well...

(Reciting aloud.)
> Veronica, dear, dear heart,
> Dear Happiness, my darling soul,
> Be as a helper to one who's dying...

Do you like this ending?

VERONICA: Would you like me to sew it up for you?

MAFFIO: Veronica, I love you such a great deal- I'll say it in front of the cripple - it doesn't matter to me. Do you want me to stay with you?

DOMENICO: Eating and drinking at someone else's expense.

MAFFIO: Do you want me to stay here with my beloved without eating and drinking?

VERONICA: I'd rather become a nun, than have you here in the house. I've chased away a good many other men on account of their arrogance.

MAFFIO: But I am Maffio, the best poet to be had in this whore of a city.

DOMENICO: Amen.

VERONICA: I'd amuse myself with you but I'd end up bankrupt in a few months.

MAFFIO: Always money, always money, you don't ever think of anything else. They even weigh up sighs in this house. One sigh - ten scudi, a moan - seven scudi, a sob - three scudi, a belch - two scudi, a fart, huh - a scudi and a half.

DOMENICO: You eat and drink your fill, but I've never seen you take out a single scudo.

MAFFIO: I don't have any. Because of that, I'm not allowed her bed. But when the Pope decides to make me Bishop of Brescia - the post is vacant, you know- if they make me Bishop, that's a hundred ducats per day guaranteed.

VERONICA: You'll certainly make an exquisite Bishop. I shall come to Brescia to hear you say mass.

MAFFIO: Oh, if they give me good wine.

DOMENICO: Just carry on getting drunk my friend. Meanwhile I'll ask our most beautiful hostess to make a little place for me in her bed.

VERONICA: I like your wanting me.

DOMENICO: You mean you accept.

VERONICA: You know that I'm a little perverse. I like to play.

DOMENICO: I'm not asking you to play.

MAFFIO: Is he really serious...With that old body?

VERONICA: Shut up. When he's naked, he looks better.

MAFFIO: Good for the fishes.

VERONICA: You don't know how tender an old body can be.

MAFFIO: He's really tender.

DOMENICO: Shall I squeeze you as much as I want you?

VERONICA: Watch out lest the fishes bite.

DOMENICO: I'll be able to kiss you as long as I want.

VERONICA: I want to too.

DOMENICO: Let's go then.

VERONICA: Yes, let's go.

MAFFIO: Let's go.

VERONICA: If you want to carry on drinking, the bottles are over there.

DOMENICO: Have a good night, poet!

MAFFIO: Why on earth do they give parties, perform heroic deeds, have tournaments, present arms and write verses to a woman when they know this woman shits?

(Lights fade up slightly on the Hospital. ANZOLA, open-mouthed watches the three eating.)

ANZOLA: Chicken...oh god...chicken...and melted butter...Saint Barbara forgive me...and the smell, the smell grabs hold of me, wrings me, grips me. I know what you're going to say - I adore the golden calf...I've smelled roast chicken and I'm ready to sell my soul for...chicken *(Putting her nose in the air.)*...chicken...chicken...I've only eaten chicken twice in my life. Saint Barbara, forgive me, twice. The first time when I was six years old and my mother served at Judge Zanin's house when they gave a party for his daughter's wedding. "Try it, have a taste"...Giannetta Zanin put a chicken thigh in my hand and when I sank my teeth into it the warm oil trickled down my chin...The second time was when I was fifteen. I'd been beaten until my blood flowed, by my stepfather and some wine merchant who took pity on me helped me and kept me in his house for three days. That evening he came into my bed, squeezed me as if he wanted to break my bones, then he ran off into the kitchen and came

284

back with some chicken he'd stolen from his wife.

(During this, lights fade down on the table. Lights up on
VERONICA, in the hospital.)

VERONICA: Poor Anzola, my poor Anzola, what shall I do with you?
ANZOLA: What will you do with me?
VERONICA: What shall I do?
ANZOLA: What will you do? But did you eat chicken every day?
VERONICA: Not every day. Do you know how much chicken costs?
ANZOLA: If I knew, it would mean that I bought it sometimes.
VERONICA: Four scudi a pound.
ANZOLA: In fact, we've never seen it in my house.
VERONICA: God how my head spins! Do you think I'll ever get better?
ANZOLA: In my opinion, you're not doing too well.
VERONICA: You're very encouraging.
ANZOLA: Your face is as white as a sheet.
VERONICA: How grey Venice is this evening! The water seems made of lead, and so still it seems stagnant. All these months the gondolas have been decked out in mourning for so many dead, but now we hear the bells less and less. Perhaps the disease is waning.
ANZOLA: No, no. They continue to die.
VERONICA: Have you said any prayers for me?
ANZOLA: I've got better things to do than say prayers for you.
VERONICA: I thought we were friends.
ANZOLA: Well, it's true that I like you...day after day being together...other people leave, you stay on...how would it be possible not to be friends? *(She thinks it over.)*...Every how many days did you eat chicken?
VERONICA: Once a month, maybe twice.
ANZOLA: Therefore every fifteen days you ate chicken.
VERONICA: Domenico didn't like chicken. He preferred fish. Sometimes he'd bring a basket of seabream, sole, black umber.
ANZOLA: Fish is for invalids. Tell me about chicken.
VERONICA: Marco once brought me a live chicken. It stayed on

285

the terrace in a daze for an hour. Then it began to run, so gay and happy that no-one had the courage to kill it. It died of old age.

ANZOLA: If it had been me, I would have seized it by a claw and hup, wrung its neck - and I'd even have eaten it raw.

VERONICA: Do you think I still have a fever?

ANZOLA: *(taking her pulse)* Yes, I think so...your heart's racing...but when will it go? No-one could kill a heart nourished on roast chicken.

VERONICA: Love has crumpled it.

ANZOLA: Have you loved many men?

VERONICA: I've had a lot of men in my bed. But I've loved, perhaps two people - Domenico Venier - the moment I met him - and Marco Venier, Enea's father.

ANZOLA: What about your husband Paolo?

VERONICA: A husband was useful to me Anzola. Then, I did think I loved him.

ANZOLA: Well, why didn't you marry Signor Domenico?

VERONICA: It was he, who didn't want to marry me. A Venier doesn't marry a courtesan.

*(Lights up on stage, where **DOMENICO** is limping about.)*

DOMENICO: I've loved you more than was permissible Veronica, permissible that is for a freethinker, for an unhappy body such as mine...And I've loved your slavery more than I wanted to. For this, I ask you to forgive me When the King of France came to visit, it was a triumph for you. But in my heart, I wept for you. There was something deeply degrading and offensive in that triumph. It was a triumph which saw you, the courtesan, nailed to the yielding city walls...However, on the other hand, you have to admit that your slavery has been a nursemaid to you. Because of it, you've had time and leisure to educate yourself and become more refined. You've been made brave and strong enough to go through the seven doors of oblivion and violence. You have succeeded, by what secret alchemy heaven knows, in combining the refined grace of the aristocracy with the astute corruption of the people...I have loved your slavery with a guilty satisfaction. Had it been my lot, I would have detested it, I confess. But yours was precious to me and I was blessed by its

286

precious nature, like a second skin which enfolded me. Each time I saw you pregnant, I dreamt of being born from you, a happy new son with my too-long nose, my watery eyes, my bad legs...but I never really had the courage to make you a mother. I considered your slavery too precious to negate in the son which you would have had. I didn't want Domenico Venier to seem like an accomplice of your adorable subjection, even if, I am an accomplice my lady, because I have encouraged and paid for your slavery - I have been a participant in your corruption...But believe me, I've done it with so much love that you can't do anything but forgive me.

(VERONICA's house. VERONICA and MARCO enter)

VERONICA: What's happening?
MARCO: Rats, dead rats, everywhere dead rats - in San Zaccaria, in San Salvador, in Castelo, the Rialto, Santa Margherita...Dead rats which explode before your eyes...What will become of us and our poor lives! They're already closing the gate...There's a terrible silence in the market. There was a meeting of the Council...soon they'll close the city gates. If you mean to leave, do it immediately. - There's always my house in Brenta if you're interested.
VERONICA: And what will you do?
MARCO: I have to stay. The captain can't desert his sinking ship...
VERONICA: Will you come and see me?
MARCO: Not if they close the city...But let's hope that it's a false alarm...Here you are, I'm leaving you a thousand scudi.
VERONICA: Is it true that you're in love Marco?
MARCO: Who told you?
VERONICA: So it's true?
MARCO: Gossip.
VERONICA: You have a new smell about you Marco, which I don't recognise...Is she young?
MARCO: She's young.
VERONICA: And are you going to marry her?
MARCO: How could I? She's a courtesan, like you.
VERONICA: A young courtesan...And tell me, does she write poetry?
MARCO: She has a virile intelligence and a great sweetness.

VERONICA: Shall I not see you any more?

MARCO: Think about saving yourself Veronica. If you need anything send me a note.

VERONICA: Aren't you going to kiss me?

MARCO: We should think about the risk of infection. Every contact is dangerous...you for me and me for you.

VERONICA: Goodbye Signor Marco Venier. You have been greatly loved.

MARCO: You should have told me that sometimes.

VERONICA: I was afraid of upsetting you.

MARCO: Me too.

VERONICA: I still love you.

MARCO: I do too.

VERONICA: And yet you make love to someone else.

MARCO: So do you. I know you often see young Maffio.

VERONICA: I don't succeed in falling in love.

MARCO: Sooner of later you'll succeed.

VERONICA: Kiss me, I beg you. I'm not afraid of infection.

MARCO: And if I were to be afraid?

VERONICA: I'd consider it an unforgivable cowardice.

MARCO: Then forgive me.

*(MARCO squeezes VERONICA tightly. Darkness.
Lights up on GASPARA.)*

GASPARA: One cow, two cows, three cows, four cows, five cows. There's nothing to see but cows in these parts...Signora Veronica is so stubborn - only thinks about writing...The villas above Brenta are beautiful, very beautiful, but good god, how boring!
(VERONICA enters.)

VERONICA: Has no-one come looking for me?

GASPARA: No-one.

VERONICA: Are you sure?

GASPARA: Absolutely sure.

VERONICA: They don't want to amuse themselves any more - no suppers, no games, no intrigues. Gaspara mine - what am I doing? And such boredom...such boredom...Did you hear that Gaspara? I sounded exactly like my mother.

(Putting on her mother's voice again.) "How boring, my little girl, how boring!" Do you remember her Gaspara, Signora Paula, with the heels of her little shoes perpetually worn out?

GASPARA: Always up and down the narrow streets.

VERONICA: Where are you going Signora Paula, in those little embroidered silk slippers...up to the Rialto, down to Santa Margherita, up to Santa Croce, down to San Marco...Signora Paula walked and walked, and she was so beautiful that everyone turned as she went by...She was more beautiful than me, isn't that true Gaspara?

GASPARA: Without a doubt. More beautiful and more sensible...because you're here dying of boredom and we don't catch sight of a single scudi! *(MAFFIO enters.)*

VERONICA: Maffio!

MAFFIO: *(reciting)*

> In this bright and blessed house
> She humbly lives,
> This, precious ragged love of mine,
> Richly ragged,
> Whose white and slender flanks,
> Shine through her tattered gowns.
> She, by day, is more beautiful,
> The less she is bejewelled....
> Just as the moon shimmers between two chimneys
> .So her face gleams from the depths of her rags.

Do you like it?

VERONICA: Maffio, what a beautiful poem. When did you write it?

MAFFIO: "The Beautiful Tramp". I don't know. It's been in my mind for a while...Won't you give me something to drink?

VERONICA: What a joy it is to see you! Sit down. How did you manage to get out of Venice with all that plague about?

MAFFIO: I don't give a damn about the plague.

VERONICA: What if you catch it?

MAFFIO: If I catch it, I catch it...I'm so fed up...Never mind, I'll let you into a secret. I've got syphilis. And do you know whose fault that is? Your beautiful Veronica's...She rejected me and I went looking for a more accommodating body. I found it. But along with

289

the body I also found something else. Whether one dies of the plague or syphilis - what difference does it make?

VERONICA: You're always joking Maffio.

MAFFIO: Do you like my poetry?

VERONICA: Very much.

MAFFIO: I like it too...yesterday I recited aloud in Piazza San Marco to about twenty beggars. At the end they wanted to carry me in triumph. Can I kiss you Veronica? Let's make peace and seal it...

VERONICA: Do you want to make me ill too?

MAFFIO: What are kisses? Nothing. You need something more than that to be infected.

VERONICA: I shouldn't even open the door to you Maffio, I know you go around insulting me. You've written things about me - infamous things...

MAFFIO: Because I desire you.

VERONICA: A fine way of showing it.

MAFFIO: You don't want me because I have no money, but I'm telling you: the Pope's given his consent. In a few days I'll be made Bishop and will have a living of a thousand scudi. Will you agree to have a Bishop with servant and carriage in your venerable bed?

VERONICA: And the French disease?

MAFFIO: It was a joke. I'm as sound as a bell. I didn't get the French disease because the beautiful gypsy didn't want me either, the bitch. So I spread it around that she's diseased. *(Laughing.)* I'd like to see the faces she'll make when her clients flee her like a mangy dog!

VERONICA: Go away Maffio, I was so pleased to see you - it would be better if you stayed away from me.

MAFFIO: You're chasing me away? You're chasing the Bishop of Brescia away?

VERONICA: I'm not chasing you away, I'm begging you to leave me alone.

MAFFIO: Give me a kiss.

VERONICA: No.

MAFFIO: *(goes off angrily shouting at the top of his voice)*
>Veronica, truly unique whore
>Lazy, cunning, wrinkled and flabby
>And mouldy and wizened and rotten and boring
>dirty bitch

Who drags herself between castle, ghetto and
customs house
Monster turned woman in human flesh
Stucco, plaster, cardboard, tanned ox-hide and plank
Phantom from Lodi, pock-marked ogre
Crocodile, donkey, ostrich, horse...

(Lights change.)

VERONICA: Domenico Venier, finally!
DOMENICO: I defied the guards to come here...the city's under
siege. There's no fresh food anymore. People are dying in the streets.
You see boat after boat laden with bodies going by...
VERONICA: Did you see Marco?
DOMENICO: Marco's well. His brother's dead of the plague.
Young Tron too.
VERONICA: Achillino's father?
DOMENICO: He was brave. He made a will. He shut himself up
alone in a room so as not to infect anyone and he breathed his last.
VERONICA: Did he leave something to his bastard?
DOMENICO: I don't know...I don't think so...
VERONICA: Maffio came here.
DOMENICO: I saw him.
VERONICA: Have you read the abusive words he wrote about me?
DOMENICO: All Venice has read them.
VERONICA: And will you publish my replies?
DOMENICO: As you might imagine, I came for just that reason.
VERONICA: I am pleased to see you...Is everything all right at
home?
DOMENICO: Everyone's in the country. I'm the only one who's
staying in town. But the plague disdains someone like me, it doesn't
pick on the old and crippled. I've come to bring you some supplies in
case things are difficult for you. Silks, cottons, a fur coat...
VERONICA: Thank you Domenico...And what do you want in
exchange?
DOMENICO: To hold you in bed.
VERONICA: How can I refuse you?...let's go.

(Lights fade. Lights up on GASPARA.)

GASPARA: Two cows, three cows, four cows, five cows, six cows...only cows out here in the countryside...If I go on counting them, I'll go mad sitting here...But why is she so late? One day to go to Venice, one day to see Signor Marco. One more day to come back...She should already be here...how long does it take? My Lady. Madonna of Mercy save my Veronica...don't let her fall into the hands of brigands, not twist her ankle, nor have her head beaten, nor run a fever, nor catch the plague...

(Black-out on GASPARA. Lights up on MARCO and VERONICA. VERONICA goes to meet MARCO.)

MARCO: Don't come near! I've got a fever and ominous swellings in my armpits.
VERONICA: I've so longed to see you...Let me hold you.
(She goes to hold him. He moves aside.)
MARCO: I told you, don't touch me!
(She manages to give him a brief caress.)
VERONICA: You're burning...
MARCO: Damned city.
VERONICA: If you'd come to the country with me-
MARCO: I would have been bored to death.
VERONICA: You've amused yourself here then?
MARCO: That beautiful girl I talked to you about, do you remember? She died in my arms a few days ago.
VERONICA: Did you love her very much?
MARCO: I looked for you in her.
VERONICA: I don't suppose you found me.
MARCO: Once, on tiptoe, you appeared in her eyes...but I was afraid of sacrilege.
VERONICA: Wouldn't it have been simpler to look for me in myself?
MARCO: If it had been so simple, I wouldn't have loved you, I wouldn't have handed you over to the King of France, I wouldn't have tolerated Domenico's presence, nor Maffio's.
VERONICA: So I'd have loved a lascivious, complicated and

292

mysterious man.

MARCO: Perhaps you too looked for someone in your lovers' eyes.

VERONICA: And who would that be?

MARCO: It would be presumptuous to say, myself. I think we shan't see each other again. And I'm not to blame.

VERONICA: Don't say that - it's only a touch of fever.

MARCO: I know the symptoms.

VERONICA: Would you like me to stay here with you?

MARCO: Absolutely not. Now go. I'm even afraid of the breath I breathe out.

VERONICA: I'll come and see you tomorrow.

MARCO: Go back to the country. I beg you...promise?

VERONICA: Just as you like. I'll come back in a week.

MARCO: The cemeteries are so stupid...with all those dead people chattering away...the nearness of the graves...it's worse than in town...there's no room to enjoy a bit of peace at night...

VERONICA: I still love you.

MARCO: Because of that you'll live...

(Black-out on MARCO. Lights up on the country house. Enter GASPARA.)

GASPARA: You're back at last! I was dreaming about you...

VERONICA: Marco is...dead.

GASPARA: One cow, two cows, three cows, four cows, five cows...count with me...The countryside has something beautiful about it...let everything become a number and wind.

VERONICA: I'm tired...Give me some water Gaspara.

GASPARA: You're pale...too pale...You haven't gone and caught the plague in the city?

VERONICA: I'm very well...I'm just tired from the journey...Give me some water.

GASPARA: One cow, two cows, three cows, four cows, five cows, six cows...most blessed Mother, save us...

(Black-out on GASPARA. Lights up on the hospital.)

ANZOLA: *(singing)*
> I had a pair of shoes made -
> Made yes, but paid for, no.
> And they're always shouting after me
> "Beautiful little blonde, are you paying, yes or no?"

VERONICA: Oh god, my head's spinning!

ANZOLA: You're so much better, you could fall ill again.

VERONICA: Why have you stayed with me all this time?

ANZOLA: If you die, I'll have your shoes.

VERONICA: Because of that! *(Laughing.)* Do you want them? Here, take them then. Anything you ask me for, I'll give you.

ANZOLA: Now I don't want them anymore.

VERONICA: I always thought you were a bit touched.

ANZOLA: I'm cleverer than you.

VERONICA: Ah yes?

ANZOLA: Yes.

VERONICA: *(going to the window)* I want to breathe a bit of fresh air. *(Alone at the window.)* The air's changed, you see? The water's rippling, the wind smells of salt...You don't see boats laden with corpses anymore...The Rialto bridge, over there's, never seemed so beautiful to me...houses, water, all perfectly clear and clean... Remember when I arrived here? I had a high fever, was ashen and crushed...How did I manage to save myself, Anzola, how? Is it really true the Lord takes the best and leaves the most stupid and perverse on earth? Marco was taken in a trice, Domenico with a little more trouble...Maffio, who's a bad seed, still lives, but tossed down over there at Ciprio, a Bishop as he wished, but penniless and riddled with syphilis...Gaspara, dead too, poor soul, counting the cows from the window...our Lord is greedy...He's never satisfied...He wants company, company, company...only you and I remain in this lazzaretto Anzola,.empty-handed, with empty eyes...

ANZOLA: Now you can leave.

VERONICA: To go where Anzola?

ANZOLA: ...Don't you know where to go? Then let's go back to the convent. A little room can be found for you.

VERONICA: To the convent? But I only know how to be a courtesan.The only thing left for me - is to beg.

ANZOLA: Well, there's nothing left to do here. The lazzaretto's closing down. I can't go back to the convent on my own.

VERONICA: Will you come begging with me?

ANZOLA: I like going round.

VERONICA: A nun and a courtesan together...a nun and a courtesan...

ANZOLA: Put your shoes on...here's your cloak.

VERONICA: Where shall we start? At the Rialto bridge?

ANZOLA: Let's go.

VERONICA: Let's go.

(Lights fade.)

END

OTHER TITLES BY AURORA METRO PRESS

"SIX PLAYS BY BLACK AND ASIAN WOMEN WRITERS"   editor: Kadija George

A landmark collection of plays for stage, screen and radio demonstrating the range and vitality of Black and Asian writing. Featuring work by:

WINSOME PINNOCK MEERA SYAL MAYA CHOWDHRY RUKHSANA AHMAD TRISH COOKE ZINDIKA

"Reading about their fears, hopes and aspirations in this entertaining way is an education in itself" Artrage Magazine

PRICE: £7.50   ISBN 0-9515877-2-2

"SEVEN PLAYS BY WOMEN: Female Voices, Fighting Lives"   editor: Cheryl Robson

A bumper collection of award-winning plays by a new generation of women writers. Features work by:

AYSHE RAIF APRIL DE ANGELIS CHERYL ROBSON JEAN ABBOTT NINA RAPI EVA LEWIN JAN RUPPE

"a testimony to the work and debate that is going on among women, artistically, theeoretically and practically. It is an inspiring document"   Clare Bayley "What's On"

PRICE: £5.95   ISBN: 0-9515877-1-4

"THE WOMEN WRITERS' HANDBOOK"
eds: Robson, Georgeson, Beck

An essential guide to setting up and running your own writing workshops. Featuring work by 15 new writers and:

CARYL CHURCHILL JILL HYEM BRYONY LAVERY

"A gem of a book. Everything a woman writer might need in one slim volume"   Everywoman Magazine

PRICE:£4.95   ISBN: 0-9515877-0-6

NEXT:

"HOW MAXINE LEARNED TO LOVE HER LEGS and other tales of growing-up" ed: Sarah Lefanu

An exciting collection of short stories from 20 new and established authors including:

RAVI RANDHAWA BONNIE GREER KATE PULLINGER MICHELE ROBERTS

PRICE: £8.95   ISBN: 0-9515877-4-9